ANIMALS
IN CELTIC LIFE
AND MYTH

Frontispiece Bronze horse and rider, from the seventh-century BC cult wagon model at Strettweg, Austria. Paul Jenkins.

ANIMALS IN CELTIC LIFE AND MYTH

Miranda Green

London and New York

First published 1992
by Routledge
11 New Fetter Lane, London EC4P 4EE

Simultaneously published in the USA and Canada
by Routledge
29 West 35th Street, New York, NY 10001

First published in paperback 1998

Typeset in 10 on 12 point Palatino by
Florencetype Ltd, Stoodleigh, Devon
Printed in Great Britain by
Butler & Tanner Ltd, Frome and London

∞ Printed on permanent paper in
accordance with American NISO Standards

British Library Cataloguing in Publication Data
Green, Miranda J.
Animals in Celtic Life and Myth
I. Title
398.24
Library of Congress Cataloguing in Publication Data
Green, Miranda J.
Animals in Celtic life and myth / Miranda Green.
p.   cm.
Includes bibliographical references and index.
1. Celts – Domestic animals.   2. Celts – Hunting.   3. Celts –
Folklore.   4. Animals, Mythical.   5. Animals, Mythical, in art.
6. Mythology, Celtic.   I. Title.
GN549.C3G74   1992
398.24′5–dc20   92–2724

ISBN 0–415–05030–8 (hbk)
ISBN 0–415–18588–2 (pbk)

For Antigone and Oedipus

(two superb examples of the affinity between animals and people)

I and Pangur Bán, my cat,
'Tis a like task we are at:
Hunting mice is his delight,
Hunting words I sit all night.

Better far than praise of men
'Tis to sit with book and pen;
Pangur bears me no ill-will,
He too plies his simple skill.

Anon
(Probably written by an Irish scholar in the ninth century AD
translated from the Gaelic by Robin Flower)

Handle-mount in the form of a cat's face, on an early first-century AD bronze bowl
from Snowdon, Gwynedd. By courtesy of the National Museum of Wales.

CONTENTS

FIGURES

PREFACE

This book has come about because of my longstanding fascination for the ancient Celts and, in particular, for Celtic myth and religion, upon which most of my previous research work has been based. In all the sources for the period of the pagan Celts (roughly 600 BC – AD 400), the role of animals in both the secular and the sacred worlds appears to have been dominant and essential. The close association between what were basically rural communities and the natural world manifested itself not only in direct economic dependence upon the land, its crops and herds, but also in the perception of a strong link between animals and the supernatural.

My evidence for animals in the Celtic world, a world which stretched from Ireland in the extreme west to Czechoslovakia in the east and which encompassed much of Europe north of the Alps, ranges between that of archaeology and that of written documents. The archaeological material consists of the remains of the animals themselves in the faunal assemblages of Celtic sites. It embraces also the iconography – the representation of animals – of both the pre-Roman and Romano-Celtic periods. The written material falls into two categories: first, there exist the comments of Graeco-Roman observers of the Celts whom they encountered, directly or indirectly, in such lands as Gaul and Britain. These have the merit of contemporaneity but the defect of bias and misunderstanding. There is always the danger that the so-called 'civilized' product of the Mediterranean world will paint a picture of a 'barbarian savage' with quaint and primitive customs, and will chronicle alien traditions in such a manner as to foster this image. The second group of documents consists of the written compilations of the oral traditions in Ireland and Wales. These have, again, to be treated with caution since they pertain only to the western periphery of the Celtic world and should not be used as sources for the European mainland. The other problem concerns chronology: the earliest vernacular writings (that is documents actually written in Welsh or Irish as opposed to Latin) date, for the most part, no earlier than the early medieval period: they

xvii

were thus compiled much later than the pagan Celtic period and, what is more, they were set down within a Christian milieu, by monks working in monasteries. From the very clear links between some of the documentary sources and information taken from the classical authors and archaeology, it is possible to infer that some of the vernacular written material does pertain to earlier, pre-Christian periods. The Insular myths abound in gods, and no reference is made to Christianity.

In this book, the role of animals in all aspects of Celtic life is explored. I should make it clear that, notwithstanding the wide geographical area inhabited by the ancient Celts, much of my source material is necessarily taken from the western regions, from Gaul and Britain, although cognisance is also taken of that from further east. The work discusses the place of animals in the economy; in hunting; in warfare; in art; and in ritual practices. The oral tradition of Wales and Ireland, with its rich mythical treatment of animals, is examined separately. The final main section details the close relationship between animals and the gods, which manifested itself in the remarkable imagery and symbolism of the Romano-Celtic period.

ACKNOWLEDGEMENTS

INSTITUTIONS

I wish to thank the following institutions for permission to publish their photographs: Bristol Museums and Art Gallery; Cambridgeshire Archaeology Unit; Danebury Archaeological Trust; National Museum of Wales; Oxford Archaeology Unit; Rijksmuseum van Oudheden, Leiden; Worthing Museum and Art Gallery; Württembergisches Landesmuseum, Stuttgart.

INDIVIDUALS

I should like to express my gratitude to people who have helped me in the preparation of this book; Barry Cunliffe, Jen Delyth, Nick Griffiths, Betty Naggar, Alison Taylor and David Wilkinson for providing illustrations; Annie Grant, David Keys and Patrice Meniel, for information; Stephen Green, for reading and commenting on the manuscript; Kath Grace, for typing the book; Paul Jenkins, for drawing most of the illustrations. To you all, many thanks.

1

THE NATURAL WORLD OF THE CELTS

Modern urban dwellers are cushioned, to an extent, from the rhythm of the seasons, from the immediate effects of good or poor harvests and of the health and fertility of flocks and herds. But in any pre-industrial and essentially rural society, the association of communities with the natural environment and their dependence on it are both close and direct. The world of the Celts was no exception. The single farm or small nucleated settlement was the home of many Celtic peoples, and even the large communal centres, like Danebury in Hampshire or Bibracte in Burgundy, were not so very far removed from the surrounding countryside.

For the Celts, the effect of this constant interaction with nature manifested itself in many ways. The pre-Roman Celtic artist, who expressed himself mainly, though not exclusively, through the medium of metalwork, chose as his themes the plants and animals by which he was surrounded in his daily life. Anthropomorphic representation was of less interest to the Celtic metalworker. Sometimes the foliate and zoomorphic designs depicted were fantastic, unreal and full of imagination, but these fantasies do not conceal the fact that the artist had a deep understanding of his subjects. The bronzesmith and blacksmith appreciated, indeed revered, the beauty and the elegance of animals and the sinuous curves of foliage, and, by exaggerating some of their features, enhanced and promoted their aesthetic qualities.

The natural world of the Celts is nowhere manifested more clearly than in the realms of religion, ritual and myth. For the Celts, the supernatural forces perceived in all natural phenomena could not be ignored but had to be appeased, propitiated and cajoled. In Celtic religion, it was the miraculous power of nature which underpinned all beliefs and religious practices. Thus, some of the most important divinities were those of the sun, thunder, fertility and water. These were the pan-Celtic deities: the celestial gods, the mother-goddesses and the cults of water and of trees transcended tribal boundaries and were venerated in some form throughout Celtic Europe. Every tree, mountain, rock and spring possessed its own spirit or *numen*.

1

The divine sun was represented by the symbol of the spoked wheel as early as the later Bronze Age: in pre-Roman and Romano-Celtic Europe, the solar force was manifest as an anthropomorphic divinity who none the less retained his original wheel motif to represent the moving sun in the sky. The spirit of the sun was capable of creating and destroying life: it could fertilize or shrivel the crop in the ground; it was a promoter of healing and regeneration, and was even able to light the dark places of the underworld. Water was acknowledged as a powerful force, again from early in European prehistory. For the Celts, the *numina* of rivers, marshes, lakes and springs were potent supernatural beings who, like the sun, could both foster and destroy living things. Water was perceived as mysterious: it falls from the sky and fertilizes the land; springs well up from deep underground and are sometimes hot, with therapeutic mineral properties; rivers move, apparently with independent life; bogs are capricious, seemingly innocuous but treacherous. All these aquatic forces were venerated, propitiated and given offerings. In the Romano-Celtic period huge, wealthy cult establishments grew up around curative springs presided over by such divinities as Sulis at Bath in Britain and Sequana near Dijon in Gaul.

Single trees, woods and groves were sacred. Before the historical Celtic period, open-air sanctuaries, like the sixth-century BC Goloring enclosure in Germany, had as their cult focus a sacred post or living tree. This tradition was maintained by communities all over Celtic Europe, from the fourth century BC until (and indeed beyond) the end of official paganism in the fourth century AD. Thus, at the third-century BC ritual enclosure of Libeniče in Czechoslovakia, there were sacred wooden pillars or trees that had been adorned with great bronze torcs or neck-rings as if they were cult statues. At the opposite corner of the Celtic world, the late Iron Age shrine of Hayling Island in Hampshire was built around a central pit holding a post or stone. The Romano-Celtic sanctuary of the Mother-Goddesses at Pesch in Germany had a great tree as a cult focus. At Bliesbruck in the Moselle, numerous sacred pits were filled with votive offerings which included the bodies of animals and tree-trunks. Romano-Celtic iconography emphasizes the importance of trees in cult expression: altars to the Rhineland Mothers and the sky-god are decorated with tree symbols. The groups of public monuments known as 'Jupiter–Giant Columns' were composed, in part, of tall pillars carved to represent trees. The ancient Roman writer Pliny refers to the sacred oak of the Druids. Epigraphy alludes to Pyrenean deities called Fagus (Beech-Tree) and 'the God Six-Trees'. The sanctity of trees seems to have been based on their height, with their great branches appearing to touch the heavens; their longevity; and the penetration of their roots deep underground. They thus formed a link between the sky, earth and underworld. In addition, trees reflected the cycle of the seasons, with

2

the 'death' of the deciduous tree in winter and its miraculous 'rebirth' with the burgeoning of new leaf-growth in the spring. The Tree of Life allegory was perhaps enhanced by the fact that animals use trees both for shelter and for food.

The sanctity of natural phenomena and of all elements of the landscape led inevitably to the veneration of the animals dwelling within that landscape. Accordingly, wild and domesticated species were the subject of elaborate rituals and the centre of profound belief-systems. The Celts depended on domestic beasts for their livelihood, on wild creatures for hunting and on horses for warfare. This intimate relationship between human and animal in so-called secular life stimulated the concept of beasts as sacred and numinous, whether in possession of divine status in their own right or simply acting as mediators between the gods and humankind. Animals were sacrificed in rituals which sometimes involved eating all or part of the carcase but, on other occasions, the animal was very deliberately left unconsumed, as an unsullied gift to the supernatural powers who had provided humans with these beasts and who demanded offerings which meant a very real loss to the community. The sacrifice of animals must have represented more than simple offerings of valuable commodities. Examination of the evidence for religion in the Romano-Celtic period, when images and epigraphy present us with clues as to how the divine world was perceived, shows us a whole range of deities whose names, cults and

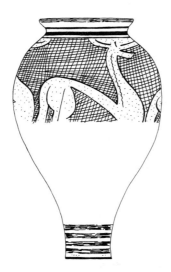

Figure 1.1 Iron Age pot with deer motif, Roanne, Loire, France. Paul Jenkins, after Meniel.

identities were intimately associated with, and indeed dependent upon, the animals depicted with them. This intimacy reached its peak in the perception of gods in human form taking on the features of the beasts themselves – hooves, horns and antlers. Moreover, sacred animals could be envisaged and depicted not only as the normal creatures recognizable within the everyday world but also as fantastic beasts whose multiple horns or composite form remind us, indeed, of the weird and wonderful creatures of the Book of Revelation: 'and behold a great red dragon, having seven heads and ten horns . . .' (Revelation 12.3).

A major theme which is explored in this book is the close link between the sacred and the mundane. It is quite impossible to separate the profane and spirit worlds, or the ritual from the secular aspects of society. Such a division is spurious and should not be attempted. It is certain that ritual pervaded most, if not all, aspects of life and was confined neither to specific ceremonies nor to formalized religious structures. The association between humans and animals expresses very clearly the conflation of cult and the everyday: the killing of animals, whether for food or for sport, had a ritual aspect; warfare was closely bound up with ceremony and religion; for the Celtic artist symbolism, sometimes overt religious symbolism, was central to his repertoire. The vernacular sources, too, show us a world where heroes straddle the realms of the mundane and the supernatural, where animals can speak to people and where divine beings can change at will between human and animal forms. These early Celtic documents open a door on a world of shifting realities and ambiguities, where animals interact closely with both humankind and the gods. To the Celts, animals were special and central to all aspects of their world.

2

FOOD AND FARMING: ANIMALS IN THE CELTIC ECONOMY

'All the . . . country produces . . . every kind of livestock'.[1] The domestication of farm animals by humans can be traced back, in parts of the Old World, to around 5000 BC.[2] By the beginning of the Iron Age, in the eighth century BC, the peoples of temperate Europe had a diverse economy which included cereal and garden crops and the rearing of animals, particularly cattle, sheep, pigs and horses.[3] This mixed farming has been a feature of many, if not most, of past European societies.[4]

There is no doubt that intensive husbandry of animals was practised in both Gaul and Britain during the Celtic Iron Age. The Celts were so good at stock-raising that the Greek geographer Strabo had occasion to comment: 'They have such enormous flocks of sheep and herds of swine that they afford a plenteous supply of *sagi* [woollen coats] and salt meat, not only to Rome but to most parts of Italy'.[5] The vernacular sources of Ireland and Wales show us a Celtic society which relied on its cattle, sheep and pigs and in which a cow or a pig represented wealth.

Figure 2.1 Bronze figurine of a bull, sixth century BC, Býčiskála Cave, Czechoslovakia. Height: 11.4cm. Paul Jenkins.

5

We have a problem in attempting to assess the stock-rearing aspect of farming during the Iron Age because almost all our information necessarily comes from bones, and these are notoriously difficult to interpret. For example, much bone waste from homes and farms has either been destroyed by acid soils or has been comminuted by the gnawing of dogs and pigs, with the result that the smaller, more fragile, bones of fish, chickens and very young animals have often vanished from the archaeological record.[6] Again, there are very few good bone reports from modern excavations: none the less, in Britain we benefit from the exhaustive bone reclamation from Danebury (Hants) and Gussage All Saints (Dorset) and their careful respective analyses by Annie Grant and Ralph Harcourt. For northern France, the work of Patrice Meniel and Jean-Louis Brunaux has enhanced considerably our knowledge of Iron Age pastoral farming.

There is a peculiar relationship between humans and animals, a rapport born of the many features they have in common.[7] Domestic animals lived and worked in a close and symbiotic association with humankind. They were tended, protected and fed but this caring was the means to a productive and profitable end – whatever was useful to humans. In a pastoral farming community, every part of an animal may be utilized: milk, wool, manure and muscle (for traction or transport) when it is alive; hides, meat, fat, blood, sinew and bone when it has been slaughtered.

There are certain general characteristics of Celtic domestic beasts and their use in Gaul and Britain. One is the small size of cattle, sheep, pigs and horses relative both to Roman strains and to present-day species. Larger, improved animals were present by the later Iron Age, possibly because of Roman influence but also perhaps because of better nutrition. At the time of the Roman occupation, both Gaul and Britain necessarily intensified their cereal production, giving cattle better fodder from the cereal waste and, at the same time, better pasture had been available by the later Iron Age because heavier soils, yielding lusher grass, were being exploited.[8] A second feature of animal utilization has been the use of beasts in ritual activity (see chapter 5). A third is the very limited use made of wild animal resources for food (see chapter 3). Hunting was practised but was clearly not a significant source of food. An exception to this trend may have pertained at Val Camonica in northern Italy, where the evidence of the rock art – if it is a true reflection of daily life – suggests that stock-rearing played a very secondary role to hunting. But even here, pastoral farming clearly fulfilled the basic needs of the Celtic Camunians, for meat, eggs, dairy products, leather and wool.[9] Some Iron Age sites used all the natural resources available to them: thus, at the Glastonbury lake village wading-birds and fish were caught, in addition to the raising of sheep for their meat and wool.[10] Athenaeus tells us that the Celts who lived near water ate fish[11] which they baked with salt and cumin.

PASTORAL FARMING AND STOCK MANAGEMENT

Generally speaking, the most common animals to be found on Celtic farms were cattle, sheep, pigs and horses. In addition, there is evidence of goats, ranched deer, farm dogs (used as guard dogs, sheepdogs and waste scavengers) and cats to keep down vermin. But within this general scenario, there were certain differences between settlements, and changes occurred through time. An interesting view of hillforts is that the function of some may have been either wholly or partially as stock enclosures.[12] Thus in the late period of Danebury (between 400 and 100 BC) the middle earthwork may have been added to form an enclosure or paddock for the protection of stock. When the outer earthwork was built, additional corralling space became available: this represents either an alteration in the system of farming in the latest phases of the hillfort, the existence of larger flocks and herds, or possibly increased tension

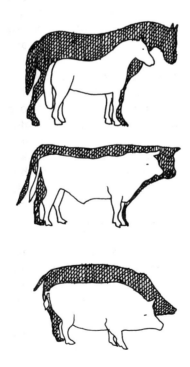

Figure 2.2 Sizes of modern and ancient Celtic animals compared (cross-hatched animals modern). Paul Jenkins, after Meniel.

Figure 2.3 Iron Age farm animals: sheep and cattle. Paul Jenkins, after Cunliffe.

resulting in the need for greater protection for stock.[13] Certainly by the first century AD stock enclosures were a feature of a great many Iron Age farmsteads in Britain,[14] and this may reflect an increasing population with a consequent requirement for more stock.

Mixed farming was carried out at most farms. In Britain, it used to be thought that there was a major distinction between the pastoral economies of the 'Highland Zone' of the north and west and the arable exploitation of the south and east. But whilst it is undoubtedly true that there was some regional specialization and that differences existed between the use of upland and valley ground, it is none the less clear that agriculture and stock-rearing were highly interactive and interdependent. Fields were cleared of grass and weeds and manured by stock before going under the plough, thus benefiting from the presence of farm animals. The beasts in turn gained supplementary nourishment from the residue of cereal production.[15]

Work in Wessex and the Thames Valley, by Annie Grant among others,[16] has thrown a great deal of light upon the integration between settlements on different soils – between high downland and valley exploitation. By the third century BC, if not before, farms in this region were developing a certain degree of specialization within a stock-rearing economy, with divergences based upon differing environments. Chalk downland sites, like Danebury, had more sheep, while low-lying gravel farms like Ashville (Oxon.) and Odell (Beds.) possessed larger numbers of cattle. There could be seasonal factors involved here. Colin Haselgrove[17] has suggested that developed hillforts like Danebury were perhaps only fully occupied during the winter months. The preference for sheep on high ground and cattle in the valleys is based entirely upon practicalities: sheep flourish on the relatively poor pasture and scarce water of chalk downland whilst the damp of the river-gravels tends to rot their feet and render them susceptible to liver-fluke. Cattle, on the other hand, thrive on the lush grass of the river valley-bottoms and need far more water than sheep do. Even so, there is evidence that cattle, sheep and pigs were all exploited to some extent in each of these environments, implying that different ground-types were used by the occupants of both downland and valley settlements and suggesting a symbiotic relationship between the communities inhabiting the different areas. Annie Grant argues convincingly[18] that an example of such interaction may be witnessed in the case of Danebury. This great fortified hill-settlement produced evidence of cattle-raising only on a modest scale (compared to the very large numbers of sheep on the site) but down in the neighbouring Test Valley are two Iron Age settlements, Little Somborne and Meon Hill, both of which reared cattle on a much larger scale. Grant's thesis is that the three sites may have been linked economically and that cattle may have been bred only at Danebury, but were kept and raised on good valley pasture on the lower ground nearby. A reverse situation may have pertained in the Thames Valley: here the Iron Age settlement at Farmoor can have had only a seasonal occupation since it would have been flooded by the river in winter. It is possible that the Farmoor community had sheep which were kept on high ground, while their cattle were sent to safe levels elsewhere during the winter. Certainly, as Andrew Fitzpatrick suggests,[19] flocks and herds of viable breeding size could not have been sustained by each and every community. So there was bound to be some interaction between settlements for their mutual benefit. Fitzpatrick envisages traditions whereby people from different communities gathered together at periodic intervals for the birth of young livestock, for the arrangements for seasonal use of uplands and lowlands and for exchange markets.

In Gaul as well as in Britain there were preferences for certain stock animals over others in particular settlements or kinds of settlement: on native farms, cattle were favoured, with pigs being less frequent. Hornaing (Nord) specialized in cattle, horses and intensive sheep husbandry. By contrast, the community at Beauvais (Oise) in the late La Tène period seems to have concentrated on pig-rearing.[20] Many trends towards one type of husbandry or another are associated with different chronological phases. In Britain and, to an extent, in Gaul, pigs became more popular in later free Celtic times, and the Roman predilection for pork is reflected by their increased frequency on Romano-Celtic sites.[21] Barbara Noddle[22] has made a comparison of the bones of the primary domestic species – cattle, sheep and pigs – from ten multiperiod (Iron Age and Romano-British) sites. Within the sample, she traces a general increase in cattle through time, balanced by a decline in sheep. At Danebury, there was no perceptibly significant change in animal husbandry traditions in its 500 or so years of occupation. However, here there seems to have been an increase in sheep whilst cattle and pigs were in decline in later periods. The paucity of pigs by the second

Figure 2.4 Bronze rein-ring decorated with knob-horned bulls' heads and bird head, second to first century BC, Manching, Bavaria. Height: 9cm. Paul Jenkins.

century BC has led Barry Cunliffe[23] to speculate that this may have resulted from the over-use and/or demise of woodland in the area (forest being the favoured habitat of pigs). Although sheep were especially dominant at this late phase in Danebury's history, the faunal remains indicate that the Danebury community had to cope with the scourge of mouth disease in their flocks.

The Iron Age economy remained mixed both in species and in methods of management throughout its duration. The advent of the new Roman culture made itself felt in many ways, but it did not alter essential indigenous patterns of animal husbandry. The Roman army liked its pork and this is reflected in the animal remains, but increased use of pigs was a trend already present in the later Iron Age, as witnessed at the pre-Roman *oppidum* of Silchester. Cattle became increasingly important in Roman times, not only for meat but also for leather. But the lack of any fundamental change between the free Celtic and Romano-Celtic traditions is shown by the fact that animals other than pigs were still mainly killed for food only when they were mature and after they had already fulfilled their other economic functions – the provision of wool, traction or milk. This is a distinctive characteristic of

10

Iron Age animal exploitation.[24] Animals in the Celtic world were some-times consumed at the optimum time for meat (i.e. at the onset of maturity or adulthood), but many were kept longer, implying that the use of cattle and sheep as meat was a consideration secondary to those of pulling-power and wool production. There were exceptions to this: pigs were raised primarily for their meat and fat and were thus generally killed when they were fully grown but their meat was still at its most tender – when the animal was about 2 years old. Weak or diseased stock might also be slaughtered young. Surplus new born animals might be killed off in the spring and extra males or barren females might be dispatched before winter came with its necessity for supplementary feeding. It was important to keep flocks and herds at their optimum level.[25]

Whilst each species of stock had particular needs (see pp. 12–21), Iron Age communities had to come up with solutions to many problems common to the maintenance of all domestic animals. One was protec-tion against predators (whether human or animal) and against the weather. This could be at least partially overcome by the building of enclosures: at Danebury, for instance, the pregnant ewes and cows may have been enclosed so that they could be kept under surveillance and receive special attention. Dogs may well have been used to protect stock. At Danebury, the many slingstones found at the hillfort may represent not conventional warfare but the protection of flocks by the driving off of predators. Slingshot could also have been used to drive flocks in particular directions – by aiming the slingstone so that it landed behind the animals.[26] Another problem to be overcome was that of winter feeding, when both flocks and herds would require supplemen-tary fodder, but Peter Reynolds[27] has stressed that it is ludicrous to imagine a mass autumn slaughter of stock simply because of the difficul-ties of winter feeding, though this used to be the accepted view. Various supplementary feeds could be used: hay was undoubtedly one; leaf-fodder gathered from local woodland another. Cattle could be fed on a mixture of barley and chaff but also perhaps unripe barley was cut with its straw and stored on rick-stands for winter use.[28]

The farming year was closely linked with the natural life of plant and animal. In autumn, winter and spring, ploughing would be preceded by manuring the fields. Spring was lambing and calving time; summer saw not only the harvest but the shearing of sheep. In late autumn, meat would be slaughtered and cured for storage; now was the time for sheep to receive such attention as hoof-trimming. In winter, supplementary food and water would be organized for wintering stock.[29]

11

THE ANIMALS ON AN IRON AGE FARM

Cattle

The cattle of the Celtic Iron Age were smaller, lighter and more slender than either Roman or modern cattle,[30] and they belonged to a now extinct shorthorn type called *Bos longifrons*. British Iron Age cattle were the progenitors of Irish Kerry Cattle and Welsh Black Cattle. At his experimental Iron Age farm at Butser in Hampshire, Peter Reynolds keeps a small herd of Dexter cattle, a type bred from Kerry Cattle in the nine-

Figure 2.5 Bronze bull-head bucket-mounts, first century BC to first century AD, from a hoard of five, found on the Little Orme, Gwynedd. By courtesy of the National Museum of Wales.

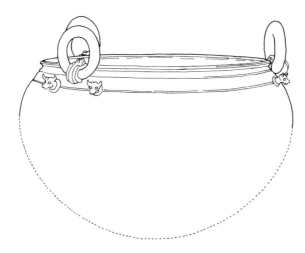

Figure 2.6 Reconstruction of a bronze cauldron with bull-head mounts, third century BC, Brå, Denmark. Height of cauldron: *c.*70cm. Miranda Green.

teenth century. They have amenable temperaments, do well on relatively impoverished pasture and are hardy winter survivors.[31] The Butser experiment set out to create a farm which reflects as closely as possible the agricultural techniques and the species of animals and crops of southern England during the later first millennium BC. As far as cattle are concerned, Peter Reynolds has answered a number of fundamental questions about the tending, management and exploitation of these beasts. A major problem of cattle-maintenance is water-supply: a cow will consume as much as an average of 16 gallons of water a day. A second problem concerns feeding: the pastures on which cattle grazed would have had to be managed and controlled, with certain grassland areas set aside for haymaking.[32] Cattle would either be kept around the farm, especially if they were used for traction (see pp. 27–9), or be herded in large enclosures or ranches,[33] particularly, perhaps, if their hides were going to be used. But at Danebury cows were probably corralled during pregnancy, for their protection and to give them extra feed, and so that, later, humans could take advantage of some of the milk produced for the calves.

Study of some Iron Age sites in Gaul and Britain throws light on some aspects of cattle management. That they were important to the Celtic economy is in no doubt: their bones are found in some numbers on most settlement sites. Danebury seems to have been a centre for breeding cattle, although they were present in far fewer numbers than sheep. The large numbers of young calves found here indicates that calving (like lambing) took place either inside or in the vicinity of the hillfort, where the cows could be tended and watched. Gussage was also a breeding-centre: excavators discovered the body of a cow that had evidently died in calving; the calf was still in an incorrect position in the womb, forefeet first, a problem which is very difficult to rectify.[34] Cattle at Danebury were killed, at the end of their useful lives, when they were turned into meat (probably rather tough), hides, sinew, bone and horn objects. Their primary use seems to have been for traction, milk or simply as a unit of wealth.[35] If cattle are not bred primarily for their flesh, their first few years are unproductive: a young ox cannot be used to pull a load nor will a cow become a milk-producer or breeder until it is mature. It would therefore make more sense to keep cattle somewhere where supplementary feeding was unnecessary while they were too young to contribute to the economy. This may account for the lack of juvenile cattle at Danebury: young animals may have been driven to the good grasslands of the Test Valley until they were old enough to be useful.[36]

In Gaul, the exploitation of cattle seems to have been essentially similar to that of southern Britain. On many north Gaulish settlements, the cattle represented by the adult bone remains are mainly cows, the bull-calves having been killed off when they were young. This occurred, for instance, at Epiais-Rhus and at Villeneuve-Saint-Germain (Aisne). Cows were kept for milk and for breeding; a few bulls would be retained to maintain the stock; the rest would be oxen raised for traction. Again, as in Britain, the animals were generally not eaten until they were too old to be useful as living beasts.[37]

Classical commentators on the Celts allude to the consumption of milk and meat, though the flesh of pig and sheep is considered more important than beef.[38] It was the Germans whom these Mediterranean writers saw as the great cattle-owners and herdsmen. Caesar says '. . . the greater part of their food consists of milk, cheese and meat'.[39] His comments could refer equally to sheep as to cattle, but Tacitus is more explicit.[40] He says that the number of cattle they possessed was the key to their status. He describes cattle as the most highly prized possessions –

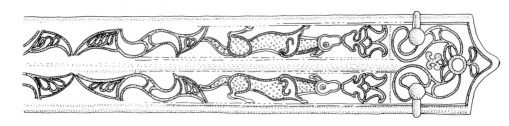

Figure 2.7 Bronze sword-scabbard engraved with bulls, fifth century BC, from a grave at Hochscheid, Germany. Width of scabbard: 5cm. Paul Jenkins.

indeed the only riches – of these people.[41] This is interesting because Tacitus is describing a society which is very like that chronicled in the early Irish literature as pertaining to Celtic communities. In Ireland, a cow and a female slave (a *cumal*) were both units of value, the main measure of wealth being cattle. Many early Irish stories tell of valuable herds of cattle, and raids between neighbouring communities were the norm. The most famous prose tale in the Ulster Cycle is the 'Cattle Raid of Cooley' (the 'Táin Bo Cuailnge'): the whole story revolves around the desire of Queen Medb of Connacht to gain as superb a bull as that owned by her consort Ailill. Her heart is set on the acquisition of the Brown Bull of Cuailnge in Ulster, described as thick-breasted, narrow-flanked, with a magnificent mane on his neck, and glaring eyes.[42] The two rulers boast of their possessions, vying with each other for supremacy, but it is cattle which mean the most to them.[43] The Ulster hero Cú Chulainn brags that he has slaughtered 'hosts of cattle, men and steeds'.[44] The great Insular pastoral festival of Beltene at the beginning of May traditionally marked the time of year when cattle and sheep were taken up to the high pasture, after purificatory fire festivals in which the herds were driven between two banks of flame.[45]

The breeding capacity of the cow was the basis of her value. Numbers were held to be important in both early Ireland and Tacitus's Germany. Interestingly, it is true for some herding societies of the present day: in Botswana, for example, the number of cattle is all-important to the Kalahari herdsman, irrespective of the condition or the fatness of individual animals.

Sheep

Two thousand years ago, a group of Celts went, with their sheep, to live on the islands of St Kilda off the north-west coast of Scotland. These sheep were the ancestors of the present-day Soay sheep which still live there and whose skeletal structure compares very closely with remains of Iron Age sheep in Britain and Gaul.[46] These animals look more like goats than sheep; they are brown with white underparts, slender, fleet of foot, and both sexes have horns. They wander widely over the land and cannot easily be controlled with dogs. Indeed, as Peter Reynolds comments, a Celtic shepherd 'followed if not pursued his flock'. Soay sheep shed their long hair in an annual moult at the beginning of summer, and Iron Age people probably tried to pre-empt this and to pluck the hair before it was scattered (see pp. 30–2).

In general, sheep were kept for wool, milk and meat but, like cattle, they were often not killed until they were old and past their best for consumption.[47] This means that sheep were valued primarily for their live contribution to the economy. The excavations at Danebury and the

15

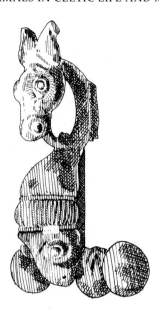

Figure 2.8 Silvered bronze brooch in the form of a horse's and a ram's head, fourth century BC, Dürrnburg, Hallein, Austria. Length: 4cm. Paul Jenkins.

work at Butser have contributed greatly to our understanding of the raising and management of sheep. Much Iron Age land must have been covered in fields, and sheep were probably grazed on these fields in rotation, where their dung could enrich the soil.[48] But if the wide-ranging Soay sheep were allowed to wander at will, then the new arable crop would have been in jeopardy from grazing, so there must have been some control or corralling system to protect the fields. Certainly, there must have been shepherds: one of the scenes on the rocks at Camonica Valley depicts a shepherd guarding his flock, armed with a long pole, perhaps a spear.[49]

Analysis of the faunal remains at Danebury shows that more than 70 per cent of the animals kept by the hillfort community were sheep. Some of them died young; a good proportion of these were killed at about a year, probably after they had been fattened on spring grass. The presence of the bones of new-born lambs indicates that the pregnant ewes were rounded up in early spring and brought in from the downs within the fort enclosure.[50] This had the added advantage that, if the neo-natal fatality rate had been high, the bereft ewes could provide milk for the people. Ewes do not lamb until they are 2 or 3 years old: decisions would have been taken as to which animals to slaughter young for meat and which ewes should be allowed to breed and to produce wool.

The predominance of sheep at Danebury reflects a situation occurring

16

elsewhere in central southern England. Normally, wool was their prime function, with meat only secondary: Iron Age Britons often had to make do with tough, elderly mutton. The downlands, with their limited water and poor grass, are ideal for sheep-rearing. The Glastonbury lake-villagers produced wool on a large scale:[51] their sheep may have been pastured on the nearest higher, well-drained soil. There was intensive sheep-rearing in many areas of Britain outside Wessex and the south-east, notably in the Welsh highlands, northern England and Scotland,[52] just as it is today. In later periods of the British Iron Age, there was a general reduction in sheep, and cattle became more dominant: at Danebury there were still a great many flocks in the second century BC, but they were ravaged by disease, as we have seen.[53]

As with cattle, there is literary evidence for Celtic sheep-rearing. Strabo[54] comments on the raising of flocks and the production of wool: he says of the Gauls, 'they have enormous flocks of sheep'. In early Ireland, sheep were clearly a major source of wealth: in the 'Táin', the flocks of Queen Medb and King Ailill of Connacht are described thus: 'Their great flocks of sheep were brought from the fields and the lawns and the level plains. . . . But among Medb's sheep was a fine ram with the value of a *cumal*.'[55]

Before we leave the subject of sheep, its close relative, the goat, should be mentioned. It is sometimes difficult to distinguish goats from sheep in the archaeological record, but the general picture seems to have been that goats were far less common. Goats are good milk-producers, and they would have been useful as browsers of weeds,[56] but they would have to have been carefully controlled, otherwise they would have destroyed the growing crops. The probability is that each farming community may have kept a few goats tethered around the farm buildings. Goats are less hardy than sheep; they dislike the damp and can be killed by cold, so they are unlikely to have competed seriously with sheep, especially in Britain and northern Gaul. They are much more at home in the hotter, drier climate of Mediterranean Europe.

Pigs

Their pigs are allowed to run wild and are noted for their height, and pugnacity and swiftness . . . they have such enormous . . . herds of swine that they afford a plenteous supply for . . . salt meat. . . . They have large quantities of food together with milk and all kinds of meat, especially fresh and salt pork.[57]

Pig-keeping is traditionally associated with the Celts. The early Welsh group of mythological tales, the Four Branches of the *Mabinogi*, tells of the first pigs or *hobeu* in Britain, gifts from Arawn king of the under-

Figure 2.9 Bronze goat figurine from the Roman legionary fortress of Caerleon, Gwent. By courtesy of the National Museum of Wales.

world to Pryderi, lord of Dyfed, and the subsequent bloody war between Gwynedd in the north and Dyfed in the south for possession of these coveted creatures.[58] Pigs seem to have been equally important in the economy and mythology of early Ireland.[59] Here, pork is frequently mentioned in the Insular literature, often being associated with the 'champion's portion'.[60] The 'Táin Bó Cuailnge' relates the story of two great bulls who were once human pig-keepers called Fruich (Bristle) and Rucht (Grunt).[61]

Pigs were and are kept almost exclusively for their meat: they are a very valuable resource in that they are able to eat virtually anything and convert a great variety of organic matter, inedible to other species, into high-quality meat.[62] It is often thought that the Celts spent much of their time hunting boar and that this was their source of pork, but it is clear from the faunal record[63] that most pig bones on Iron Age sites are those of the domestic pig. None the less, Peter Reynolds has made the point[64] that the piglets of wild pigs are easily tamed, so perhaps wild and domestic pigs were sometimes treated similarly and even interbred.

Iron Age pigs were probably maintained semi-confined, herded rather than kept in sties, and allowed to forage in the woodland to which they are particularly suited.[65] They are adaptable creatures and ideally should have access to wooded areas, so that they do not compete unnecessarily with humans for land and food.[66] Pigs actually contribute to the management of woodland in that they keep down unwanted shrubs and undergrowth. But they are also useful in agriculture: if they are turned out onto the fields in spring and autumn, they will break up, turn over and manure the soil before the ploughing.[67] Being good scavengers, they will clean up after the harvest and aerate the earth ready for the new cycle of crop-sowing.

In Gaul, pigs were consistently important throughout the Iron Age, though other species might fluctuate in popularity according to time.[68] In Britain, pigs were never as common as in Gaul, but they generally increased towards the end of the Iron Age and during the Roman occupation.[69] Pigs breed fast and, if the herd were carefully managed, it would be possible both to keep sufficient breeding-stock to maintain the herd and to rear the remainder for slaughter in prime condition (at about two years old).[70] Many of the males would have been killed while they were still young, but the sows were kept alive longer for breeding. This occurred on a number of Iron Age settlements studied by Patrice Meniel in northern Gaul.

Danebury is again a useful type-site for the analysis of pig-rearing practices in southern Britain. Pigs were not very numerous here but

Figure 2.10 Romano-British clay pig-figurine, Birrenswark, Scotland.
Reproduced by courtesy of the Trustees of the National Museums of Scotland.

19

were present in some proportion during the entire period of occupation. Though Danebury is on downland, there is heavy clay soil nearby which would have supported woodland and therefore pigs. But by the second century BC there was significant local decline in pigs (contrary to evidence elsewhere in southern England), perhaps the result of a decrease in the quantity or quality of the local forest.[71] The bone evidence at Danebury conforms, however, to the general pattern of usage seen on other British sites. Pigs must always have been invaluable as a steady source of meat, even if other species were sometimes consumed for preference. But in Gaul, the pig played a much greater role in the human diet.

Horses

Horses were the common companions of humans by around 1600 BC in much of Europe.[72] At Camonica Valley in north Italy, the rock carvings date from the Neolithic to the Iron Age. Here, horses are first depicted in any numbers in the very last phase of the Bronze Age (c.1000–800 BC). The images show horses as display animals or as mounts for warriors, and they are depicted pulling funerary wagons to the tombs of the high-ranking dead.[73]

Celtic Iron Age horses were small and light compared to Roman horses (see chapter 4). The livestock at the Butser experimental farm includes the Exmoor pony, which is not dissimilar to the small, fast and tough horses of the British and Gaulish Iron Age.[74] On Celtic farms they were used for riding (perhaps for rounding up herds), as pack or draught animals, and they were also eaten. The evidence from Danebury, Gussage All Saints and from some Gaulish sites suggests that horse-breeding did not take place within the confines of farmland, but that horses were rounded up and trained as and when required (indeed the slings found at Danebury could have been used in the hobbling of horses). That horses were not bred on these sites is suggested by the paucity of the bones of young horses in the faunal record.[75] The Danebury animals were mainly male, and the implication is that the mares were allowed to run free with the herd. But in the latest phase of the hillfort's occupation, there seems to have been a shift in horse-management practices: young horses are represented in the bone assemblage, indicating that breeding did now take place on site.

Sometimes there is evidence as to how horses were used. The animal is relatively common on some Gaulish settlements, such as Chevrières and Creil in the Middle Oise.[76] On such Gaulish habitation sites, horses were killed young, probably for food;[77] but at Danebury horses, like cattle, were generally eaten only at the end of their useful lives.[78] Horses could be employed to pull light loads: the analysis of the wear on the

Figure 2.11 Bronze figurine of a horse, fifth to fourth century BC, Freisen, Germany. Length 12cm. Paul Jenkins.

horse bones at Gussage indicates that here they were used as draught-animals or pack-horses,[79] perhaps for hauling carts of produce. Donkeys were known only in the very late Iron Age in Gaul, as at Hornaing (Nord); it is possible that they were introduced by the Romans.[80] They would have been used, as today, as beasts of burden.

In early Celtic Ireland, during the first millennium AD, it is clear that horses, like sheep and cattle, were considered as symbols of pastoral wealth: Cú Chulainn of Ulster boasted that he had slaughtered 'hosts of cattle, men and steeds'.[81] The Táin speaks thus of the horses belonging to the royal court of Connacht, Ulster's enemy: 'From grazing lands and paddocks their horses and steeds were brought to them. Medb had a splendid horse which was valued at a *Cumal*'.[82]

21

Figure 2.12 Romano-Celtic stone relief of a mare with suckling foal, Chorey, Burgundy. Miranda Green.

Other farm animals

Deer

It is usual to classify deer as a wild species, hunted both for sport and to protect arable land from its depredations (chapter 3). But the bones of red and roe deer found on some habitation sites could represent something more than sporadic hunting. The so-called ranch boundaries of later prehistoric Britain could reflect deer management as well as cattle-herding. It is possible to envisage an annual round-up of deer within these boundaries, followed by any culling deemed necessary or advantageous.[83]

Chickens and other birds

Domestic fowls were known in Hallstatt and La Tène times in temperate Europe: remains of chickens dating to the sixth century BC have been found at the Hallstatt stronghold of the Heuneberg in Germany. Fowls were common in the Mediterranean world from at least the sixth cen-

Figure 2.13 Wooden carving of a stag, second century BC, from a *Viereckschanze* at Fellbach-Schmiden, Germany. Height: 77cm. Paul Jenkins.

tury. The chickens of the Celtic Iron Age were Red Jungle Fowl, imported from India or the Far East.[84] Chickens were kept for their eggs and flesh, especially during the later Iron Age in Gaul and Britain. They are often poorly represented archaeologically, since their fragile bones are easily fragmented or destroyed by dogs or pigs. But in Gaul the bones occur in the protected context of graves, where they are found to be of moderate size, smaller than those of the Roman period. A silvered metal model of a cockerel comes from the Gallo-Roman sanctuary at Estrées-Saint-Denis (Oise) (figure 2.14).[85] A brooch in the form of a hen comes from the much earlier context of the princess's grave at Reinheim, dating to the fourth century BC (see chapter 6). In Britain, chickens arrived later than in Celtic Europe. Caesar[86] indeed stated that the

23

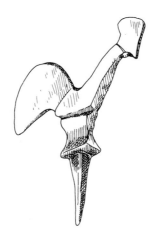

Figure 2.14 Bronze fowl from a Romano-Celtic sanctuary at Estrées-Saint-Denis, France. Paul Jenkins.

Britons shunned geese and chickens as food. But none the less, remains of domestic fowl are found among food debris in Iron Age Britain, for example in the late period at Danebury.[87] The keeping of chickens greatly increased during the Romano-Celtic period.

Geese and ducks were kept on some farms. Peter Reynolds[88] considers that they are likely to have been greylag geese and mallard ducks. Both birds appear as funerary offerings in Gaul.[89] Pliny refers to the keeping of geese among the Morini of the Netherlands.[90] In the Romano-Celtic period, both geese and ducks are represented in religious iconography (see chapter 8).

Dogs and cats

Strabo[91] mentions the export of British dogs for hunting. Certainly (see chapter 3), they would have been invaluable in sniffing out, bringing down and retrieving prey, and also in protecting their masters from savage beasts such as boar and bear. Faunal remains, iconography (mainly of the Romano-Celtic period) and vernacular Celtic literature all indicate that there were many different types of Celtic dog, from the deer-hound so splendidly represented at the Lydney sanctuary[92] to small terriers and lapdogs (figure 2.15).[93] Classical writers mention both large and small hunting-dogs and stress that British dogs had an especially fine reputation. Greyhounds are specifically mentioned in the early Welsh literature: they formed some of the many gifts presented to Pwyll by Arawn, lord of the Otherworld, in the First Branch of the

Figure 2.15 Romano-British bronze figurine of a dog, Kirkby Thore, Cumbria.
Paul Jenkins.

Mabinogi. Two greyhounds accompany Culhwch, when he sets out in all his splendour to visit his cousin Arthur, in 'Culhwch and Olwen'.[94] The guardianship aspect of dogs in Celtic life is amply illustrated by one of the stories of the early life of Cú Chulainn: he kills the hound of Culann the Smith and, in recompense, pledges himself to act as guard dog in its place (see chapter 7).

Around the farm, dogs were useful not only as guard dogs but also as scavengers. A range of dog types and sizes is represented at Danebury.[95] At Camonica Valley, sheepdogs are depicted,[96] although Reynolds has argued that dogs are ineffective in controlling the way-ward Soay sheep. Dogs would help to keep the farmyard free of vermin, especially rats, which would threaten the stored grain. But in addition, there is evidence that dogs were eaten,[97] both on habitation sites and as part of ritual feasting, as at the sanctuary of Gournay (Oise). Dog pelts were also utilized: there is archaeological evidence for skinning at the Iron Age cemetery of Tartigny (Oise) (chapter 5).[98] Diodorus Siculus remarks of the Celts: 'When dining, they all sit not on chairs but on the earth, strewing beneath them the skins of wolves or dogs'.[99]

There is evidence for cats in the British Iron Age, indeed the earliest record for the domestic cat in Britain. Cats, including a small kitten, lived at Danebury. At Gussage All Saints, there were several cats, mainly juveniles: five new-born kittens died here and were disposed of together. The presence of young animals indicates that they were bred

Figure 2.16 Bronze mirror-handle with cat's head terminal, first century BC
to first century AD, Holcombe, Devon. Height: 37.2cm. Paul Jenkins.

on site, perhaps primarily to keep down mice and rats. But equally,
some cats may have been pets.[100]

ANIMALS IN AGRICULTURE

Crop and animal husbandry were interdependent on Celtic farms.
Arable land needed to be fertilized by the dung of grazing animals, and
its nutrients replenished after harvest. The by-products of cereal production were used to feed cattle, especially in the winter months.
Animals were used in many ways on a farm: pigs or cattle could be let
loose to eat the stubble and churn up the ground after each harvest,
prior to the next season's ploughing; sheep or cattle could graze on
grasses and weeds growing on the fields before they were sown. Cattle
pulled the plough and, together with horses, pulled the carts laden with
produce.[101]

Manuring

The utilization of dung from farm animals could be effected in one of
several ways: the animals could be turned out onto harvested or fallow
fields, thus fertilizing arable land before ploughing and at the same time
resting the normal pasture, or beasts (and this applies particularly to
sheep) could be penned up in particular areas for a period of intensive

26

manuring.[102] A third way is by the collection of dung from byres in which animals were kept in winter, which would then be spread over the fields before early spring ploughing.[103] Certainly one or other method would be used before either autumn, winter or spring ploughing. If an animal is corralled overnight, most of its dung can be collected without too much effort; Peter Reynolds's calculation of dung production per cow per day is an average of 25kg.[104] At Danebury, the dung of sheep, which is manure of high quality, was invaluable in its addition of nutrients to the thin chalk downland soils.[105]

The benefits of manuring were recognized long before the Iron Age. The dung of goats, sheep and horses was probably valued most, followed by that of cattle and pigs. As well as being applied directly to the fields, manure could first be burned and its ash spread onto the arable land. Burning dung was also a useful source of fuel: this practice is widespread in Europe and beyond, from India to Iceland. It was a common source of fuel in Scandinavia and northern Britain.[106] Traditionally, dung is collected by women and fashioned into 'cakes' or 'bricks' for burning. I have witnessed women rolling dung in this way on the edge of the Nile at Tel el Amarna in southern Egypt. That dung was likely to have been put to this use in Iron Age Britain is suggested by the identification of dried-out cow-dung at the pre-Roman Iron Age site of Hawk's Hill in Surrey.[107] The dung was probably stored for a while before use, since the drier it was the better it would burn and, in any case, fresh dung damages the grass on which it lies.[108]

Ploughing, reaping and threshing

The Bronze Age rock art of Scandinavia and Camonica Valley depicts scenes of ploughing, using a simple plough or ard drawn by a pair of cattle. One Camunian scene shows two oxen drawing the plough, accompanied by the ploughman, who is walking behind. Two other men are also depicted, one in front of the animals, the other behind the ploughman. The individual at the animal's head carries a kind of mattock or hoe, as does the person at the rear of the group; the leading man also bears a twig or branch (figure 2.17).[109] Reynolds has observed a similar scene in present-day rural Spain, where peasants break up the clods of earth before and behind the plough and where one man walks by the animal's head to brush off flies with a kind of fly-whisk or swatter. In the Camunian scene, the ploughman carries a stick, which is generally interpreted as a goad, to keep the cattle moving. But in Spain a stick is used by the ploughman to free the point of the plough periodically, as it becomes bogged down in heavy soil.

The evidence for Iron Age ploughs is scanty, because they were made of wood and do not generally survive, though by the third century BC in

Figure 2.17 Ploughing scene, on a Bronze Age or Iron Age rock carving at Camonica Valley, north Italy. Paul Jenkins, after Anati.

Britain, ard-shares were tipped with iron and these parts sometimes turn up as finds on sites.[110] We do have the evidence of the rock art, where the plough is depicted as a simple angled spike or 'ard'. Wooden ards like those carved on the rocks are found preserved in the waterlogged conditions of peat-bogs, especially in Denmark: the Donnerupland ard, found in a Danish marsh, has been reconstructed and used in experimental farming, where it was found to be extremely efficient.[111] In Britain, evidence for Iron Age ploughs exists mainly in the form of score-marks; an ox-drawn ard was used at Danebury.[112] The simple plough or ard was an uncomplicated implement consisting of a wooden shaft ending in a spike set at an angle, sometimes iron-tipped, which simply stirred and made furrows in the soil. The ard is distinctive in possessing no mouldboard or coulter for turning over the earth. However, there is some evidence from the later Iron Age that fairly heavy soils were none the less being exploited.

Cattle or horses could be used in ploughing: the bone evidence of horses suggests that they were sometimes used for this purpose.[113] Again, a later Iron Age Camunian rock-art scene depicts a plough pulled by horses.[114] But most farmers undoubtedly used cattle for traction (figure 2.18). The presence of middle-aged or elderly cattle on archaeological sites implies that they were worked before they were eaten. Such is the case at the habitation site of Variscourt; and at the sanctuary of Gournay, the cattle had undoubtedly been used as working animals before they were sacrificed to the infernal gods.[115] For successful ploughing, it is necessary to have a pair of specially trained animals, with the correct size to power ratio. Peter Reynolds has calculated that the average Celtic field (for which there is archaeological evidence in Britain) can be ploughed in a single day.[116] The cattle used for traction were probably kept apart from the herd, controlled and specially tended.

At the Butser experimental farm, two of the slender, long-legged

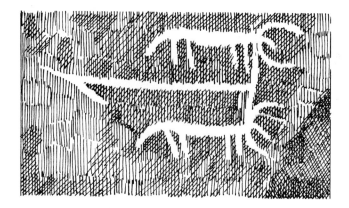

Figure 2.18 Rock carving at Camonica Valley, depicting two oxen pulling
a plough. Paul Jenkins.

Dexter cattle were trained as a working pair for ploughing. It takes about
two years to train these animals to work in unison as a team, yoked
together, to pull a light ard.[117] Reynolds has found that cattle are
difficult to train and can be quite intractable, requiring a considerable
period of handling before being introduced to each other, the yoke or
the plough. What is interesting about the work at Butser is the conclusion that many plough teams may well have been cows rather than
oxen, because they are more amenable to training. The two animals
could be yoked together by either a neck or a horn yoke: both methods
were used in the Iron Age and are indeed both still employed in modern
peasant farming.[118]

Animals were also required for their pulling-power at harvest time.
Certainly, by the Romano-Celtic period, reaping-machines pulled by
horses, donkeys or mules were known in northern Gaul and depicted
on such stone sculpture as that from Reims and Buzenol-Montauban.[119]
After the corn had been cut, oxen or horses would be needed to carry
the harvested crop away from the fields to the farm for processing and
storage. The scenes on the rocks at Camonica show a number of light,
four-wheeled wagons pulled by horses or cattle (figure 2.19). These
vehicles could represent the transport of corn, hay or other produce.[120]

After harvesting, the grain had to be extracted from the raw corn.
Although threshing can be carried out efficiently with flails, it can also
be done by allowing farm animals to trample over the harvested corn.[121]
Right through the farming year, therefore, from the initial manuring of
the fields and ploughing to the harvest and even after, animals were
closely linked with humans in nearly every aspect of crop production.

Figure 2.19 Wagon-pulling scene on a rock carving at Camonica Valley.
Paul Jenkins.

WOOL

Their wool is rough and thin at the ends, and from it they weave
the thick *sagi* [coats] which they call *laenae*; but the Romans have
succeeded even in the more northerly parts in raising flocks of
sheep (clothing them in sheepskin) with a fairly fine wool.[122]

So wrote Strabo of wool production in Celtic Gaul. There is no doubt
that the raising of sheep for wool was an important aspect of the Iron
Age economy. Unlike milk, wool production is not dependent on either
the age or sex of the animal. The faunal evidence indicates that large
numbers of sheep were kept for wool and only killed for food long after
the optimum time for meat had passed.[123] In any case, compared to
cattle and pigs, the meat yield of sheep is small. Wool production
continued to be important during the Roman period.[124] Strabo comments upon the fame of Gaulish and British woollen blankets, and the
Emperor Diocletian, at the end of the third century AD, levied a huge tax
on the *birrus Britannicus*, a kind of woollen duffel-coat, and the *tapete
Britannicum*, a rug used on saddles and couches.[125]

There must have been a well-organized wool-cloth industry during
the Iron Age. Flocks would have been carefully managed and their size
may have been strictly controlled. If an inhibition on mating was
deemed desirable, the sexes could be separated by means of corralling or
the rams could be fitted with an apron-like device to stop them from
serving the ewes.[126]

If we assume that Iron Age sheep were basically of Soay type, then their wool could have been gathered either by plucking or by shearing. Soays shed naturally during June, so, if they were plucking wool, the farmers would have needed to gauge the best time to gather it, just before it was rubbed off naturally.[127] One sheep would produce only about 1kg of wool in a year, and a small family of two adults and three children might need as many as twenty Soay sheep to keep themselves in clothes and blankets.[128] Barry Cunliffe suggests that the sheep may have been plucked with the bone combs which are so common on Iron Age sites and which are generally designated 'weaving combs'.[129] During the Iron Age there was an important technological advance in wool-winning with the invention of iron shears, which meant that the entire fleece could be removed and the farmers no longer needed to rely on the somewhat haphazard business of plucking during the annual summer moult. Shears are common on Continental Iron Age sites[130] but may not have been introduced into Britain until the Roman period.

To the Romans, Celtic wool was rough and coarse, but Diodorus Siculus mentions variegated colours, which could have been natural or dyed.[131] Soays are brown and white, but selected breeding may have produced particular colour traits. Very few remains of Celtic fleeces or wool are known archaeologically, but a complete fleece (arguing the use of shears) was found at Hallstatt in Austria, and a bog in north Germany has produced another, dating to around 500 BC. Wool fibres were

Figure 2.20 Clay ram figurine, found with the burial of a Romano-British infant, at Arrington, Cambridgeshire. By courtesy of Cambridgeshire County Council.

embedded in the bronze of a funerary couch at the tomb of the Hallstatt prince at Hochdorf in Germany.[132] The wool would have been hairy and relatively stiff, but some finer wool could have been produced by controlled breeding.[133] Soays have medium-heavy kemp hairs and a finer underwool; sheared fleeces result in a mixture of the coarse kemp hairs and the fine, soft underwool. Interestingly, although the texture of wool possibly did improve during the Roman period, some yarn which survives from the Roman fort of Vindolanda in north Britain, with its exceptional waterlogged preservation of organic remains, shows that the same hairy fibre was sometimes still being used.[134]

The shed wool of naturally moulting sheep probably led to the accidental discovery of both felting and spinning in antiquity: the wool would be rubbed off onto bushes by sheep and this process might sometimes have led to the winding of the discarded wool into long strands. Once the sheep had been plucked or sheared, the wool was cleaned and carded with bone or antler combs: the act of combing would ensure that the fibres lay straight. After that the wool was ready to be spun: spindle-whorls and bobbins survive on many Iron Age sites, including Glastonbury, which produced a great deal of evidence for wool production.[135] The yarn was then woven into cloth on a vertical loom: weaving involves the interleaving of horizontal weft yarns over and under the stronger, vertical warp threads. The loom itself is merely a frame on which the warp yarn can be held taut.[136] Loom-weights of clay or stone are common finds. Sites like Glastonbury have revealed evidence for all the stages of cloth-making: combs, spindle-whorls, bobbins and loom-weights.[137]

FOOD WITHOUT SLAUGHTER

Milk and cheese

'The greater part of their food consists of milk, cheese and meat': so commented Julius Caesar about the Celt-related Germanic tribes he encountered during his conquest of Gaul in the mid-first century BC.[138] Strabo remarks that the British Celts used milk but did not make cheese.[139]

Milk could be obtained from cattle, sheep or goats. Sheep give a poor milk yield relative to that from goats, but goats are less easy to keep in a temperate climate and, since sheep were kept anyway for their wool, it is likely that they were milked as well.[140] We know of an Insular Celtic festival, Imbolc, on the 1st of February, which celebrated the early spring lactation of ewes.[141] The high neonatal mortality rate for lambs evidenced at Danebury meant that the milk of the corralled and bereft ewes was available for human consumption.[142]

Most milk was probably taken from cattle. The Dexter cattle raised at Butser were found to give an adequate milk supply even when fed on relatively poor pasture.[143] But certain factors need to be taken into account when cattle are reared for milk, especially during the Iron Age. Firstly, a milch-cow requires a great deal of water. Secondly, Celtic cows were smaller than modern species and gave milk for only a short time after calving.[144] If milk was required as a regular and important source of food, the management of cows and calving would have been a major preoccupation of the pastoral farmers. Cows mature at about two and a half years old; they will then calve virtually every year for five or six years after that. A cow gives her maximum yield when she is between 7 and 10 years old.[145]

Peter Reynolds observed that his Dexter cattle lactate for around ten months. If humans wished to take advantage of cows' milk, then either the calves could be weaned early (stoppers could be placed in the udder to prevent the calf from suckling, or cow and calf could be separated), or

Figure 2.21 Handle of bronze vessel, in the form of a cow and calf, sixth century BC, from the Hallstatt cemetery, Hallstatt, Austria. Length of cow: 14.4cm. Paul Jenkins.

they could have been culled for meat: culling occurred at certain Gaulish settlements, such as Villeneuve-Saint-Germain.[146] Certainly during the Iron Age and Romano-Celtic periods, there was some dependency upon cows' milk: for the community at Danebury, it was a source of protein along with meat. In the Roman period, the people living at Portchester in Sussex kept cattle that were mainly female, and the supposition is that they were exploited for milk.[147]

Milk is an important food, especially in temperate Europe. This is because it is a rich source of vitamin D, the other main source of which – sunlight – may be conspicuously scarce in this region. North Europeans, unlike some other peoples of the Old World (notably West Africans, Chinese and the peoples of Southeast Asia), are able to digest milk-sugar (lactose) because they possess the enzyme lactase. Iron Age Celts were therefore probably able to use milk in its liquid, unconverted form. They may, also, have made yoghurt and, despite Strabo's comment about the Britons, it is almost certain that they produced cheese. In his *Natural History*, Pliny[148] alludes to cheese-making among the Gauls, and observes that the Romans ate cheese imported from the provinces, particularly from the area of Nîmes. He especially mentions goat's cheese. Both wicker baskets and leather containers could have been used in the cheese-straining process.[149] Butter may also have been made, and used in cooking and flavouring. Both cheese and butter were presumably discovered in antiquity by accident: by chance observation of curdling milk in the case of cheese, and by the agitation of milk in the case of butter.

Eggs

The evidence for chickens, ducks and geese on Iron Age habitation sites and in graves suggests that these birds were kept for their eggs. They would have been a significant source of protein and a welcome variation in the diet of Celtic communities. Eggs were actually found as part of the grave-goods buried with the Celtic warrior chieftain and his chariot at La Gorge Meillet (Marne).[150] Deities depicted in Romano-Celtic iconography carry eggs: the healer-goddess Sirona at Hochscheid in Germany is depicted carrying a bowl containing three eggs; and the Genii Cucullati portrayed at Cirencester (Glos.) bear eggs as fertility symbols.[151]

Honey

The use of honey as a sweetening agent, for preserving and for fermenting to make mead must have been well known to Iron Age Celts. Beeswax may also have been recognized as useful, perhaps as a sealant for containers. Archaeological evidence is sparse, but there are sufficient indications for us to assume not only the collection of wild honey but also some knowledge of apiculture. Mead is attested, for instance, by the 'mead-vat' found in the grave of the Hochdorf Hallstatt prince, a huge bronze cauldron containing the sediment of 400 litres of mead.[152] A number of pottery containers found on Iron Age sites may well have been holders for honey or wax. That bee-keeping was practised in Iron Age Britain is evidenced by the discovery of the head of a worker-bee preserved in peat at the bottom of an Iron Age sump at Hardwick (Oxon.). Waterlogged wood from the site has yielded a radiocarbon date of 220±90 BC. The first century AD site of Caldecotte in Buckinghamshire has also revealed evidence of apiculture.[153]

The early Irish tales speak of honey and the making of mead.[154] Honey was used in cooking and there are Insular literary references to meat rubbed with honey and salt and cooked over an open fire. Salmon was also baked in honey. The name of the mythical Queen Medb of Connacht may be associated philologically with mead intoxication. Mead was drunk at the great sacred Celtic festivals, and the official name of the assembly hall at Tara (a royal court over which Medb presided) is Tech Midchuarta, the House of the Mead Circling. Classical writers refer to a honey drink which may or may not have been fermented to produce mead. Diodorus Siculus[155] says that the Celts washed honeycombs and used the washings as a drink.

BUTCHERY AND MEAT-EATING

> Their food consists of a small number of loaves of bread together with a huge amount of meat, either boiled or roasted on charcoal or on spits. They partake of this in a cleanly but leonine fashion, raising up whole limbs in both hands and biting off the meat, while any part which is hard to tear off they cut through with a small dagger which hangs attached to their sword-sheath in its own scabbard.[156]

There is no doubt that meat and meat products formed a substantial part of the Celtic diet. In addition to meat itself, the marrow could be extracted from the bones, the brain and tongue from the skull, and the bones then boiled for stock. Blood would have been important both for its dietary salt content and pigs' blood for the making of black-pudding, known by the Romans as *botellus*.

The Celts ate a wide range of meat, including beef, mutton, pork, poultry, venison, horse, hare and dog meat.[157] Recent studies of Iron Age communities in Gaul show that the type of meat most frequently eaten varied with each settlement. Among the Gauls generally, pork was consistently favoured,[158] though there were local preferences for beef at, for instance, Variscourt and Villeneuve (Aisne).[159] We have to be careful in assessing choice from the bones alone, since of course one ox will provide much more meat than one sheep or a single pig. The optimum time for butchery is when an animal achieves adulthood, which means at 3 to 4 years for beef-cattle and 2 years for a pig or sheep. But there is a great deal of evidence (see pp. 7–11) that the choice was made to utilize the living animal for work, milk or wool and to kill it only when its useful working life was over. Pigs, of course, were the exception: they both were and are raised almost solely for meat, and they would only have been spared longer than their prime culling time if they were needed for breeding. At the late La Tène site of Beauvais (Oise), where the bones were particularly well preserved, pig-bones were especially abundant, thereby making a valid study of killing-trends possible. Most of the pigs here were culled at between 1 and 2 years old. The males were slaughtered earlier than the females, partly because breeding sows would have been valued but also perhaps because the males were more aggressive and therefore troublesome to maintain.[160] Other than pigs, animals were generally killed earlier than in middle or old age only in exceptional circumstances: unnecessary males, barren females or surplus young might be culled because they were not contributing to the economy. Gaulish dogs were sometimes killed for food at the optimum time for meat,[161] suggesting that they were actually favoured for their flesh and not just eaten at times of food shortage. This happened at the sanctuary of Gournay, but here there could have been a ritual element in the choice of dog meat. Older horses which had been used first as working-animals were eaten, but sometimes on Gaulish sites there is evidence that they, too, were killed young for their food. At Epiais-Rhus in northern France, the skins of the horses were removed (perhaps for use as floor or bed coverings) and the good portions of meat taken.

Figure 2.22 Bronze boar figurine, with elaborately ornamented dorsal ridge, second or first century BC, Lunçani, Romania. Paul Jenkins.

Sheep were sometimes killed for their meat, at 2 or 3 years old. At Beauvais, some young lambs were culled, but at Hornaing (Nord) they were kept until they were 6 years old, presumably because wool production took precedence over meat provision.[162] Most cattle were eventually eaten, even if they had worked first: the cows were sometimes culled younger than oxen, implying that the use of cattle for traction could have been of greater importance than milk. Clearly the cows were not being used to pull ploughs here. At Villeneuve-Saint-Germain, for example, some cows were slaughtered quite young.[163]

The southern British site of Danebury has yielded a huge number of animal bones, making it possible to gain some idea of the meat-eating habits of the community.[164] Danebury people ate pork, beef, mutton and horsemeat. Pig bones were not present in large numbers, although pigs were bred on the site: many of the Danebury pigs were despatched as juveniles, with a small proportion of mature sows kept from the pot until their breeding-lives were over. Few of the abundant sheep at Danebury were killed at the time of their optimum meat-yield (2 years), but some were culled at a year, probably after they had been fattened by the spring grass. Most sheep were kept to old age for their wool. Cattle at Danebury were again mostly slaughtered only when they were too old for work. The same was true of horses, which were killed for food when they were no longer useful. Horses were eaten elsewhere in southern Britain, for instance at Ashville (Oxon.), but the practice was comparatively rare this side of the Channel.

The situation elsewhere in the south of England generally reflects the patterns seen at Danebury: sheep were often not killed for meat until they were old; the same was true for cattle, even in the Roman period when there was an increased requirement for beef and hides. Pork was not nearly as popular in pre-Roman Britain as in Gaul,[165] but pigs steadily increased in Britain through time until, by the Romano-Celtic period, much more pork was consumed. This may have been due, in part, to Roman tastes.[166] It is interesting that, despite the fact that pigs were not particularly favoured in the diet of British Iron Age communities, pigs and pork feature strongly in the early Welsh and Irish stories. The *hobeu* given as presents to Pryderi by Arawn, in the *Mabinogi*, were so highly prized that they were the cause of a full-scale war between Dyfed and Gwynedd.[167] In Ireland, pork was supreme and carried deep symbolic meanings. Time and again, the 'hero's portion' was the subject of dispute between warriors, each of whom considered the choice cut was his due.[168] This tradition of the champion's portion is also described by classical observers of the Celts. Diodorus Siculus has this to say: 'Brave warriors they honour with the finest portions of meat.'[169] Diodorus goes on to comment that this Celtic custom had its parallel in the epic tales of Homer.

Figure 2.23 Detail of bull-head terminal, on an iron firedog, first century BC/first century AD, Barton, Cambridgeshire. Paul Jenkins.

There is not a great deal of evidence for the eating of wild animals (chapter 3), though hunting was practised. Venison was probably con-sumed: mention has already been made of possible deer-ranching. In the early Irish sagas, a haunch of venison was occasionally offered as the champion's joint at the ritual feast, instead of pork.[170] Of other hunted species, hare was most frequently consumed. Likewise, there is little evidence for fish-eating, though negative data are probably misleading because fish bones are so small and fragile as to be difficult to identify, even when they have survived. But fishing is depicted occasionally at

Val Camonica, and fish-hooks were among the grave-goods found with the sixth century BC Hallstatt prince at Hochdorf in Germany.[171] Evidence for fish consumption, however, comes both from the vernacular literature and from the classical commentators. In Ireland salmon was eaten: it was sometimes prepared with honey, as we have seen. The classical author Athenaeus says of the fishing practices of the Celts: 'Those who live beside the rivers or near the Mediterranean or Atlantic eat fish in addition, baked fish, that is, with the addition of salt, vinegar and cumin.'[172]

Butchery techniques, curing and cooking

Gaulish communities had preferences not only as to species, but also as to cut. Sometimes ribs or legs were favoured, sometimes the shoulder, sometimes the head and brain. The heads of animals were frequently split to extract the brain or tongue. During the Iron Age the bones were carefully separated by cutting through the ligaments, often using a sharp knife, but at the late Iron Age site of Beauvais, both knives and choppers were used. Certainly during the Roman period, heavy cleavers were wielded to separate the carcase into joints by cutting through bones.[173]

Techniques of slaughtering often leave no traces on the bones which survive on Iron Age sites. Often the animal's throat must have been cut, and pigs were probably sometimes bled to death so that their blood could be collected and used separately. At the sanctuary of Gournay, the oxen sacrificed to the infernal gods were killed by a blow to the nape of the neck,[174] but this represents a highly ritualized slaughter and need not have been the norm. We do not know whether there were specialist butchers on large settlement sites: the probability is that everyone did their own killing and butchering.

After the meat was killed and jointed, it would either have been cooked for immediate consumption or cured and kept to be eaten later. Meat could be dried, smoked or salted.[175] Strabo mentions the salting of pork by the Gauls.[176] This meat-curing was probably carried out during the late autumn, after surplus animals had been culled.[177]

Cooking was mainly by means of spit-roasting or boiling, though some pork was grilled.[178] Diodorus comments on Celtic cooking practices: 'Beside them are hearths blazing with fire, with cauldrons and spits containing large pieces of meat.'[179] The Irish and Welsh stories frequently allude to cauldrons, and the Irish god, the Daghdha, had an enormous cauldron in which whole oxen, sheep and pigs were boiled.[180] Cooking utensils are sometimes attested archaeologically, most frequently in the form of cauldrons. The massive vessels at, for instance, Llyn Fawr (Mid Glam.) and Llyn Cerrig Bach on Anglesey, were found in religious contexts and were probably used for ritual feasting.[181] The Danebury excavators discovered iron hooks for suspending a cauldron over the fire (figure 2.24), two iron spits for skewering meat, and the remains of joints of beef and pork.[182] The curious flesh-hook decorated with swans found at Dunaverney in Co. Antrim[183] was undoubtedly designed for spearing pieces of meat as they boiled in the cauldron (figure 2.25).

Figure 2.24 Iron hooks for suspension of a cauldron over a cooking-fire, from the Danebury Iron Age hillfort, Hampshire. By courtesy of the Danebury Trust.

The useful carcase

After an animal had been slaughtered and its meat consumed, the inedible parts of its body were put to good use. The hide or pelt could be

Figure 2.25 Bronze 'flesh-fork' ornamented with swans and crows, seventh century BC, Dunaverney, Co. Antrim, Northern Ireland. Length: 60.7cm. Paul Jenkins.

used for clothing; the bones made into needles, combs and a host of other tools; the gut could be made into containers and its sinews into rope or string.

Hides and pelts

The production of leather and fur, like wool, was not influenced by an animal's age or sex. Leather was an important commodity in Celtic life. Strabo[184] refers to the export of hides from Britain to the Roman Empire. Cattle hides must have been in the greatest demand: leather was used for containers, shoes, clothing, saddles and harness, fish-net floats and boats. Originally the river coracles of Wales and the Irish sea-going curraghs were made of hides mounted upon a wooden framework. Pliny[185] refers to the Britons using boats of osier covered with stitched hides. Julius Caesar[186] alludes to the use, among the Veneti of north-west Gaul, of leather sails. Rawhide was utilized for the manufacture of rope, slings and whips.[187] Pigskin was sometimes used as well as cattle leather;[188] the early Irish stories tell of pigskin jackets worn by charioteers.[189] Dogskins were prepared at Villeneuve.[190] Cú Chulainn's charioteer Laeg, described in the 'Táin Bó Cuailnge', wore a 'skin-soft tunic of stitched deer's leather, light as a breath'.[191] Once the Roman army was established in Celtic territory, it made increased demands for hides, not only for armour, footwear and harness, but also for making leather tents. Cattle were probably herded in ranch-like enclosures, perhaps sometimes primarily for their hides. In any case, once an ox or cow reached the end of its useful life, it would be slaughtered, eaten and its hide used. Cú Chulainn wore a 'heroic deep battle-belt of stiff, tough tanned leather from the choicest parts of the hides of seven yearlings . . . and a dark apron of well-softened black leather from the choicest parts of the hides of four yearlings'.[192]

There is evidence of tanning at some sites such as Villeneuve (Aisne).[193] Before the Roman period, it was done by means of smoke and oils. There is no pre-Roman evidence for vegetable tanning, which requires pits for long soaking.[194] Leather is occasionally preserved, usually because of its immersion in a waterlogged deposit. The Danish

Iron Age bog-body, Tollund Man, wore a leather cap and girdle.[195] In the Roman period, shoes and other leather items are found in such contexts as wells. The Roman fort of Vindolanda in north Britain produced a great deal of evidence for leatherworking.[196] One of the most remarkable early Iron Age finds is at Hallstatt in Austria, where hide objects used by the salt miners in the mid-first millennium BC were preserved by the salt itself. Bags and shoes survived, and a splendid cowhide hod, with the hair still attached, was used for carrying salt (or the salt miner's lunch); it closely resembles a modern duffle-bag.[197]

Although pelts of wild and domestic beasts were utilized (figure 3.8), there is comparatively little evidence for the use of the wild, hunted species. However, Diodorus Siculus states that 'their custom is to sleep on the ground upon the skins of wild animals'.[198] The 'Táin' refers to the use of skin coverings as bedclothes: a charioteer asks 'put the skin covering under my head and let me sleep for a while'.[199] Bears must have been hunted for their thick pelts, but almost the only archaeological evidence consists of the late Iron Age chieftain buried at Welwyn in Hertfordshire, who lay on a bearskin. The Hallstatt prince interred at Hochdorf was laid on a bronze couch, on a bed of horsehair, wool and badgerskin, the fibres of which were preserved embedded in the metal.[200] Fox fur was used to make an armlet for Lindow Man, who was ritually murdered by strangulation and buried in a marshy pool in Cheshire sometime between the fourth century BC and the first century AD.[201] Dog pelts were used, for instance at Villeneuve and at Beauvais,[202] and we have the evidence of Diodorus Siculus[203] to the effect that the Celts sat on the 'skins of wolves or dogs' when dining.

Bone, horn and gut

Bone assumed a lesser importance in metal-using societies than in the Neolithic and earlier times. But it was none the less used for small artefacts, like needles or toggles. Bone and antler were made into combs for plucking and carding wool. Weaving-shuttles, spindle-whorls and musical pipes could also be fashioned from bone.[204] It was a useful resource since it was present anyway in the food debris and did not have to be specially obtained.

Horn casings were made into drinking-horns and spoons. The horn was softened by immersion in boiling water and the outer keratinous sheath then removed from the useless bony core, which was discarded. Pliny refers to the 'northern barbarians' using aurochs horn for drinking-vessels; and Caesar mentions the same practice among the Germanic tribes.[205] On some British sites, goats may have been kept for their horns: horn-cores are sometimes found chopped from the skull.[206]

Figure 2.26 Bronze goat figurine, with exaggerated horns, Romano-British, Dumbuck, Dumbartonshire, Scotland. Maximum height: 6.1cm. Reproduced by courtesy of the Trustees of the National Museums of Scotland.

There is evidence of horn-working in Roman London, where horns were hacked off the head with a cleaver.[207]

Gut was used for making containers, for instance for sausage or black-pudding; for making bow-strings and fishing-lines.[208] Even the lowliest part of the animal was found to have a role to play in the economic aspect of Celtic life.

3

PREY AND PREDATOR: THE CELTIC HUNTER

Our knowledge of hunting practices among the Celts comes from a number of sources. First, such classical writers as Strabo, Caesar and Arrian refer to hunting in Celtic communities, who had a fine reputation for their prowess. Caesar[1] remarks of the related Germanic peoples he encountered in the Rhineland, that 'all their life is spent in hunting and in the practice of the art of war'. Second, there is a certain amount of iconography, where hunters and their quarry are depicted. A rich source is the rock art of Camonica Valley in north Italy, which displays numerous scenes of stag-hunting, snaring and trapping. Third, we have the faunal evidence of wild and therefore hunted species in the bone assemblages of Iron Age sites. Here it is the negative evidence which is most evocative, indicating that hunting must have played a very minor role as a source of food.

THE HUNTER'S QUARRY

The three sources of evidence alluded to above provide a wide variety of information as to the kinds of beasts which were hunted by the Celts. They included the larger, mainly herbivorous creatures such as the stag, boar and wild aurochs and the smaller, carnivorous fur-bearers, like the badger, fox and stoat. The hare was also surprisingly popular as prey.

Caesar refers to the hunting of the aurochs, a kind of large wild cattle (now extinct), among the Germans.[2] He describes how keen the Germanic tribes were on hunting the creatures, catching them in pits. The horns were particularly prized and used as drinking-vessels. Caesar recounts how the hunters who killed the greatest number of aurochs brought the horns into a public place as evidence of their prowess, and won praise from their peers. Archaeological evidence for the aurochs is scarce, though it was certainly still in existence during the Iron Age in western Europe. One example from this period comes from a grave at Rouliers in the Ardennes, where the phalange of an aurochs was buried in the tomb of a man.[3] The baseplate of the Gundestrup Cauldron bears

Figure 3.1 Third century BC bronze deer, Rákos Csongrád, Hungary.
Height: 3.7cm. Paul Jenkins.

a scene in repoussé of a huge dying bull (figure 5.1) being attacked by two huntsmen accompanied by hounds.[4] It is most likely that an aurochs is depicted here.

Other creatures which were prolific during the Iron Age, but where there is little evidence that they were hunted, include the wolf and the bear. Wolf phalanges have been found at the Iron Age site of Villeneuve-Saint-Germain in northern France.[5] Wolf teeth were perforated as ornaments at the Hallstatt Iron Age site of Choisy-au-Bac (Oise);[6] and wolf was found at the sanctuary of Digeon (Somme), which is distinctive in having a number of wild animal deposits.[7] Wolves were important in coin symbolism (see chapter 6);[8] and a terracotta trumpet-mouth in the form of a snarling wolf's head comes from Numantia in Spain.[9] Bears are very rare in the archaeological record. Bear teeth come from the cemetery of Mont-Troté in the Ardennes, where they were used as necklace-beads.[10] Interestingly, a Romano-Celtic bear-goddess, Artio, is known from Muri near Berne in Switzerland (figure 8.13),[11] on a bronze group where a goddess is accompanied by a large bear.

45

Two animals which stand out, at any rate in the iconography, are the boar and the stag. The boar has often been seen as the Celtic hunted beast *par excellence*, but Patrice Meniel[12] warns us that this image is a cliché (immortalized by Asterix's companion Obelix) which is based upon a muddled statement by Strabo,[13] who describes large fierce pigs which roamed free and which were extremely savage when approached. This, together with the known Celtic predilection for pork, has given rise to the concept of the Celts continually going off on wild-boar hunts, in order to provide meat for feasting. But the evidence of animal bones from archaeological sites suggests that hunting for food was not an important activity. Except in the case of very young animals, it is perfectly possible to distinguish pigs from boars in the bone assemblages of Iron Age sites: boars are much bigger and more robust than pigs. What is clear from a study of this material is that boars were not generally eaten: they were not a common source of food. If they were hunted, they were not brought back to settlements and consumed. Perhaps they were feasted on at hill sites in the forests. Evidence for domestic pigs is very abundant, but boar bones are rare.[14] Where boars do occur on Iron Age sites, the lack of cut-marks on their bones implies that the carcases were not butchered.[15] At the sanctuary of Digeon, where many wild species were present, boars formed part of the assemblage, probably as the result of some kind of ritual, perhaps involving sacrifice (see chapter 5).[16]

However, despite the dearth of evidence for boar-hunting from the faunal deposits on early Celtic sites, the image of the importance of the boar-hunt is by no means confined to Strabo and may be inferred also from the evidence of iconography and of other classical writers. Thus, on a bronze cult-wagon of perhaps second or first century BC date from Mérida in Spain, a boar is depicted being hunted by a mounted sportsman.[17] Again, a bronze group from Balzars, Liechtenstein, depicts soldiers with a boar and stag: this was modelled between the third and first centuries BC.[18] At Matzhausen in Bavaria (figure 3.3), a long-necked flagon dating to around 400–300 BC is decorated with an incised hunt scene which includes boars and stags pursued by a hunting-dog.[19] Boars are important generally in Iron Age iconography: they appear on the Gundestrup Cauldron;[20] and boar figurines are common, either as statuettes or as helmet crests (see chapters 4 and 6). The first-century BC bronze boar from Hounslow near London (figure 5.12) almost certainly surmounted a helmet.[21] By contrast, figurines from Lunçani in Romania (figure 2.22) and Báta in Hungary may have been freestanding statuettes or they may have decorated battle-standards. Boar images occur on coins (figure 3.4) and as sword-stamps,[22], reinforcing their imagery of ferocity and indomitability by means of their erect dorsal ridges. Among classical writers referring to the boar-hunt as an important sporting

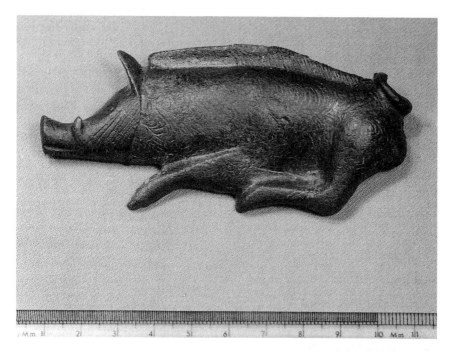

Figure 3.2 Bronze plaque of slain boar from the first-century AD shrine of Muntham Court, Sussex. By courtesy of Worthing Museum and Art Gallery.

activity, Arrian alludes to boars as a favourite quarry, which required great skill from the huntsman and courage from his horse and dogs.[23] Martial refers to the existence of boar-traps to lessen the risk to the hunter.[24]

The stag was hunted by the Celts but, once again, the evidence of the bones is at variance with other forms of data, notably the iconography. However, there is more faunal evidence for Iron Age stag-hunting than for hunting boars.[25] Large ungulates such as deer can cause grave damage to crops, and it is probable that this was the primary reason that they were hunted by farmers. The density of forest cover in Gaul and Britain during the pre-Roman periods was certainly significantly greater than now. Indeed, Caesar refers to the thick woods of north-east Gaul. But though deer are essentially woodland creatures, they can adapt to sparser forest cover, using what shelter there is by day and foraging by night. Stags were hunted in Compiègne[26] and at other sites in the Oise region.[27] At the Digeon shrine, ten stags were slaughtered[28] and their skull caps with antlers attached were utilized, probably for some ritual, perhaps shamanistic purpose, as head-dresses. In Britain, there is some evidence for stag-hunting,[29] sometimes apparently for ritual purposes:

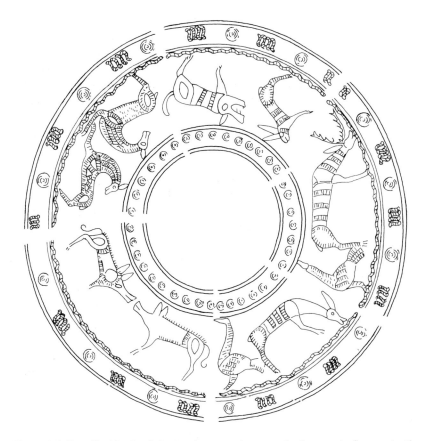

Figure 3.3 Detail of incised decoration on a long-necked ceramic flagon, in the form of geese, boars, a dog, deer and a hare, fourth century BC, Matzhausen, Germany. Height of pot: 23.8cm. Miranda Green.

deer bones and antlers occur in Iron Age ritual shafts.[30] The first period at the Danebury hillfort in Hampshire (between about 1000 and 500 BC) is indicated by a series of pits which follow the line taken by the later defences. One of these contained an undoubtedly ritual assemblage of carefully selected species, including red and roe deer.[31] Antlers were found in a ritual pit at Newstead in southern Scotland.[32] At Wasperton in Warwickshire, a Romano-Celtic ritual pit contained a deposit of two sets of antlers with parts of the skull caps attached, arranged to form a square. These had been placed beneath a layer of burnt material; and in the centre of the square a fire had been lit.[33]

Iconography displays hunted stags (figure 3.5) or the stag-hunt itself; the seventh-century BC bronze cult wagon model from Strettweg in Austria depicts what is probably a ritual stag-hunt; two stags with enormous antlers are accompanied by foot-soldiers and horsemen; the central figure is a goddess who holds a vessel of liquid above her head, as if in benediction.[34] On an early Iron Age pot at Sopron in Hungary, dating to the seventh or sixth century BC, a scene depicts mounted horsemen with spears hunting a stag.[35] Similarly, the Matzhausen pot (figure 3.3) shows deer, an antlered stag and other wild beasts chased by a hunting-dog.[36] A figurine of a wounded stag, dating to the first century BC, comes from Saalfelden in Austria.[37] A Romano-Celtic sculpture from the mountain shrine of Le Donon (Vosges) portrays a stag in company with his hunter (see pp. 60, 64).[38]

The most interesting illustration of stag-hunting occurs at Camonica Valley, where the rock art of the Bronze and Iron Ages abounds in stag symbolism. Camonica Valley is a natural corridor, rimmed by high mountains, which was habitually used by herds and was therefore potentially a rich kill-site. On the Naquane rock, a seventh-century BC stag-hunt scene consists of hunters, of whom one is ithyphallic, surrounding a half-human, half-stag creature with huge antlers (figure 3.13).[39] This is one of many Iron Age hunting scenes at Camonica, where stags are pursued by huntsmen, sometimes on horseback, and accompanied by hounds.[40] Here the divine element in the stag-hunt is most prominent: the stag is quarry but also divinity. Some carvings show hunters in prayer grouped around a trapped stag.[41] On a Naquane representation, a group of armed figures dances round a large stag which

Figure 3.4 Celtic coin depicting stag and boar, Maidstone, Kent. By courtesy of the National Museum of Wales.

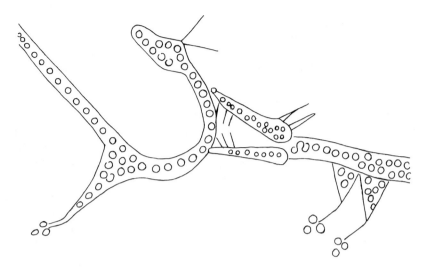

Figure 3.5 Detail of pot with incised and stamped decoration, in the form of a deer attacked by a dog or wolf, third to second century BC, Lábatlan, Komáron, Hungary. Height of pot: 40.2cm. Miranda Green.

stands before a temple.[42] Another scene depicts the worship of a stag with huge antlers, surrounded by people and other, smaller stags, as if the central animal is divine.[43]

Classical writers make some allusions to stags and stag-hunting. Arrian mentions the use of horses for wearing down stags until they become exhausted.[44] This observation is borne out by some of the iconography, where the hunters are mounted. Julius Caesar[45] shows an amazing credulity in his description of elks in Germany which, he says, have no joints to their legs but sleep leaning against trees and, if they fall over, cannot get up and are thus easy prey for hunters.

Curiously enough, the hare appears to have been the animal most commonly hunted for food, according to the faunal evidence. This is despite Caesar's assertion that the Britons regarded hares as taboo for food.[46] Touget (Gers) has produced a stone statue of a hunter-god bearing a large hare in his arms (figure 3.11).[47] Arrian refers to hunting hares, using dogs both to flush out the quarry and to bring it down into the trap or snare.[48] Hares like open spaces, fields and pastures, where they can see a long way and can rely on speed to carry them away from danger. They feed at night, generally lying under cover during the day. In those Iron Age sites of northern Gaul which have been the subject of recent study by Patrice Meniel,[49] the hare is especially important among wild species represented in faunal assemblages. This is particularly marked since the bones of hare are more fragile and easily destroyed than those of more robust creatures like deer but, even so, they are represented in greater numbers than the bigger animals. In an early La Tène site in Compiègne, hare formed 7 per cent of the bone material, compared to red deer 2 per cent and roe deer 1 per cent. At Tartigny a grave produced the remains of a dog, a horse and a hare in association, as if a hunter's burial were represented.[50] In a Gaulish Compiègne village the proportions of dog, hare and horse are again high.[51] All species of what might be termed game are comparatively rare on Celtic sites, whether settlements, graves or shrines. Animals other than the stag and hare appear in extremely small numbers in real terms. Their presence may be attributed either to their value as fur-bearers or to their involvement in ritual. The settlement at Villeneuve-Saint-Germain contained what is considered to be a rich deposit of bones representing fur-bearing animals: out of 70 bones of wild species, 60 were of fox or badger. Wolf and stoat were present in only very small numbers and, clearly, had been less systematically hunted.[52] The ritual element in the use of fur-bearing wild animals is especially interesting: a deposit of five weasels' heads comes from what must have been a sacred deposit at Bordeaux.[53] An odd assemblage comes from an Iron Age ritual pit at Winklebury (Hants), consisting of a red deer and twelve foxes. Special pit-deposits like this were generally placed at the bottom of storage pits before they were finally filled with rubbish and loose soil (see chapter 5).[54] Some of the Gaulish sanctuaries, such as Digeon, Mirebeau and Ribemont, were found to contain remains of foxes, but these are very rare.[55] Fox-hunting is depicted at Camonica Valley.[56] The Iron Age Cheshire bog-body Lindow Man was ritually murdered some time in the late first millennium BC, and placed in a marshy pool wearing nothing but an armlet made of fox-fur.[57] This suggestion of a ritual association with foxes is perhaps borne out by the presence of Celtic personal names linked with the word for fox. The name Louernius means 'Son of the Fox', and belonged to an Arvernian chief: Athenaeus[58] comments upon his immense wealth and his practice of holding great festive gatherings

Figure 3.6 Potsherd decorated with a frieze of stamped hares, fourth century BC, Libkoviče, Czechoslovakia. Length of hares: *c.*2cm. Miranda Green.

in a huge enclosure at which he liberally distributed largesse in the form of treasure to his people. The name Louernius crops up again, on a set of third-century AD pewter tableware at Appleford (Berks.) and on an altar at the Cotswold shrine of Uley, in the fourth century AD. Anne Ross[59] is of the view that the Celts revered the fox for his fiery coat and cunning nature.

Other species occur only very occasionally in the archaeological record: wild cat is represented at Camonica Valley[60] but is very uncommon in faunal remains. Beaver teeth appear at the Rouliers Iron Age cemetery;[61] frog or toad bones have been found in grave contexts, as at 'La Croisette', Acy.[62] Sometimes a wild and presumably hunted species – the bear for instance – will appear only in sepulchral or sacred contexts and never on a settlement site.

There is some evidence for the hunting of wild birds: wild duck was found at the Gournay (Oise) sanctuary; thrush and blackbird at the Ribemont shrine.[63] There were partridge bones at the 'La Noue Mouroy' cemetery at Acy-Romance.[64] Of particular interest is the raven, which is heavily overrepresented at some sites, for instance at Winklebury and Danebury, both Hampshire hillforts. The body of a raven with wings outspread was buried at the bottom of a pit, which also contained a pig, at Winklebury.[65] Ravens were buried in pits at Danebury, their numbers being far in excess of their normal representation in proportion to other wild birds.[66] Crows and ravens could have been hunted because they were a threat to crops, but there is more likely to have been a ritual element in these deposits (see chapter 5).

REASONS FOR HUNTING

Why were wild animals hunted in the Celtic Iron Age? The faunal evidence from bone assemblages indicates that wild species formed an extremely small part of the diet of these communities, so food was not a primary reason (chapter 2). There is some evidence for butchery, so at least some of the herbivores were eaten. Other reasons for hunting included the desire for fur, the need to protect farmland from the destructive activities of such animals as deer, and finally – and this is likely to have been the primary reason – for sport.

The hunting of the larger animals – like stags and boars – may well have been a sporting pastime for the aristocratic élite, who would have seen hunting as a simulation of and practice for warfare. This may partly account for the small number of such beasts represented in the faunal assemblages of Iron Age settlement sites and the absence of butchery marks on boar bones.[67] Barry Cunliffe says that if hunting took place at all at Danebury, it must have been merely for sport, since wild-animal bones are so rare.[68] Arrian, writing in the second century AD, speaks of

Figure 3.7 Bronze figurine of crow or raven from the Romano-Celtic sanctuary of Woodeaton, Oxfordshire. Betty Naggar.

hunting as a sport for the wealthy[69] and refers to hunting among the Celts as a noble pleasure rather than a livelihood, though he says that for the Celts hunting was not just a noble pastime but a daily exercise of skill and courage, involving several levels of society.[70] The idea of hunting as an activity of the élite would fit in well with the hunting methods employed by the Celts, which involved horses (expensive creatures to maintain) and specialized hunting-dogs. Weapons of war could indeed be used with equal effect in hunting: Strabo remarks that the Celts used a spear-like stick both for hunting birds and in war.[71]

There is evidence both from classical writers and from archaeology that wild animals were hunted for their skins (see also chapter 2). Diodorus Siculus[72] speaks of the use of wild beasts' pelts by the Celts for bedding and of wolfskins for covering house floors. The young late Iron Age chieftain whose remains were interred in a rich grave at Welwyn (Herts.) was laid on a bearskin.[73] The earlier Iron Age Hallstatt prince buried in the fantastically rich barrow at Hochdorf in Germany was laid to rest on a bronze couch covered in a badgerskin.[74] Wild animals are poorly represented in the skinning debris (tail and paw bones) of Gaulish sites, but there is some evidence for wolf, badger, fox, polecat

Figure 3.8 Stone image of a man (rear view shown) possibly wearing an animal pelt, Cirencester, Gloucestershire. Betty Naggar.

and stoat. Though bears were plentiful during this period, their skeletons are not generally found in the faunal assemblages: their skins must therefore have been removed away from the settlements, if they were used at all.[75] We have seen (pp. 44–5) that occasionally the teeth of bear and wolf were used as ornaments and it is possible that such creatures were hunted specifically to provide decoration for the dead. Foxes may have been hunted for their pelts, as is shown by Lindow Man's fox-fur bracelet. But the fox remains at the sanctuaries of Mirebeau and Ribemont indicate from butchery marks on the bones[76] that foxes were sometimes consumed. The strange deposit of red deer and twelve foxes in a pit at Winklebury in Hampshire[77] must surely indicate the hunting of these creatures for a primarily ritual purpose (see chapter 5). At Danebury, there is evidence that both badgers and foxes were trapped for their fur.[78] Interestingly, at the settlement of Villeneuve-Saint-Germain, the tail and paw bones of animals (indicative of skinning) were found on a part of the site which was kept separate from the areas of food preparation.[79] The small numbers of fur-bearing animals represented on Celtic sites probably does not reflect reality. Wolves, bears, badgers, foxes must all have been hunted with some frequency, but the skeletal evidence is rare, implying that there must have been many instances where skinning took place away from the settlements themselves, presumably at the kill-sites.

Wild and hunted food animals are relatively rare on Iron Age sites, such species being often represented by less than 5 per cent of all animal bones. We have seen that boars are not commonly found in the faunal material and that, if they do occur, the lack of cut-marks suggests they were not butchered and consumed on settlement sites. Of all the hunted animals, the hare seems to have been most popular, even though Caesar says that hares were not eaten in Britain.[80] At Epiais-Rhus (Val d'Oise), the animals hunted for food were mainly hare, followed by roebuck, red deer, stag and boar. In the villages of Compiègne and in the settlements of the Somme region, again the hare was the wild animal most frequently consumed. Patrice Meniel[81] makes the point that, although wild animals are few on northern Gaulish sites, they are none the less consistently present in small quantities on all the sites investigated. In Britain, at the Meare lake village (Som.),[82] a wide range of wild resources was utilized, including boar and deer, marsh-birds and such fish as pike and eel. Wild game birds, like geese, swans and ducks, were also snared at Danebury.[83] Generally speaking, there is little evidence that fish were commonly eaten in the Iron Age, though the rock art of Camonica Valley depicts the occasional fish being netted or harpooned.[84] However, fish bones are fragile and are not readily preserved on archaeological sites. The unequivocal message conveyed by the archaeological evidence is that hunting was peripheral to the Iron Age economy and, in terms of food, served only to supplement and add variety to a meat diet whose requirements were generally met by farming.[85] Interestingly, whilst there is a great deal of evidence of culinary sacrifices and ritual feasting which involved meat, evidence from many of the Celtic shrines – such as Gournay, Hayling Island and many others – suggests that wild beasts were not used at all.[86]

HUNTING METHODS

The hunter's companions

Both classical commentators and iconography throw light on the way game was hunted by the Celts. There were different kinds of hunting: the peasant wishing to rid himself of pests threatening his crops would perhaps use dogs, traps and snares. The knight-hunter, maybe practising the art of war, would use swift horses and sometimes specially bred and trained dogs. The main method employed in the pursuit of large and fast game certainly involved horses and big, aggressive dogs. The best type of horse for long-distance endurance would be lean and tough.[87] Thus the hunter could follow his prey on horseback over long distances. The use of horses in hunting is reflected iconographically: the seventh-century BC Strettweg cult-wagon carries bronze figurines of horsemen and foot-soldiers in the company of two stags, in a ritual hunting scene.[88] The Iron Age rock art of the Camonica Valley includes scenes of mounted hunters in pursuit of or surrounding stags; other game, such as wild goats, were followed in a similar manner.[89] A pot dated seventh to sixth-century BC from the Hungarian site of Sopron depicts a stag hunted by mounted spearsmen. The Camonica hunters are shown armed with spears and shields, just like warriors,[90] and they often hunted in pairs. One representation is of a horseman, led by an armed servant, hunting with a long curved stick, rather like a hockey stick.[91] This is especially interesting since Strabo alludes to the use the Celts made, when they were hunting birds, of a spear-like stick 'with a range greater than an arrow'.[92] Strabo also comments on the use of bows and slings. The spear or lance was a weapon commonly used by huntsmen, especially on horseback. The second- or first-century BC bronze wagon-model from Mérida in Spain depicts a spearman on horseback chasing a boar. He wears greaves like a soldier.[93] According to Camonican iconography, the lance was the favourite weapon for despatching animals once they had been snared.[94] If he was a rider, the hunter would probably have belonged to the upper echelons of society. So too, perhaps, would the falconers; there is a hint that falconry may have been employed in hunting during the La Tène Iron Age: bronze brooches from the Dürrnberg hillfort in Austria (figure 3.10) depict birds of prey wearing collars.[95] Certainly hawks were familiar to the Celts of the early vernacular legends; gifts exchanged between Pwyll, lord of Arberth, and Arawn, king of the Otherworld, in the First Branch of the *Mabinogi*, include horses, greyhounds and hawks.[96]

Dogs played an important part in hunting: Strabo[97] refers to the export of British hunting-dogs to Rome. He describes them as small, rough-haired, strong, swift and keen-scented. The continued fame of British dogs is demonstrated by a later writer, a Roman poet of Carthaginian origin, Marcus Aurelius Olympius Nemesianus, who wrote a poem called the 'Cynegetica' ('The Hunt') in about AD 283–84. He includes these lines in the poem: 'Besides the dogs bred in Sparta and Molossus, you should also raise the breed which comes from Britain, because this dog is fast and good for our hunting.'[98] Claudian describes British dogs as strong enough to break the necks of great bulls.[99] Representations at Camonica Valley depict captured wild animals surrounded by packs of dogs. Here there is evidence that the

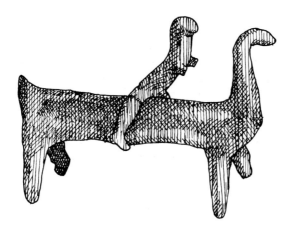

Figure 3.9 Clay figurine of horseman, sixth century BC, Speikern, Germany.
Length of horse: 8.7cm. Paul Jenkins.

Camunians trained their dogs to drive beasts into snares.[100] Arrian discusses the use of horses and hounds in hunting:[101] he alludes to the employment of both these creatures in wearing down prey until it was too tired to run further, when the hounds would flush small game out of cover. Arrian comments upon Gaulish dogs called *vertragi*, whose name, he says, derived from the Celtic word for 'speed'. He describes them as being muscular, with lean flanks, broad chests, long necks, big ears and long muzzles. Strabo[102] remarks that horses and dogs each enjoyed privileged status among the Celts because of their usefulness in the hunt.

There is some archaeological evidence for the presence of large, perhaps specially bred hunting-dogs. Some of the Danebury dogs were sufficiently large and robust to have been used for hunting quite large prey. The dogs found in the subterranean shrine of second- or third-century AD date in Cambridge[103] were probably hunting-dogs; they were sacrificed along with a horse and a bull. The later Romano-Celtic shrine at Lydney (Glos.) was dedicated to a British god Nodens: many images of dogs were found on the site (chapter 8) including a superb bronze deer-hound (figure 8.2).[104] It is very likely that some dogs were specially bred and trained for their aggressive temperaments. The close association between horses and dogs is reflected in some Iron Age bone assemblages, where their remains are found together in what may be ritual deposits, perhaps associated with a hunting cult. This occurred at Danebury often enough to be statistically significant,[105] as also in cemeteries in the Compiègne region of northern Gaul and elsewhere. A grave

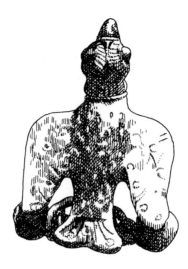

Figure 3.10 Bronze brooch in the form of a bird of prey wearing a collar, fourth century BC, from a grave at the Dürrnburg, Hallein, Austria. Length: 3.2cm. Paul Jenkins.

in the cemetery at Tartigny (Oise) may have been a hunter's tomb: here, remains of a dog, horse and hare were found, carefully selected for deposition in the grave. The dog was about a year old and, in a rather gruesome ritual act, it had been skinned and eviscerated. The horse was represented only symbolically, by the placing of its mandible in the tomb.[106]

Traps and snares

Traps, pits, snares and lassos were all employed in the hunt. Caesar, speaking of German hunting methods, alludes to the capture of the wild aurochs by digging pits into which the animals fell and were trapped.[107] Martial refers to the use of boar-traps, which lessened the danger to hunters.[108] Modest hunting, perhaps undertaken by peasants rather than the aristocracy, both for food and to protect the crops, seems to have been particularly dependent upon snares, lassos and traps.[109] All these methods are depicted on the rock art of the Iron Age Camunians. Some scenes show aquatic or marsh-birds caught by snares and then dispatched with a spear or axe. The Camunians set snares for small animals, like fox and hare, and the dogs would often do the rest.[110] The negative evidence of archaeology is reflected in the rock art, in that fishing is rarely depicted by the Camunian communities. But

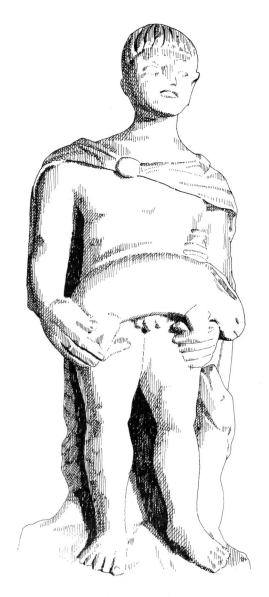

Figure 3.11 Stone statue of a hunter-god with knife, hound and hare,
Romano-Celtic date, Touget, Gers, France. Height: 75cm. Paul Jenkins.

there are a few carvings which record the catching of fish using harpoons or traps.[111]

THE IMAGE OF THE HUNTER

The image of the Celtic hunter is projected by the iconography . Often he is armed like a warrior with his spear, sword and shield. He is on horseback or unmounted and he is frequently accompanied by his dogs. In the vernacular sources of Ireland and Wales, we are presented with the description of the hunter as a nobleman with his thoroughbred horse, greyhounds and hawks. Such a man is Manawydan, the superhuman hero of the Third Branch of the *Mabinogi*, and Pwyll of the First Branch (see chapter 7). The Mérida waggon shows us a naked, mounted warrior with greaves, spear and hunting-dogs. The Strettweg stag-hunters have shields; the hunters on the bronze group from Balzars (Liechtenstein) wear leather armour; the stone hunter-god at Touget (Gers) (figure 3.11) is naked but for a cloak and a sword. He is accompanied by a large hound and holds a hare in his arms. The Camunian hunters have spears and shields, horses and dogs: these images are especially interesting since some of the hunters are portrayed as ithyphallic, suggesting a link between virility, fertility and the hunt (see figure 3.13). This is quite comprehensible in that hunting is an aggressive, masculine, conquering activity pitting man against the forces of wild nature. Perhaps, too, the use of the thrusting, penetrating spear reflects male potency. In the Baringo region of Kenya, spears are symbolic of young manhood and sexual prowess.[112]

HUNTING AND THE SUPERNATURAL

The relationship of the hunter to his prey is equivocal and ambiguous: this is reflected in some of the iconography. There is no doubt about the desire of the hunter to overcome and kill his quarry. But there is also respect and the animal must in some manner consent to its death in order that the harmony of nature be maintained. So the weapons would have to be made in the correct manner and the right rituals observed. This is exactly the kind of attitude to wild animals displayed in the hunting communities of the North American Indians. This may be why some of the hunter-gods depicted in Celtic iconography display a close, even tender relationship between hunter and hunted: the Touget huntsman[113] carries his hare in his arms, not by the ears or slung over his shoulder. The hunter at the Vosges sanctuary of Le Donon rests his hand affectionately on the antler of the stag standing fearlessly next to him.[114]

Figure 3.12 Stone figure of a horned hunter-god with torc, bow and billhook, Romano-Celtic date, La Celle-Mont-Saint-Jean, Sarthe, France. Paul Jenkins.

Classical sources, the vernacular Welsh and Irish tradition, archaeo-zoological evidence and iconography all make a very positive and direct link between hunting and the supernatural. Religion and the hunt were closely associated. Killing wild animals was dangerous, an activity which required the will of both the victim and the gods. The hunter needed to protect himself from his prey and also from the risk of unbalancing nature by taking a life. Hunters entered into a kind of relationship with their quarry, and because the slaughter of animals was sometimes necessary in order that a community might survive, the hunt itself became a composite symbol of death and resurrection or regeneration. There was thus a seemingly direct exchange of life for death.[115] Arrian states that ancient Celts never went on hunting expeditions without the blessing of the gods.[116] In a sense, hunting itself was a form of ritual activity which needed both permission and assistance from the divine powers.[117] Since hunting could be either for sport or for food, the hunter-deities could themselves be associated with war or with abundance. Arrian's comments on the attitude of the Celts to hunting make it clear that the activity was perceived as a theft from the natural world: thus hunting had to be redeemed by a reciprocal payment, a life for a life. So Arrian explains that hunting cult-practices consisted of payment made in the form of offerings in respect of the different creatures hunted. The wealth thus annually accumulated was used to buy a domestic animal to sacrifice to the superna-tural powers. Arrian alludes to a hunter-goddess to whom this sacrifice was made, together with the first-fruits of the hunt, on the occasion of the goddess's birthday. This account of hunting sacrifice is interesting: in order to fulfil the 'life for a life' bond, a domestic beast was exchanged for a wild one. Perhaps the deity regarded this as a more valuable offering than one of her own wild creatures. The necessity, in religious terms, of substituting one life for another is described elsewhere of humans, by Julius Caesar, who speaks of the Gauls' habit of sacrificing humans in time of war.[118]

There are other literary allusions by Graeco-Roman commentators concerning hunting and the gods. Like Arrian, Diodorus Siculus[119] refers (indirectly this time) to the offering of the first-fruits of the hunt, when discussing the Celtic practice of offering up the decapitated heads of their enemies to the gods: 'they nail up these first fruits (severed heads) upon their houses, just as do those who lay low wild animals in certain kinds of hunting.' Strabo[120] describes a horrific form of Celtic human sacrifice, whereby huge wicker images of men were built, filled with humans, cattle and different species of wild beast (presumably specially caught for the purpose), and burnt as sacrificial offerings.

Though the archaeozoological or faunal evidence of wild animal re-mains from Celtic Iron Age sites is so sparse, certain deposits are closely associated with ritual (see chapter 5). Sanctuaries like that at Gournay, with their evidence for ritual feasting, are significantly lacking in the bones of wild beasts, indicating perhaps a deliberate avoidance of such creatures as religious food. But one sanctuary, Digeon (Somme), does show evidence of ritual activity which was specifically associated with wild creatures. The most spectacular behaviour represented at this shrine concerned the apparent massacre of a number of stags in order to make use of the skullcaps with antlers attached.[121] If the interpretation of this evidence is correct, then it looks as if the head and antlers could have been worn, perhaps in fertility or hunting ceremonies, where a shaman-priest dressed up as a deer in order magically to attract the herd and promote a successful hunting expedition.

In Britain, wild animals were associated with ritual shafts and pits.[122] A pit at Newstead in southern Scotland contained sets of antlers, deliberately placed there as if for a religious purpose.[123] Two pits at Ipswich in Suffolk each contained a piece of hare fur; a ritual shaft at Ashill, Norfolk, contained a deposit of antlers, pots and boar tusks;[124] and there are other examples of this kind of functionally inexplicable behaviour. In Romano-Celtic Chelmsford, a young boar was buried entire, perhaps as a foundation-offering, to bring good luck to a building; at Sopron in Hungary, an Iron Age ritual deposit contained a complete boar, packed into a stone-lined grave.[125]

The supernatural element in hunting is prominently displayed in the iconography of the Celtic Iron Age and Romano-Celtic period. The veneration of an essentially rural people for the natural world manifests itself in art, where motifs and designs based on deer, boars and birds abound. Boar images are particularly common as figurines or as war emblems (see chapter 6).[126]

The imagery of Camonica Valley is particularly rich in hunting symbolism. Stags are depicted with immense antlers, perhaps evocative of supernatural status; the hunted stag was a divinity as well as prey. In the Bronze Age, the Camunian stag-god appears in the rock art as a god of hunting. The divine stag, worshipped in its own zoomorphic form during this period, was semi-anthropomorphized in the Iron Age. The ambiguity of hunted animal as god is easy to comprehend in the terms of the ambivalent attitude towards the hunt already discussed. The victim might evoke feelings of both veneration and guilt at the taking of a life from wild nature. On one image at Naquane, one of the main group of Camunian images, a set of armed figures dances round a large stag which stands before a temple. The stag is perhaps about to be killed by a hunter-spirit.[127] On another scene, people surround and pray to a huge stag accompanied by other deer of 'normal' size.[128] The implication is that the bigger animal is divine. This apotheosis is demonstrated still more strongly by a third representation which portrays a creature that is in semi-human, semi-stag form, with enormous tree-like antlers (figure 3.13).[129]

Figure 3.13 Rock carving of a god in the form of a half-human, half-stag figure, Camonica Valley, north Italy. Paul Jenkins.

What of the hunter-gods themselves? The images we have depict divine huntsmen who in some ways closely resemble human hunters. But in other respects there must be differences. The Touget hunter is naked, as is the Mérida boar-hunter; this would not be a sensible way of going to the hunt especially if he were facing dangerous game. But Celtic warriors sometimes fought naked, and there may thus have been a close symbolic link between hunting and warfare. The god at Touget carries a hare, which perhaps he had killed with the sword hanging at his belt, and the large hound at his side perhaps flushed out the prey from cover. The accoutrements of the Le Donon god are similarly significant. He is armed with lance, knife and chopper; his mastery over the forest is demonstrated by his clothing – his wolfskin cape and his boots, which are decorated with the heads of small animals. His stag quarry stands next to him. In Britain, the god Nodens at Lydney may have been a hunter: he was equated on dedications with Silvanus, the Roman woodland god, and one of the offerings at his shrine was a model of a hunting-dog.[130] At the Nettleton Shrub (Wilts.) temple,[131] the presiding god was Apollo Cunomaglus (Hound-Lord), implying the presence of a hunting cult; Apollo had a role as a huntsman in classical mythology. In north Britain, Cocidius was worshipped as a local hunter-god, often depicted with horns to demonstrate his affinity with the animal world.[132] It is interesting that Cocidius could be equated both with Silvanus and with Mars, thus showing the very close link perceived to pertain between war and hunting.

The vernacular Welsh and Irish myths show very clearly the close relationship between the hunt and the supernatural (see also chapter 7). In these myths there are countless allusions to hunting, usually as an activity of nobles. Hunters frequently have encounters with beings from the Otherworld. Thus in the *Mabinogi*, Pwyll meets Arawn, king of Annwn, while both are out hunting. Again, Manawydan and Pryderi are hunting in Dyfed when they and their dogs meet an enchanted boar from the Otherworld.[133] In Irish mythology, such heroes as Finn and Cú Chulainn hunt magic boars and stags which entice them to the realms of the supernatural powers. Sometimes these animals are emissaries, but on occasion they are gods transformed into animal form.[134] Flidhais, an Irish goddess of wild things, including deer, may have been a divine huntress, like Arduinna and the Roman Diana. Certainly the Welsh Mabon, in 'Culhwch and Olwen', is a hunter-god.[135] The idea seems to have been that the divine hunt brought not simply death and the end but immortality through the act of shedding blood. Certainly in the myths, a blow can be the catalyst which transforms an animal back to its original human form. It may be the case that the mythology which associates superhuman heroes with the hunt reflects the archaeological evidence, with its scarcity of faunal remains relating to hunting activity. Accordingly, at least some hunting may have been strictly the preserve of noblemen. Equally, hunting may have been hemmed round by bonds, taboos and rigid rules. Because hunting was a serious matter, involving the destruction of part of nature, it may have been perceived as an activity in which the gods must play the key role.

4

ANIMALS AT WAR

A crucial role in Celtic warfare was played by animals. Horses were employed in cavalry and in chariot-units, and lesser equines – mules, ponies and donkeys – were used as draught- and baggage-animals. Dogs may also, on occasions, have been used as fighting animals. Horses and dogs fought together in the war between Ulster and Connacht, as chronicled in the 'Táin Bó Cuailnge',[1] and Pliny alludes to the custom of crossing dogs with wolves to produce a fearsome battle-animal.[2] Certain beasts were regarded as symbols of ferocity, aggression and battle, because of the valour or bellicosity of their dispositions. But this chapter is necessarily first and foremost concerned with horses. Celtic warriors were renowned for their skill as cavalry and chariot-fighters and it was, at least partly, because of this that horses enjoyed such a prominent position as status symbols and objects of veneration in the Celtic world. 'Horseback produced history's first revolution in land transport.'[3]

The use of horses for riding, which allowed warriors to cover ground very fast, transformed methods of warfare. Owning horses – then as now – involved a certain level of wealth, since feed and maintenance were relatively costly. This led to social divisions, between those who could afford to keep and ride horses and those who could not. This hierarchy of 'knights' and the rest is evident not only in the world of the Celts but also in the Near East much earlier, at around 2000 BC, and in recent American Indian societies after AD 1600. There can be no doubt that the introduction of horse-riding had an enormous impact on civilization.[4]

The three main uses of horse-riding in antiquity were for sport, hunting and warfare. The efficient control of a horse depends upon the use of a bit, which rests on the sensitive gum between the incisors and premolars, enabling the rider to apply pressure to the soft mouth of his mount. The oldest surviving bit dates to about 1500 BC, but a horse whose teeth bore the evidence of wear from a bit was buried in the Ukraine in about 4000 BC.[5]

Figure 4.1 'Jangle' from bronze horse-harness, the earliest piece of evidence for horse-harnessing in Wales, 850 BC, from the Parc-y-Meirch Hoard, Gwynedd. By courtesy of the National Museum of Wales.

Ann Hyland has recently published a fascinating study of the horse in the Roman world,[6] but her observations are more wide-ranging and she makes a number of useful general points about horses and warfare which pertain to many ancient societies. She comments that war-horses do not need to be particularly fast, but they have to be compact and able to bear loads without undue stress. Short, stocky beasts with an adequate ride, speed and capacity for endurance would thus be especially suitable. Ponies are not good in battle: they are unstable and uncomfortable to ride, but we know that certain Celtic tribes did use ponies, sometimes even riding without saddles. Horses are not naturally aggressive creatures, but they can become so in a war situation, particularly stallions, who can be trained to use both feet and teeth against an opponent. They are intelligent, with some ability to reason and to learn. They can forage on the march and they are brave.[7]

Horses were being used for transport in Mediterranean Europe by at least the mid-second millennium BC. From the eighth century BC in much of northern Europe, including Hungary, Switzerland, south Germany,

Belgium and Britain, there is archaeological evidence of a new and very distinctive group of metal types associated with bridle-bits and bones of horses. This is the first indication of the tradition of riding in temperate Europe. The cemetery of Court Saint Etienne in Belgium, and the deposits at Llyn Fawr (Mid Glam.) and Heathery Burn (Dur.) in Britain are examples of the sporadic nature of the distribution outside the main central European cluster of evidence for horse-riding, and these discoveries represent not large-scale migration but rather local contact and the activities of raiding parties from Middle Europe. So we can say that by the eighth century BC warriors were fighting on horseback in much of the Celtic world.[8]

During the Hallstatt period of the earliest Celtic Iron Age, from around 750–700 BC, there is evidence of aristocratic horsemen wielding long iron swords. Some of these martial princes were buried in rich graves on wagons pulled to the tomb by horses. One such was the chief interred with great ceremony at Hochdorf in Germany in the sixth century BC: he had been covered in sheet-gold; even his shoes were of gold; and he wore a neckring decorated with rows of tiny horsemen, similar to the belt worn by another sixth-century warrior at Kaltbrunn,[9] which was ornamented with horse motifs. Certainly Hallstatt iconography reflects the concerns of an aristocratic, horse-riding society who habitually fought on horseback. A grave at Hallstatt itself contained a sword-scabbard (figure 4.2) decorated with images of foot-soldiers and horsemen with spears, wearing trousers or breeches, short tunics and helmets; one of them is depicted spearing an enemy who lies by his horse's front hooves.[10] Many objects belonging to the Hallstatt tradition display iconography associated with horsemanship. A pot from a barrow at Sopron-Varhély, probably belonging to the late seventh century BC, bears an incised figure of a horseman.[11] A sheet-bronze lid from a bucket or *situla* at Kleinklein in Austria (figure 4.3) is decorated in repoussé with horsemen riding ithyphallic horses with radiate manes.[12]

Figure 4.2 Detail of engraving on a bronze and iron scabbard, showing warriors on horseback, 400–350 BC, Hallstatt cemetery, Hallstatt, Austria. Length of scabbard: 68cm. Paul Jenkins.

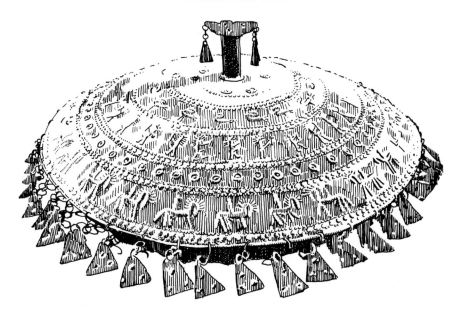

Figure 4.3 Sheet-bronze bucket-cover decorated with horsemen and infantrymen, Hallstatt Iron Age, Kleinklein, Austria. Diameter: 35.7cm. Paul Jenkins.

Mounted warriors are present on the bronze cult-wagon at Strettweg: here the horsemen are naked, with oval shields, spears and pointed helmets; and they ride slender, graceful beasts (frontispiece).[13] *Situlae* may depict horses and horsemen: the vessel at Vače in Yugoslavia shows war-horses being led by their masters.[14] A clay figure of a horseman comes from Speikern in Germany (figure 3.9)[15] and, at Hallstatt, a bronze axe dating to about 600 BC bears the figure of a horse and rider, probably a warrior, on the top of the blade.[16]

THE CELTIC HORSE

Gaulish and British horses were small compared to those of Italy.[17] Domestic horses appeared in Gaul during the course of the Bronze Age:[18] pre-Roman equines, including types of pony, are depicted in French rock art. Horse-breeding formed an important part of Celtic culture: since Celts were, as a race, larger than Latins, efforts were made by the Gauls to upgrade their indigenous stock by crossing with Italian stallions, to produce larger, Gallo-Roman horses for warfare.[19] But in pre-Roman Gaul and Britain, small, pony-like animals were used both as war-horses and as baggage-beasts. Unsuitable as ponies are as war-mounts, these smaller animals were often ridden in battle, especially in

Britain where the native stock was retained because of the isolation of the British Isles; in Gaul, however, interbreeding with Italian stock was producing larger breeds which could be used in war alongside indigenous ponies.[20] The horses at Danebury (Hants) were small and pony-like; the majority of those whose remains were found were male and some were killed (for food) when they were 2 years old or older. They were used both for riding and as pack-animals.[21] Interestingly, in Britain, there is little archaeological evidence for riding after the late first century AD, but in Ireland, the horse-trappings found indicate that it continued there for some centuries longer.[22]

Celtic horses, whether they were used for warfare or in peacetime activities, required careful feeding: with grass in summer, hay in winter and 'hard-feed' (barley or other cereal grains) all the year round. In addition, a kind of broad bean, the so-called 'Celtic bean', was fed to horses, because it was high in protein.[23]

Horses were used both in domestic and in military contexts as

Figure 4.4 Late Iron Age bronze horse, dedicated to the god Rudiobus, Neuvy-en-Sullias, Loiret, France. Paul Jenkins.

70

draught-animals, but they could not be used to pull very heavy loads since horse harness was not designed for this purpose until the Saxon period. Accordingly, oxen would have been the main traction-animals on farms, whilst horses would be employed far more for riding and warfare.[24] The Gauls imported big draught horses from Italy which were heavier than their native ponies.[25] Caesar alludes to a heavy draught-horse bred in Gaul,[26] and a kind of heavier pony was also used in Britain. Horses at Danebury and Gussage All Saints (Dorset) were harnessed to pull light loads.[27] Hallstatt chiefs were buried on wagons that had been pulled by two horses. Baggage-beasts were essential in warfare, and indigenous Celtic ponies were employed in this capacity. Ponies function more efficiently in cold, damp conditions than the mules and donkeys characteristic of the Mediterranean world. Ponies are especially suitable as pack-animals since they are able to bear heavier loads, relative to their size, than horses.[28]

Harness was both functional and designed for display in battle. Richly ornamented and elaborate horse-gear is in evidence from the Hallstatt Iron Age until the first century AD, when the flamboyantly decorated horse-trappings were buried in the Polden Hills hoard (Som.).[29] Both simple and two-piece bits were used by riders to control their mounts. Stirrups are unknown at this period, but spurs were used: they were placed in tombs, such as that at Goeblingen-Nospelt;[30] and one panel on the Gundestrup Cauldron[31] depicts horsemen with spurs (figure 4.5). A good, firm saddle is important to a mounted warrior, to keep him upright during charges and intricate manoeuvres. The Gundestrup Cauldron shows a cavalryman on a saddle with two horns rising up at the front and back, which would keep the rider rigidly in position and incapable of being dislodged by a swerve or blow.[32] But Caesar remarks of his campaigns across the Rhine that the Germans considered it shameful to ride in saddles and that they were happy to fight any number of saddled horsemen. From this, it may be assumed that the Celtic cavalry in Caesar's army (see pp. 74–9) had saddles.[33] The use of leather *bracae* or trousers, depicted for instance on the scabbard at Hallstatt and on the Gundestrup Cauldron, would have helped keep the cavalryman in the saddle. Metal or leather chamfreins (head-armour) were worn on occasions by war-horses. The later Iron Age Torrs Chamfrein from Scotland was a metal mask, to which horns were added later.[34] The earliest example of a chamfrein in north-west Europe is that depicted on the thirteenth-century BC bronze horse at Trundholm in Denmark,[35] which pulled a cult wagon in Bronze Age solar rituals.[36]

It is interesting to note that farriery (horse-shoeing) was developed in the Celtic world and spread to the Roman world from there, though shoeing was not widespread until after the Roman period. Both Iron Age and Roman sites have yielded horseshoes.[37]

Figure 4.5 Plate from gilded silver cauldron, depicting a Celtic army scene, from the second- to first-century BC cauldron found at Gundestrup, Jutland, Denmark. Paul Jenkins.

ATTITUDES TO HORSES IN THE CELTIC WORLD

The evidence of literature and archaeology points to the high status accorded to horses in Celtic society. Many divinities were closely associated with them (chapter 8), and faunal remains from Iron Age sanctuaries such as Gournay-sur-Aronde (Oise) and Ribemont-sur-Ancre (Somme) point to reverential treatment of dead horses (chapter 5). At Gournay, seven horses which had died naturally were accorded special burial in the ditch.[38] At the Ribemont shrine, the close association between man and horse is indicated by the presence of an ossuary, a kind of structure built from the long-bones of humans and horses.[39] Rivers in Gaul contain ritual deposits of horse skulls, found in the same places as prestigious weapon-offerings.[40] The esteem with which horses were regarded stems, above all, from their use by the aristocracy as war-horses or for display. At Camonica Valley, the rock art of the early Iron Age implies that ownership of horses was a luxury, reserved for leaders, warriors and hunters, and only these higher members of society are depicted riding. Camunians are first depicted on the rocks on horseback in the seventh century BC, fighting with swords, daggers and shields.[41] It is suggested that horses may sometimes have been kept at Danebury as status symbols[42] and, at the Iron Age site of Gussage, all the horses found were unbutchered, perhaps indicative of a taboo on the consumption of horsemeat,[43] although horses were eaten elsewhere.

Other indications of the prestige enjoyed by horses include lavish harnesses and the fact that horses are not particularly useful in economic terms, being expensive to maintain and unsuitable for heavy traction.[44]

Classical writers endorse the notion that Celtic horses had high status, especially in association with warfare: a passage in Polybius's *Histories* describes a series of duels imposed by Hannibal on his Celtic prisoners-of-war on his arrival in Italy; the prize for the winning fighter included a cloak and a horse.[45] At the Battle of Orange in 105 BC, the Teutonic tribe of the Cimbri made a vow to their gods, dedicating to them all their spoils, sacrificed enemies, weapons and horses on the battlefield.[46] Caesar[47] describes the *equites* or knights as the noble stratum of Celtic society; the literal translation of the term *equites* is horsemen, and the definition of a nobleman was someone who possessed a horse and arms. These knights were the cream of the Celtic warriors, who formed the cavalry contingent of the army.[48] A number of classical writers, including Strabo,[49] allude to the Celtic custom of headhunting in battle: 'when they are leaving the battlefield, they fasten to the necks of their horses the heads of their enemies.' Brunaux[50] suggests that headhunting may have been the prerogative of horsemen. Certainly, this association between horses and severed heads is confirmed by iconographical evidence from the Lower Rhône Valley: a stone frieze from Nages (Tarn) is carved with alternating galloping horses and human heads (figure 4.6); and at nearby Entremont, a sculpture depicts a horseman with a severed human head slung from his harness.[51]

THE IMAGE OF THE HORSEMAN

In the La Tène Iron Age, depictions of horsemen appear on coins, jewellery, pottery, sculpture and metalwork. Mounted warriors and charioteers, both male and female (figure 4.13), are frequent motifs on Celtic coins;[52] a silver coin from Scarisoara in Romania has a mounted soldier on the reverse.[53] The southern Gaulish sanctuary of Roquepertuse was decorated with human skulls, perhaps those of battle-victims; here also were stone images of war-gods, and a stone frieze dating to the third or second century BC is carved with four horse heads.[54] One panel of the Gundestrup Cauldron (figure 4.5) depicts various contingents of a

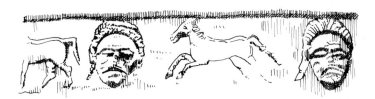

Figure 4.6 Stone frieze of alternating horses and severed heads from the pre-Roman *oppidum* at Nages, Provence, France.

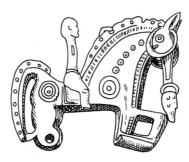

Figure 4.7 Iron Age bronze brooch in the form of a horseman, with a severed human head beneath the horse's chin, Numantia, Spain. Paul Jenkins.

Celtic army, including foot-soldiers, horsemen and trumpeters with their boar-headed carnyxes.[55] A pot made in the first century BC and discovered at Kelvedon in Essex is stamped with images of spiky-haired horsemen (perhaps with the lime-washed hair alluded to by classical writers on Celtic warriors), bearing hexagonal Celtic shields and curious crook-shaped objects.[56] A brooch from Numantia in Spain (figure 4.7) depicts a naked, mounted warrior with his horse trampling a severed human head.[57]

In the Romano-Celtic period, Celtic warriors were still depicted, but mainly in the form of gods (chapter 8): thus the sky-god is shown on horseback (figure 8.7), riding down the monstrous forces of evil represented by a giant which is half-human, half-serpent.[58] Among the tribes of eastern Britain, a Celtic version of Mars appears transformed from his Roman guise to that of a native horseman. He appears thus as Mars 'Corotiacus' (a native sobriquet) at Martlesham in Suffolk, and on a bronze figurine at Peterborough. Several little votive figures of horsemen were offered at the shrines of Brigstock in Northamptonshire. Stone warriors on horseback are represented, for instance at Margidunum (figure 4.8).[59] A recent acquisition by the British Museum consists of a bronze figurine of a war-god mounted on a proud, high-stepping horse. It was discovered on the Nottinghamshire/Lincolnshire border near the Roman site of Brough and close to the Fosse Way. The rider wears a helmet, short tunic with leather thongs, and greaves. The horse is more carefully modelled than his rider, and his ornamental harness can clearly be seen. The high-stepping stance perhaps reflects the horse's participation in a procession or parade.[60]

THE CELTIC CAVALRY

Evidence of Celtic horsemanship and the use of the horse in battle comes from iconography and, above all, from the comments of classical

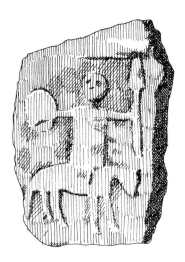

Figure 4.8 Romano-Celtic stone relief of a mounted warrior, Margidunum, Nottinghamshire. Maximum width: *c*.10cm. Paul Jenkins.

writers, of whom Caesar is our most informative source (pp. 77–9). Strabo[61] echoes the sentiments of many authors in his remark that the Gauls and the Germans excelled in cavalry and that the best Roman horse was recruited from them. It is highly probable that Celtic horsemen (like those of Numidia and Spain – both also noted for their cavalry) had ridden from childhood. It was in 390 BC that the Romans first encountered Celtic cavalry, when they were faced by invasion from the area of the Po Valley and Rome was sacked by a huge Celtic army with thousands of horsemen. In 218 BC the Carthaginian Hannibal, invading Italy, had a large cavalry force which was composed of Spanish, Celtic and North African horse. We are told that the Celts fought in the Hannibalic wars as mercenaries, for whichever side (Roman or Carthaginian) offered the best pay and prospects at any given time. At the Battle of Cannae (a disastrous defeat for the Romans), the Phoenicians won, although they were inferior in numbers, because of the superb quality of their cavalry.[62]

The deployment of cavalry can be extremely effective, but its use is constrained by a number of factors. Because of the varying seasonal availability of forage, cavalry naturally operate best in the period of late spring to late autumn. However, forage alone is not sufficient; a supply of corn is also needed.[63] A second important factor concerns the choice and training of the horses. Animals would be selected for their character and temperament: they must have high spirits but not be too individualistic; they must be amenable to training and obedient. Cavalry horses

Figure 4.9 Celtic silver coin decorated with triple-phallused horse and solar
wheel, Bratislava, Czechoslovakia. Paul Jenkins.

would be trained not to react to the smell of blood or to noise, and to
manage the crossing of both rivers and rough ground.[64] Tacitus
recounts the fate of a Roman officer Aulus Atticus, at the battle between
the Roman forces and the Caledonian Celts at Mons Graupius in AD 84.
Atticus's horse panicked and bolted straight into the enemy lines.[65] Ann
Hyland speaks of the danger of a frightened rider transmitting his fear to
his mount.[66]

Methods and use of cavalry forces

The Celts used cavalry units in a number of ways: they could act as
advance or reconnoitring troops; they guarded marching columns; they
challenged and taunted; they ambushed foraging Romans; they cut off
supplies; and in pitched battles, they harried and outflanked. A favourite method of fighting was to charge, hurl javelins and then dismount to
fight hand to hand. Cavalry operate best in open country: Tacitus
describes Celtic cavalry tactics in wooded areas of Britain, where troops
dismounted and led their horses until the trees thinned.[67] There is
conflicting testimony as to how much actual fighting was done on

horseback. Polybius[68] states that Iberian and Celtic cavalry were not really a coherent squadron of horse, but merely mounted warriors who dismounted once they arrived on the battlefield. But this is not borne out by other writers who describe cavalry charges; and iconography does depict horsemen actually fighting from their horses.

There are several instances where Julius Caesar[69] alludes to the Britons' use of cavalry and chariots together for mutual support. Chiefs and nobles gradually abandoned chariots for horseback, as their skills increased, except for Britain, where chariots were retained long after they became obsolete in Gaul. Caesar speaks in detail of cavalry tactics in Britain, Gaul and Germany. In Britain, mounted forces were used to harry the Romans as they landed from their boats in shallow water.[70] He recounts how British cavalry charged the Romans while they were off-guard, fortifying their camp.[71] The Roman general complained that the Britons fought in scattered groups rather than closely knit units, with reserves posted at intervals so that the various sections could cover one another's retreat and with fresh troops to replace tired soldiers.

Vercingetorix used his cavalry to cut off the Romans' supply lines and prevent them from foraging.[72] While the Romans were building siege-works against the fortifications of Vercingetorix's stronghold at Alesia,[73] they were continually harassed by Gaulish cavalry. An interesting tactic used by the Arvernian leader more than once was his deployment of cavalry and light infantry as mixed units.[74]

Caesar describes a particular form of cavalry-fighting in which his German adversaries were trained:[75] horsemen went into battle supported by an equal number of infantry, each foot-soldier having been carefully selected by the cavalryman for his personal protection. In any crisis, the infantry surrounded an injured, fallen horseman and guarded him. These unmounted warriors were able to keep up with rapid advances or retreat of horse by running alongside, clinging to the horses' manes. In addition, German cavalrymen trained their horses to stay in one spot once they had dismounted, in order that they could be swiftly reunited with their mounts when necessary.[76]

Another method of fighting on horseback is described by Pausanias[77] in his account of the Celtic invasion of Greece in the early third century BC. He alludes to something called the *trimarcasia*, saying that *marca* was a Celtic word for horse. The *trimarcasia* consisted of a group of horsemen, composed of a nobleman and his two grooms. The servants stayed behind the army ranks, ready to supply their master with a fresh horse should his be injured. If the lord were himself killed or wounded, one groom replaced him in the cavalry action, while the other took him back to camp if he were still alive. The idea of the *trimarcasia* was thus to maintain the original number of horsemen in an engagement.[78]

Caesar himself was a superb horseman, who clearly understood the

Figure 4.10 Incised decoration on a pottery vessel, depicting horseman, seventh century BC, Sopron, Hungary. Maximum diameter of vessel: 63.2cm. Paul Jenkins.

potential of cavalry. He not only utilized Gallic horsemen for his own troops, but he was keenly interested in the Gauls' use of cavalry against the Romans, and in his *Gallic Wars* he chronicles its importance over and over again. He comments, for instance,[79] that some tribes, like the Nervii, had virtually no cavalry, but that the Sontiates of Aquitaine[80] and the Aedui[81] were very strong in their horse regiments. The German and British cavalry also greatly impressed him.[82] Caesar discusses at length the role played by the Gallic cavalry in the war between himself and Vercingetorix, the Arvernian leader of the great uprising against the Romans in 52 BC. Vercingetorix had paid particular attention to cavalry provision when preparing for rebellion.[83] For the Alesia campaign,[84] he ordered the entire cavalry force of 15,000 to assemble at Bibracte, in the territory of the Aedui. Caesar[85] was only too well aware of the superiority of Gaulish horsemen. As an example of courage and brash confidence, the Roman general describes an oath sworn by Gaulish cavalry officers[86] that any one of their number who did not ride twice through the Roman marching columns should consider himself exiled and would never see home and family again. But Vercingetorix[87] was deeply concerned by the terrible losses being inflicted on his horse regiments and at one point he sent all the mounted forces away from Alesia into safety, under cover of night. At the final attempt of Vercingetorix's forces to

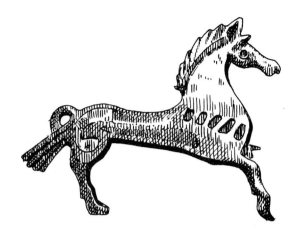

Figure 4.11 Romano-Celtic bronze brooch in the form of a horse, York.

relieve the besieged stronghold, the Arvernian chief's army consisted of 240,000 infantry and 8,000 horse.[88]

The Romans' use of Celtic cavalry

The Romans themselves never fully developed their own cavalry arm: instead, they recruited regiments of horse from those of their provinces which possessed a strong indigenous tradition of cavalry fighting, most particularly Numidia, Spain, Germany and, above all, from Gaul. Gallic cavalry was renowned throughout the empire for its superb horsemanship: Strabo's comments about its excellence have already been noted.[89] In Gaul, the regions which provided the most cavalry included Narbonensis, Belgica and Lugdunensis.[90] Caesar says that he raised his horse mainly from Narbonensis and from the Burgundian Aedui.[91] By AD 70 British horse were being recruited as well. In the Roman army, native cavalrymen were generally levied with their own mounts. Up to the Flavian period (later first century AD), many Roman auxiliary cavalry units were raised as a national troop which was then posted abroad, thus retaining its integrity as an ethnic unit. However, in time of war, replacements had of necessity to be levied on the spot, thus diluting the unit's ethnicity.[92] But the Romans had to exercise caution in transferring cavalry around the empire: moving horses from hot to cold regions works reasonably well, but horses adjust badly to increased heat and so care would have been taken not to move – say – Gallic or British horse to the east.

Caesar repeatedly describes his own use of Gaulish and German cavalry whom he greatly admired. On one occasion, he recounts how he

Figure 4.12 Bronze harness-mount inlaid with red enamel, first century AD, Santon Downham, Norfolk. Height: 7.9cm. Miranda Green.

ordered the Gauls to provide him with cavalry to use against the Germans.[93] He speaks of another campaign in which he engaged a Gallic horseman to take a letter through the enemy (Gallic) lines to his general Cicero.[94] In the revolt led by Vercingetorix, Caesar used German horse as reinforcements, perhaps because nearly all of Gaul was hostile to him.[95]

HORSES AND CHARIOTS

'Standing on their chariots with their richly harnessed horses, the warriors must have been very impressive sights.'[96] Chariots must have been attractive to the Celts as much for display as for function in battles. The evidence for chariot-warfare falls into three categories: the evidence of archaeology, the testimony of ancient Graeco-Roman writers, and the vernacular sources of Ireland and Wales.

The evidence of archaeology

The two-wheeled chariot was probably introduced to Celtic Europe from Western Asia. In the Near East, the fast, light, manoeuvrable chariot is associated with cultures from the mid-second millennium BC.[97]

In the seventh and sixth centuries BC, some of the earliest Iron Age warriors were buried with four-wheeled wagons or carts (see p. 68). They were interred in wooden mortuary chambers, beneath large barrows. Hochdorf in Germany is a good example of this tradition; Vix in Burgundy is another.[98] Representations of such carts are depicted on seventh-century rock carvings at Camonica Valley. The horses themselves were not usually buried, though exceptionally they might be slaughtered and buried with their dead chief, but sometimes three sets of harness are found in these princely graves, as if two were for the wagon team and the third for the chief's own charger. The yokes found at Hradenin in Czechoslovakia provide a particularly rich example of such harness. These four-wheeled wagon-burials were gradually replaced by the interment of light, two-wheeled chariots, in the Rhineland, the Marne and elsewhere in France and then in Britain. Chariot-burials occur too in eastern Europe, in Hungary and Bulgaria.[99]

In the La Tène phase of pagan Celtic tradition, the two-wheeled chariot was employed in warfare, in parades and displays and in burial of an aristocratic warrior-élite. In Gaul, chariotry was practised until the second century BC, but in Britain, where it persisted much longer,

Figure 4.13 Female charioteer driving a human-headed horse, on a gold coin of the Redones, first century BC, France. Diameter 2cm. Paul Jenkins.

Caesar was surprised to see chariots operating in the mid-first century BC.[100] The archaeological evidence consists of iconography, the remains of chariots and their fittings, found in such deposits as Llyn Cerrig Bach, and, above all, from the chariot-burials, to which I will return.

Hellenistic reliefs, at places like Pergamon in Asia Minor, represent Galatian chariots among the Celtic trophies depicted on triumphal arches.[101] From these images and from actual remains of chariots, it is possible to piece together a reconstruction of a typical Celtic Iron Age chariot. The vehicles were made of iron, bronze, wicker and wood, built to be as light and agile as possible; they were drawn by two pony-like beasts. The harness was richly decorated with bronze ornament, sometimes inlaid with coral or enamel. To allow the charioteer fine control over his horses, the reins passed over a wooden yoke through a series of bronze rings or terrets. The bridge-bits or snaffles contained three main elements: a central bar with rings at each end. A reconstruction in the National Museum of Antiquities of Scotland shows the warrior standing in the chariot armed with his spears, while the charioteer squats in a crouch for greater stability and control, holding the reins.[102] As well as spears, a warrior might be equipped with a long iron sword or a sling. Bows and arrows seem to have been used only rarely.[103]

Indirect evidence for chariot warfare exists, independent of the vehicles themselves. Barry Cunliffe[104] has suggested that the entrance courtyard of the east gate of Danebury could have been a chariot park. In addition, the site contains corral areas which would have made good pasture for chariot-ponies. Some fine bronze fittings found here could well be from chariot-pony harness. At the Brigantian stronghold of Stanwick, Yorkshire, a mount in the form of a schematized horse could have been a chariot-fitting (figure 4.14): it is a superb example of Celtic art, which captures the essential spirit of a horse's face in a few brilliantly modelled lines.[105]

It is the chariot-burials which provide a fascinating insight into the Celtic chariot-warrior and the rituals associated with his death. The tomb of La Gorge Meillet (Marne) was discovered in 1876: it consisted of a pit about 1.7 metres deep, dug into the chalk subsoil and containing a two-wheeled chariot decorated with rich bronze fittings inlaid with coral. The vehicle had been buried with the body of a warrior, who had been laid out on the chariot-platform, with his weapons on the floor beside him. He was a young aristocrat who wore a gold bracelet and was accompanied by his long iron sword, four spears with iron blades, and a bronze helmet. Provision was made for the dead man in the afterlife or for the Otherworld feast: he had eggs, a fowl, joints of pork and a knife to eat them with; and a superb Etruscan-made flagon held his wine. Another chariot-burial, at Somme-Bionne (Marne), contained similar remains of an elaborate feast, including joints of wild boar, pig, duck

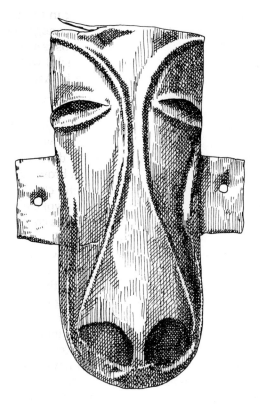

Figure 4.14 Bronze mount in the form of a horse-mask, first century AD, Melsonby, Yorkshire (originally from Stanwick). Height: 7.5cm. Paul Jenkins.

and a peculiar deposit of a number of frogs placed in a pot.[106] This burial dates to about 420 BC.

Rare examples exist of the interment of horses in a chariot-grave. At the end of the La Tène period (first century BC), two tombs were built at Soissons and elaborate rituals took place: in one burial, the chariot was found with the dead man, accompanied by what resembled a funeral cortège (figure 5.8): the two horses for the chariot were present but in addition there were two bulls, two goats, a ewe, a dog and some pigs. In a second Soissons grave were the remains of a chariot, an inhumation, two horses, two oxen, two goats, three sheep, four pigs and a dog. In both tombs the horses were small and apparently not sufficently robust to pull the heavy carts implied by the surviving fittings. Like the horses, the other beasts were all buried whole and had therefore not formed part of the funeral feast. They were presumably sacrificed in honour of the dead men, who must have been important members of their community. This high status is perhaps implied also by the slaughter of the

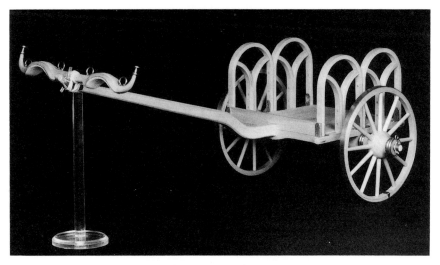

Figure 4.15 Reconstruction model of a chariot, based on fittings from Llyn Cerrig Bach, Anglesey. By courtesy of the National Museum of Wales.

horses themselves, which, though of considerable value, were given up to the dead.[107]

In Britain, the chariot-burials of East Yorkshire do not normally contain the horse team itself, but occasionally the animals are present, as at the King's Barrow, where the body, chariot and a pair of horses were all interred.[108] A pair of rich burials at Garton Slack was discovered in 1984 during gravel-digging. Here, a male and female of high rank were each interred with a dismantled chariot. The man was a warrior, who was accompanied by his sword in its scabbard, seven spears and a fragmentary shield; the woman's grave was very lavishly furnished, with precious bronze objects such a mirror and a cylindrical container which may have been a work-box.[109]

Uses of chariots in war: the ancient sources

As we have seen, the Continental Celts used chariots until the second century BC: various Mediterranean commentators on the Celts remark on this 'barbarian' form of warfare and display. Athenaeus[110] speaks of the Celtic chieftain Louernius, who rode in his chariot over the plains, distributing gold and silver to the thousands who followed him. Bituitus, the king of the Arverni was displayed in the Roman triumph of 121 BC in multicoloured array, riding in a 'silver' chariot 'exactly as he had fought'.[111] Diodorus Siculus comments on the Gauls thus: 'for their journeys and in battle they use two-horse chariots, the chariot carrying both charioteer and chieftain.'[112] He goes on to describe how, when they met the enemy's cavalry in battle, they cast their javelins and then descended to fight on foot with their swords. The chiefs would stand in front of their army and chariot-lines, challenging their opposite numbers. The chariot-drivers were apparently poor but free men, presumably the landless men described by Caesar. In the definitive conflict between the Romans and the Gauls in north Italy in 225–224 BC, the Celts employed 20,000 cavalry and chariots to the Romans' 70,000 horse.[113] At the Battle of Telamon (225 BC) the chariots were positioned on the wings.

In Britain, as alluded to earlier, chariot warfare continued several centuries after such methods had become obsolete on the Continent. It was a vital part of the British battle-machine.[114] The last reference to the use of war-chariots in Britain occurs in Dio Cassius's description of the Severan campaigns against the Caledonii of northern Scotland in AD 207.[115]

Julius Caesar's testimony on British chariot-warfare is detailed and informative. He ruefully remarks, 'thus they combine the mobility of cavalry with the staying-power of infantry.' He frequently comments that they used a combination of chariots and cavalry: 'they had sent on ahead their cavalry and the chariots, which they regularly use in battle.'[116] Again, he mentions how the Britons ambushed the Romans while they were reaping grain, surrounding the legion with horses and chariots, and throwing them into confusion.[117] On one occasion[118] cavalry and chariots were used together in order to block the progress of the Roman army at a river. The Britons had a trick of drawing the Roman cavalry away from the support of their legion and then jumping down from their vehicles to fight on foot, giving them an advantage over the enemy.[119] In discussing the Catuvellaunian king, Cassivellaunus, Caesar's most formidable British opponent, the Roman general describes the native chieftain's 4,000 chariots. Whenever the Roman cavalry went into the fields for grain, Cassivellaunus sent his charioteers out of the woods, where they had been concealed, and attacked them.[120]

Caesar's detailed account of the Britons' charioteering skills deserves to be quoted in full:

> At first they ride along the whole line and hurl javelins; the terror inspired by the horses and the noise of the wheels generally throw the enemy ranks into confusion. Then when they have worked their way between the lines of their own cavalry, they jump down from the chariots and fight on foot. Meanwhile, the drivers withdraw a little from the field and place the chariots so that their masters, if hard-pressed by the enemy, have an easy retreat to their

ranks. . . . Their daily training and practice have made them so expert that they can control their horses at full gallop on a steep incline and then check and turn them in a moment. They can run along the chariot-pole, stand on the yoke and return again into the chariot as quick as lightning.[121]

The chariot in war thus combined several functions. Battles involving chariots would have been formal engagements on selected ground.[122] Conflict was highly ritualized, beginning, as Caesar describes, with insults, boastful riding up and down, clashing of weapons, challenges to single combat and only then a full-scale battle-charge. This all involved a great deal of social interaction and display.[123] In a pitched battle, a great deal of chariot warfare was psychological: especially to an enemy unfamiliar with such tactics, the noise and speed of the horses and their rumbling vehicles driven full-tilt, the rain of the javelins, all combined to cause panic. The first line of the enemy was especially vulnerable to being trampled beneath the horses' hooves.

Chariots in early Ireland: the vernacular literature

Some of the earliest Insular literary records, which may well pertain to pagan Celtic traditions, contain fascinating allusions both to chariots themselves and to chariot warfare. The 'Tochmarc Emer', the story of the Ulster hero Cú Chulainn's wife Emer, describes a fine chariot built of wicker and wood, on white bronze wheels, with a gold yoke, a silver pole and yellow plaited reins.[124] In the most famous of Ulster tales, the 'Táin Bó Cuailnge', both Queen Medb of Connacht and her bitter adversary Cú Chulainn possess chariots. Medb instructs her charioteer to yoke up her chariots ready to make a circuit of her camp and survey her armies.[125] The young Cú Chulainn, a superhuman, semi-divine hero, breaks twelve chariots before finally finding one – that of his king Conchobar of Ulster – to carry him.[126] Just before his death, Cú Chulainn yokes up his chariot for his final confrontation with Medb: he has two chariot-horses, the Black of Saingliu and the Grey of Macha. The clairvoyante Grey cries tears of blood at the foreknowledge of his death.[127]

The 'Táin' is full of allusions to chariots and, interestingly, makes specific reference to the shrunk-on iron tyres which were an invention of Celtic Iron Age smiths.[128] The following is a description of Laeg, Cú Chulainn's charioteer, his chariot and his horses:

> The charioteer rose up then and donned his charioteer's war-harness. The war-harness that he wore was: a skin-soft tunic of stitched deer's leather, light as a breath, kneaded supple and smooth not to hinder his free arm movements. He put on over this

his feathery outer mantle, made (some say) by Simon Magus for Darius king of the Romans. . . . Then the charioteer set down on his shoulders his plated, four-pointed, crested battle-cap, rich in colour and shape; it suited him well and was no burden. To set him apart from his master, he placed the charioteer's sign on his brow with his hand: a circle of deep yellow like a single red-gold strip of burning gold shaped on an anvil's edge. He took the long horse-spancel and the ornamental goad in his right hand. In his left hand he grasped the steed-ruling reins that give the charioteer control. Then he threw the decorated iron armour-plate over the horses, covering them from head to foot with spears and spit-points, blades and barbs. Every inch of the chariot bristled. Every angle and corner, front and rear, was a tearing place.

The body of the chariot was spare and slight and erect, fitted for the feats of a champion, with space for a lordly warrior's eight weapons, speedy as the wind or as a swallow or deer darting over the level plain. The chariot was settled down on two fast steeds, wild and wicked, neat-headed and narrow-bodied, with slender quarters and roan breast, firm in hoof and harness – a notable sight in the trim chariot-shafts. One horse was lithe and swift-leaping, high-arched and powerful, long-bodied and with great hooves. The other flowing-maned and shining, slight and slender in hoof and heel.[129]

ANIMALS AS SYMBOLS OF WAR

This chapter has necessarily been focused upon the role of horses in Celtic warfare. These were the animals which were directly concerned with fighting, in cavalry and chariot units. But there were symbolic ways also in which beasts were associated with war. Such creatures as geese, ravens and, in particular, boars were linked with weapons and with warriors because of their aggressive traits which evoked the idea of conflict and combat (chapter 6).

Diodorus Siculus refers to the wearing of horned or animal-crested helmets by the Celts.[130] This increased the men's stature and made them appear more fearsome to the enemy. Such helmets are known archaeologically: a superb horned helmet comes from the river Thames at Waterloo Bridge (figure 4.16); and one of the panels of the Gundestrup Cauldron (figure 4.5) depicts soldiers wearing boar- and bird-crested helmets.[131] A goose surmounts the helmet of an Iron Age goddess depicted by a bronze figurine at Dinéault in Brittany.[132] The third- or second-century BC helmet from Ciumeşti in Romania (figure 4.17) bears the figure of a raven on the top.[133] This piece is especially interesting because the wings are hinged so that when its wearer ran towards the

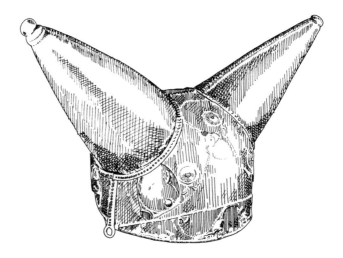

Figure 4.16 Bronze horned helmet with enamel inlay, first century BC, from the river Thames at Waterloo, London. Width between horns: 42.5cm. Paul Jenkins.

enemy, the raven's wings would flap up and down in a realistic and unnerving manner. The war symbolism of birds is interesting. The goose evoked concepts of aggression and alertness and was thus an appropriate image of war. Indeed, the bones of geese are found in the graves of eastern European Celtic warriors.[134] But the raven or crow was the bird of battle *par excellence*. These birds are cruel – hence the collective term 'an unkindness of ravens' – and scavenge on dead flesh, so they symbolize both the pitilessness and the carnage of war. The association of ravens with combat and destruction is found above all in the vernacular tales of Ireland, where the goddesses of war, the Morrigna and the Badbh, could change at whim from human to raven form, squawking dreadful omens and terrifying armies by their presence. 'Badbh Catha' actually means 'Battle Crow'. Sometimes these women appear as old hags hunched in black rags and so take on the semi-guise of carrion birds while retaining their human form. One of the perceived characteristics of ravens was their ability to prophesy the future, especially the outcome of battles: the armies to whom the war-goddesses appeared as birds took their presence as a prediction that they would be defeated. When the Ulster hero Cú Chulainn is finally killed, he has such a fearsome reputation that it is not until one of the raven-goddesses alights on his shoulder that his enemies believe he is dead and dare to approach and behead him.

There is an interesting raven story from antiquity concerning a battle between the Celts and the Romans under Valerius Corvus, in which a

Figure 4.17 Iron helmet with bronze crest in the form of a raven with hinged wings, third to second century BC, Ciumeşti, Romania. Height: 25cm.
Paul Jenkins.

crow or raven, sacred to the Celts, attacked the adversary of Valerius and pecked out his eyes: the Roman general thenceforth took the cognomen of 'Corvus' (Crow). A curious depiction on an Etruscan pot at Citta della Pierce consists of an image of a Celtic warrior, a raven pecking at his eye.[135]

Boars are perhaps the most immediate symbols of war. They are aggressive, indomitable and awesome creatures at bay, strong, fearless and destructive: the Celts therefore adopted them as battle emblems, placing them as motifs on weapons and armour (see chapter 6). A warrior at Somme-Bionne (Marne) was buried with his chariot and food, which comprised not only the usual pieces of pork (from domestic pigs) but also joints of wild boar, which is an unusual culinary find (chapters 2, 3). As images on war gear, boars would have acted as apotropaic signs, to protect the warriors and ward off blows. Thus the boar appears on Iron Age sword-stamps;[136] and on the shield from the river Witham in Lincolnshire (figure 4.18) there was the image of a schematized boar, with a pronounced snout and long legs.[137] A boar-crested helmet (figure 4.19) both protected the wearer and made him frightening to look at. Nearly all these war emblems of boars share the feature of an exaggerated dorsal ridge, standing up stiffly erect from the creature's back. This recalls the Irish story of Diarmaid's foster-brother, who is an enchanted boar, and whose poisoned spines stand out like spears (chapter 7). The stress on the dorsal bristles in Iron Age art is a way of expressing the

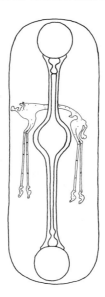

Figure 4.18 Bronze shield originally bearing boar motif, and with its outline still visible, second century BC, river Witham, Lincolnshire. Miranda Green.

Figure 4.19 Bronze helmet-crest in the form of a boar, Gaer Fawr, Powys. By courtesy of the National Museum of Wales.

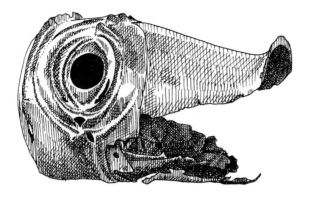

Figure 4.20 Bronze carnyx (trumpet) mouth in the form of a boar's head, first century AD, Deskford, Grampian, Scotland. Length: 21.5cm. Paul Jenkins.

ferocity of an angry boar and thus, by implication, of the warrior himself.

Celtic battles were noisy, terrifying affairs, with neighing horses, rumbling chariots, shouts, screams of pain and rage, and clashing weapons. But added to this was the clamour of the carnyx, the Celtic trumpet, whose mouth was in the form of the head of a boar or, more rarely, a wolf.[138] These carnyxes are depicted on the Gundestrup Cauldron;[139] sometimes the actual trumpets have been found. A bronze example of the mid-first century AD comes from Deskford (Grampian) in Scotland (figure 4.20): it has a snarling, open mouth containing a pig's palate and an articulated wooden tongue[140] which would vibrate when blown and which no doubt made a ghastly braying shriek, contributing to the din, confusion and sheer terror of the battlefield.

5

SACRIFICE AND RITUAL

Ritual behaviour involving the deliberate killing of animals was endemic in Celtic society: the evidence for this activity is manifest in sanctuaries, graves and habitation sites, the last context indicating that the ritual was not an élite one and that it is impossible to separate symbolic from economic behaviour. Rituals involving animals did not, of course, first take place during the Celtic Iron Age. In Britain, for instance, there is abundant prehistoric evidence: the deposition of animals in the ditches of Neolithic causewayed camps, and the 'head and hooves' burials of the Neolithic and Bronze Age are examples.[1] Sometimes the animals involved in Celtic ritual were eaten or partially eaten; sometimes whole or parts of bodies of beasts were offered to the gods. It is possible to observe a complex but systematic behaviour-pattern in animal ritual. The results of such activity are interpreted as ritual since they are repetitive, have no explicable function in terms of 'rational' behaviour and sometimes involve a considerable economic loss to the community.[2] In any ritual, there is a strong element of formalized, repeated action, prescribed and circumscribed by certain rules and taboos, which are adhered to and handed down. It is crucial to recognize that for the Celts ritual behaviour was not marginal but central to everyday life.[3] This is why such behaviour manifests itself not just in sacred places nor within the context of funerary activity, but in the places where people lived their daily lives. Thus in southern Britain and elsewhere (see pp. 100–5) grain-storage pits in hillforts and isolated settlements were the centres for complicated ritual activities involving animals.[4]

There are many possible explanations for animal ritual. Animals were considered important in religion because they played a central and crucial part in life. Cattle, for instance, were a symbol of wealth. They were used as draught beasts; their flesh was eaten; their hides used to make leather; and their milk drunk or made into cheese. Animals were important as food, in hunting and in warfare and were thus of equal importance in death and religion.[5] In sanctuaries, ritual feasting and offerings of food to the dead involved the butchery of animals. In the

Figure 5.1 Baseplate of the Gundestrup Cauldron, depicting the hunt or sacrifice of a great bull. Diameter of baseplate: 25.6cm. Paul Jenkins.

disused storage pits of southern Britain, the burial of animals may have been magico-religious acts which represented the deliberate loss to their rural communities of potential wool, milk, manure, traction, meat and offspring.[6] Here, then, fertility rites may have been carried out to ensure that the gods were involved in acts of reciprocity and that the divine powers would continue to provide for humankind.

It is important to remember that much of the ritual which must have taken place does not survive in the archaeological record. Holocausts, where the complete body of an animal was burnt, might leave no trace. In addition, it is sometimes difficult to detect a difference between evidence for animal ritual and ordinary food refuse. Among the Iban of Borneo,[7] food ritual involving animals takes place on house verandahs and would be archaeologically indistinguishable from normal butchery and food consumption. Indeed, animals involved in ritual in many societies would be eaten either as part of or after their ritual usage.

THE MEANING AND NATURE OF SACRIFICE

The ancient Italic Tables of Iguvium (Umbria) allude to rites of passage or gate ceremonies involving the sacrifice of animals. These rites were complex and precise: the town could only be purified by means of appropriate animal sacrifices at each of its three gates. Thus at one entrance, three oxen and three pregnant sows were killed; at the second, three oxen and three sucking-pigs; at the third, three white-faced oxen and three ewe-lambs.[8] This is a fascinating insight into the intricacies of sacrifice and its purpose: entrances were especially vulnerable and had to be protected. Fertility ritual can be inferred from the involvement of sows, sucking-pigs and ewe-lambs – all either pregnant or young animals. Oxen were present in all three gate rites, perhaps because of their agricultural importance.

Our evidence for the pre-literate Celtic world is very imprecise compared to the extraordinarily detailed data of the Iguvium Tables, but there are hints of similarly important and complicated sacrificial rituals involving the destruction of beasts. Indeed, at Camonica Valley, the rock art shows scenes of sacrifice, with an animal, an altar and a temple.[9] In terms of precise parallels with early Umbria, we can point to the Gaulish sanctuary of Gournay (Oise), where elderly oxen were sacrificed to guard the entrance to the shrine and where parts of their bodies flanked the gateway.[10]

Sacrifice involves the permanent removal of otherwise useful or valuable objects from daily life, for offerings to the forces of the supernatural. For the Celts, as for other peoples, a sacrifice had somehow to be destroyed in order for it to pass over into the Otherworld. Metalwork was bent or broken or cast into an inaccessible place such as a marsh or river. Animals had to be killed in order to reinforce life. The life-force of a sacrifice could not be released into the supernatural world unless its links with this world were first severed. This is a case of 'rendering unto God the things that are God's'. By being given over to the supernatural world, the sacrificial victim served to shift these Otherworld forces towards the earth and focus them on the person or persons who performed the ritual.[11] The idea seems to have been that a death released new life and force, the sacrifice establishing a channel of communication between this world and the realm of the supernatural.

The sacrifice of an animal could have a number of different purposes. Classical writers do not allude a great deal to Celtic animal sacrifice, perhaps because it was a commonplace activity and familiar, too, in their own Mediterranean world. Where they do mention such activity,[12] the reasons given for sacrifice include augury and divination – both magical devices for foretelling the future by observing the actions of animals and birds in life and in the throes of death. In the Battle of Orange of 105 BC, the Cimbri are reported to have promised the gods all the spoils of the battlefield, enemies and animals and weapons.[13] Animal sacrifices could be thank-offerings, as in this case, or they could be acts of propitiation – for a cure from disease, to ask for fertility for oneself, one's livestock or

Figure 5.2 Ritual burial of a goat in a disused Iron Age grain storage pit,
Danebury, Hampshire. By courtesy of the Danebury Trust.

crops. Alternatively, they could be divinatory – to provide people with
an understanding of happenings and processes beyond their earthly
control. They could also be acts of communication between people and
the gods. Thus the underworld deities could be appeased by a chthonic
sacrifice, the burial of an animal in the ground, so that its juices and
flesh would become one with the earth itself and penetrate deep underground. Barry Cunliffe suggests[14] that the sacrifices buried in grain-
storage pits in south-east Britain, could be translated into water-burials
elsewhere: both evoke similar ideas of reaching the regions of the
underworld. A sacrifice might be given wholly to the gods or divided
between the divine powers and humans. Thus some pieces might be left
uneaten (the gods' portion) and others consumed. There is some evidence, as at Bliesbruck (Moselle) for instance, that the best bits were
consumed by people in ritual feasts and the less palatable portions
(offal, intestines) were offered to the divine forces. This kind of apparent
cynicism was common also in Greek religion.[15]

The deposition of animals by sacrificial ritual was an important way of
communicating with the gods.[16] In sanctuaries where ritual feasting
took place, the consumption of food within a sacred space represented a
kind of conviviality between the consumers and the divinities of the

Figure 5.3 Plate of the Gundestrup Cauldron depicting a triple bull-slaying scene. Paul Jenkins.

holy ground.[17] Among the Iban of Borneo 'animals play an important part as intermediaries, both as messengers of the gods and as vehicles for human supplication to the spirit world'.[18] The gods of the Iban are perceived as using animals as go-betweens, to allow humans to see into the future. Humans make contact with the gods by such ritual activities as cock-fighting and by the consumption of sacrificial meat. Birds, with their sky domain, are perceived as a link between the living Iban and their ancestral spirits.

The importance of animal sacrifice and ritual for the Celts and for other peoples, as a means of communicating with the supernatural, prompts the question as to what the animals represented. It is possible that beasts were perceived as being close enough to humans to be substitutes for human sacrifice.[19] The Celts did practise human sacrifice but not very often, and it may be that animals were more frequently used instead. After all, animals share a great many characteristics with humans. What is interesting about Celtic animal sacrifice is that by far the majority of animals killed belonged to domestic species, those creatures which shared man's life and aided him in his work, bore him in battle, fed and clothed him.

The organization of animal sacrifice may have been quite complex:[20] many different individuals would have been involved in any given ritual. Of these, the most important were firstly the person or group of persons who provided the sacrificial victim and who were, presumably, the main beneficiaries of the ritual, and secondly, the person(s) who performed the rite of sacrifice itself. These may have been professional functionaries, religious specialists who took charge of the rituals, from the reception and slaughter of the victim to the prayers, chanting and communication with the forces of the supernatural who received the gift. Caesar[21] tells us of one such group of religious officials, the Druids, who, he says, were in charge of public and private sacrifice in Gaul. The professional sacrificers must have been accorded high status, because their job was to handle sacred objects. It is interesting to speculate as to the precise moment at which an animal became holy: when it was chosen by the initiator, when it was handed over to the priest or only when it had been killed. Once an animal had been selected for sacrifice, it may have attained a kind of separateness and sanctity. The religious functionaries in charge of sacrifice had a strange, ambiguous job: they were high-ranking priests with an ability to form a close contact with the supernatural world, but they also dealt with the fairly messy matter of slaughter. It may be that there existed colleges of functionaries of differing ranks, the lower echelons of whom dealt with the practical side of sacrifice. But we know that Roman priests, the *haruspices* ('gut-gazers') for instance, certainly handled entrails and livers themselves.

SELECTION, CONSUMPTION AND RITUAL FEASTING

An interesting aspect of animal-sacrifice concerns the criteria of selection. In many religions, the appearance, species, sex and age of beasts for sacrifice are important factors determining choice. Appearance is something we cannot generally trace archaeologically. That it may have mattered is implied by Pliny's comment in his *Natural History*[22] that the two bulls chosen for sacrifice by the Druids on the occasion of the mistletoe festival on the sixth day of the moon were white. The Tables of Iguvium stipulate that for one of the gateway purification ceremonies, the three oxen sacrificed had to have white faces. This stress on whiteness may have been related to purity.

In terms of age, species and sex, certain inferences can be made from faunal assemblages on religious and sepulchral sites in Gaul and Britain. For example, pigs in some Gaulish cemeteries were young.[23] At Skeleton Green (Herts.) it seems that male animals were buried with men and birds with women.[24] At the sanctuary of Gournay, certain animals were old when sacrificed: the oxen (figure 5.4) were kept as long as ten years or more before slaughter and burial by the entrance.[25]

At Gournay, certain animals (the cattle and horses) were not eaten but buried as offerings to the chthonic or infernal gods, while young pigs and lambs were consumed in ritual feasts. There are many indications that certain animals were deliberately chosen for consumption and others left uneaten. The idea may have been that offerings to the infernal powers were left to rot, to seep into the earth and replenish it.

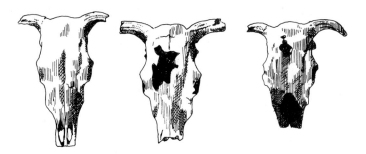

Figure 5.4 Skulls of oxen sacrificed at the Celtic sanctuary of
Gournay-sur-Aronde, Oise. Paul Jenkins.

In some sanctuaries, part of the animal was eaten, part left for the gods: 'divided between gods and men and consumed by the latter'.[26] Sometimes the killing and consumption of animals may have been accompanied by rituals whose purpose was to make reparation for the death of the animal (see chapter 3).

In all animal sacrifice or ritual for which there is evidence on Celtic sites, there is a distinction between consumed and unconsumed animals. At Bliesbruck the remains of beasts buried in pits were the domestic species generally eaten by Celtic communities (pig, cattle, sheep). There is difficulty, therefore, in distinguishing between daily life and ritual, by the assemblage alone. But the deposits are positioned deep within the pits and the shafts were then filled very rapidly, both activities arguing a non-functional pattern of behaviour which may reflect ritual practice. In the storage pits of southern Britain, by contrast, 'special deposits' of whole or parts of animals are distinctive in that they were definitely not eaten, a 'rare and uneconomic practice' but one which occurred consistently. There is a sharp contrast between these deposits and the waste products of butchery.[27] People deliberately chose not to eat certain animals but rather to offer them to the gods, thus occasioning a considerable economic loss. Although much is made of the economic loss that uneaten animal deposits imply, and whilst this is undoubtedly true in some respects, there may have been a balance between religious and economic factors on some occasions. At Danebury in Hampshire, the most important animal in the economy of the hillfort was the sheep, yet in the many 'special deposits' in grain-storage pits, fewer are of sheep than of – say – the economically less useful dog or horse.[28] This could have been a deliberate method of minimizing loss. Another way was to bury deposits of parts of animals, something which occurred at Danebury and elsewhere. Thus one could appease one's gods and feed one's family at the same time, so satisfying religion and reason.

In sanctuaries and graves, there is evidence both for offering uneaten meat to the gods (or to accompany the dead to the Otherworld) and for extravagant ritual feasting, where the animal was sacrificed for the living rather than for the dead or the divine. Brunaux has described religious functionaries as follows: 'Gallic sacrificers were perhaps no more than a specialized form of butcher.'[29] Even butchery can be ritualized, not simply carried out functionally.[30] Cooking, whether boiling, roasting or grilling, may also have been an integral part of sacrifice and ritual. In the circumstance of the sacred feast, meat could only be consumed within the context of ritual behaviour, which might involve special ways of despatching and preparing meat, just as pertains in Middle Eastern countries at the present day.

Meat-eating was widespread in sanctuaries, presumably as part of ceremonial feasts. Sometimes the animal appears to have been killed elsewhere with selected joints only brought into the shrine. This occurred at Gournay, where only certain portions of lambs were consumed. But often the killing, as a sacred act, would take place within the sacred space. There may also have been certain ritual activities which leave no trace in the archaeological record: there may have been blood-letting, for instance, for libations of blood to the gods; rituals associated with skinning; and prayers which preceded consumption. The devoured victim was sacred and the act of eating holy food was a kind of

Figure 5.5 Possibly sacrificial burial of an Iron Age horse found with a human in a grave during excavations for the extension of the Jubilee Line, at Stratford Langthorne Abbey, East London, in November 1991. By courtesy of London Underground and the Oxford Archaeological Unit.

sacrament, which helped transfer the supernatural power to the consumer. We must remember also that any uneaten remains would have to be disposed of within the context of the religious ceremony,[31] just as in Anglican acts of Communion the officiating priest will consume any wine that has not been used after it has been consecrated.

An interesting point about Celtic ritual feasting is the lack of wild species (see chapter 3), which are virtually unrepresented in these activities. This must be deliberate: domestic animals must have fulfilled some religious criterion that wild beasts did not. Maybe feasting was something which represented gifts from humans to gods, since humans were responsible for creating and tending domestic herds, whilst wild animals were perhaps perceived as belonging to the gods. Wild animals were sacrificed, as at the Digeon (Somme) shrine (see p. 125) but the wild species did not form part of the ritual meal.

Feasting ceremonies, as opposed to offerings of entire animals or joints of meat, leave traces of butchery on the bones. At some sanctuaries, there is further evidence: at Mirebeau (Côte d'Or), bones and broken pots strewed the floor of the shrine, redolent of a great feast or series of meals taking place within a sacred area.[32] Feasting also took place at the sites of graves, perhaps performing similar bereavement rites to the wakes which accompany some modern funerals and which are essentially for the living rather than for the dead. Brunaux[33] suggests that the elaborate animal-headed firedogs (figure 5.6) found in some rich Iron Age graves, and which were probably used to contain hearths, may have been associated with the role of animals in ritual feasting and sacrifice.

SACRED SPACE: PITS, GRAVES AND SANCTUARIES

Pits

In Britain and in parts of Continental Europe, there is a consistent and repeated ritual activity which associates animal burials with pits, wells or shafts. Most striking is the behaviour of Iron Age communities in southern England, who used pits dug into the chalk for the storage of grain. What seems to have happened is that once a pit came to the end of its useful life and was no longer required, elaborate, pre-closure thanksgiving ceremonies took place, indicated archaeologically by the deposition of whole or parts of animals. This act of burial was a non-rational act, involving a serious economic loss, as we have seen, but it was none the less repeated in many pits and on a number of sites in southern Britain. The animals, often known as 'special deposits', were usually positioned, sometimes very carefully, at the bottom of pits before they were finally filled with rubbish and soil. Pits containing

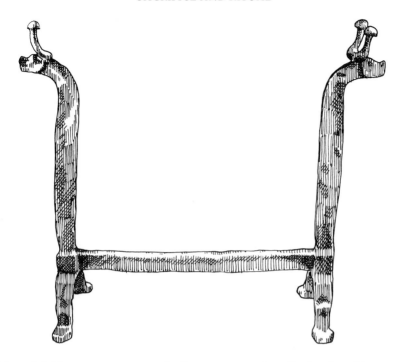

Figure 5.6 First-century BC or early first-century AD iron firedog found in a grave at Baldock, Hertfordshire. Paul Jenkins.

'special deposits' are always situated in the interior of occupation sites, rather than on the periphery. Through time there is a shift in the type of site in which such pits occur: thus in later periods, the 'special deposits' of animal burials decline in open settlements but increase sharply in the hillforts.[34]

The special or abnormal deposits of animals in pits fall into three main categories: they may consist of complete or partial articulated skeletons, bearing no signs of butchery for consumption, and sometimes beheaded; or they may be represented by skulls, which were not split to extract the brain, as was the normal economic practice; or they may comprise articulated limbs. In all three groups, the remains represent the loss to a community of the normal economic benefits of animals, whether for consumption, for animal products or for breeding. This loss was deliberate and presumably reflects valuable offerings to the gods.

The animals which were sacrificed in this manner were nearly always domestic species or birds. An exception occurs at Winklebury (Hants), where a deposit of twelve foxes and a red deer was laid down. There are a number of reasons for these 'special deposits' to be considered abnormal and therefore arguably the result of ritual activity: one is the absence of evidence for consumption, in the form of butchery; another is that the animals represented by special deposits do not accurately reflect their proportions in the general animal population: thus horses are overrepresented, sheep underrepresented, and so on. A third reason is the presence of multiple burials, where two or more complete animals were interred together. It is surely too much of a coincidence to suppose that the animals died naturally at the same time, and deliberate sacrificial slaughter is a much more persuasive explanation.[35]

It is worth while to examine these 'special deposits' in British grain-storage pits in a little more detail. Whilst much of the current and recent research has been stimulated by the excavations at the Danebury hillfort (Hants), occurrences at other sites in southern Britain indicate that animal burials in pits were a recurrent phenomenon. Whole skeletons were present, for instance, at Ashville (Oxon.) and Maiden Castle (Dorset); skulls at Meon Hill (Hants) and Camulodunum (Essex). At Twywell (Northants) two pigs and a dog were buried together; a dog and a man at Blewburton (Oxon.). Several times at Danebury, dogs and horses were interred together, and on one occasion a cat and a sheep shared a pit.

Danebury is particularly rich in animal remains and it is this site which has provided the greatest opportunity to study the curious ritual activity reflected by special animal deposits. The pits at Danebury are narrow-mouthed, flaring out at the base.[36] About one-third of the pits contain special deposits of animals (figure 5.7). It may be, however, that some of the others may once have contained organic offerings – grain, slices of meat, vegetables or liquor – which have vanished, leaving no archaeological trace. Certainly, some pits contained iron tools, which were themselves arguably offerings. The very high proportion of special animal deposits at Danebury is in part due to the exceptionally large number of bones yielded by the site altogether.[37] The ritual associated with pits and animals may be quite elaborate: in an early pit, dating to before the defended enclosure was erected (i.e. pre-500 BC) were two dogs, associated with other bones, which were covered with chalk blocks.[38] In another, later, pit were an eviscerated horse and a pig, again associated with large blocks of chalk. Several of the animal bodies at Danebury were found with stones and slingstones, used for defending the stronghold in time of war. Annie Grant has suggested that, although many deposits of domestic beasts reflect a considerable economic loss to the community, there may none the less have been economic considerations at work.[39] Thus, whilst sheep are the most important secular commodity at Danebury, these animals appear relatively rarely as special pit-deposits. Conversely, horses and dogs occur with relative frequency as ritual burials, even though they are of less economic importance. What Grant suggests is that it may have been precisely

Figure 5.7 Ritual burial of a horse and a dog in a disused Iron Age grain-storage pit, Danebury, Hampshire. By courtesy of the Danebury Trust.

because these animals were less significant as food that they were singled out for use as special offerings to the gods. Indeed, where there are partial animal burials, it may be argued that only part of an animal carcase was sacrificed and the other part was consumed, thus allowing gods and humans to share the largesse.

To understand the placing of offerings in storage pits, it is perhaps helpful to think of corn storage itself as, in a sense, a ritual or religious act, whereby the grain was given into the safe-keeping of the chthonic or underground gods. Thus it is quite comprehensible to envisage thank-offering ceremonies taking place before a disused pit was finally closed. Such a ritual act would be at one and the same time one of gratitude, appeasement and a rite of passage at a time of change. What we seem to be witnessing is the manifestation of a magico-religious belief associated

103

with animal husbandry, in which the gods were thanked for protecting the corn by means of fertility-offerings symbolic of the renewal of the earth. The animals which rotted in the ground, their blood and vital juices seeping into the earth, nourished the earth-gods in whose territory the pits were dug. Storage in pits was a very efficient method of keeping corn dry and vermin-free, unspoilt and ungerminated. This efficiency was acknowledged with gratitude as being of divine origin.

In addition to the discrete phenomenon of grain-storage pit ritual in central-southern England, there is evidence in Iron Age and Romano-Celtic Britain that shafts and wells were also sites of ritual activity involving animals.[40] These vary through time: for instance, bird deposits are particularly important in Iron Age shafts, pigs in pits belonging to the Romano-Celtic phase. In the Iron Age, the shafts tended to be deeper, more indicative of careful, systematic ritual deposition. The votive offerings which they contained are connected with perceptions of natural and domestic fertility.[41] In the Roman period, wells are particularly associated with dogs: at the Romano-British town of Caerwent, the tribal capital of the Silures, five skulls were placed in a well; numerous dogs were cast into a deep well associated with a shrine of the first century AD at Muntham Court (Sussex); and the remains of sixteen dogs, together with a complete Samian bowl, were placed in a second-century well at Staines near London.[42] It is very probable that dogs were linked with some chthonic or underworld ritual (see pp. 111–13). Bird remains in wells are interesting: most curious of all is the deposit of ravens or crows set between pairs of tiles at Jordan Hill, Weymouth, a dry well associated with a Romano-Celtic temple.[43]

Ritual pits as sacred places for animal-burial occur in Continental as well as in British contexts. The Czechoslovakian site of Libeniče is a long, subrectangular enclosure dating to the third century BC. Inside was a central pit containing a standing stone and several postholes; devotees descended into the pit at the time of feasting by a stairway, and performed animal sacrifices. Before each ceremony, the bottom of the sunken structure was carefully prepared and a layer of earth spread out. It is thus possible to count the number of sacrifices which took place on successive occasions: there were twenty-four. The sanctuary seems finally to have been destroyed by fire.[44] The *oppidum* of Liptovska Mara was another cult site in Czechoslovakia, where the sacral activity was focused on a large pit containing burnt remains of domestic animals, associated with pottery, jewellery and carved wood. This sacred site dates to the middle to end of the first century BC.[45]

In Gaul, a number of sites have yielded evidence of animal ritual involving pits. In Aquitaine, deep pits of the mid-first century BC contained cremations and animal bones, including those of toads. In Saint Bernard (Vendée) one shaft contained the complete trunk of a cypress,

antlers and the figurine of a goddess.[46] The *vicus* or civil settlement at
Bliesbruck (Moselle), which was occupied during the first to third centuries AD, contained hundreds of holes and pits filled with layers of
'offerings', including remains of animals, attesting to ritual behaviour.
The pits were all lined with stones and their sole apparent purpose was to
receive sacrificial deposits. Unlike the southern British pits discussed
earlier, they had no overt primary function but seem to have been
constructed as a religious act. Each pit contained several thousand bones,
which fall into two groups: some were the result of ritual feasting, shown
by their being thrown into ashy earth full of charcoal, along with other
material. The second group of bones was deposited in a structured,
ordered manner and represents the joints of meat, articulated bones,
heads or complete bodies of animals offered to the presumably chthonic
deities of the land.[47] Many of the meat-offerings at Bliesbruck seem to
have been the less palatable parts of the animal, particularly the spinal
columns, implying once again that the choice pieces were consumed by
humans in ritual feasting. By contrast, groups of sacred pits at
Argentomagus (Indre) contain the best portions of meat – shoulder and
leg joints.

One of the most interesting series of pits on Gaulish sites is a group
found within the sacred space of Gournay (Oise). Here, Jean-Louis
Brunaux excavated nine pits grouped in threes and a larger pit which
was constructed to receive the carcases of sacrificed oxen, which were
left there for six months or more to decompose before being placed on
either side of the sanctuary entrance, in an apotropaic, guardianship
ritual (figure 5.4). This kind of burial is interpreted by Brunaux as a
chthonic and fertility ritual, perhaps similar to that represented by the
'special deposits' of southern England, in which an animal was received
into the earth to nourish it.[48]

Graves

In the middle of the first century BC Julius Caesar refers to a burial rite
which he had heard of in Gaul but which he describes as being before
his time and obsolete at the time of writing:[49] he comments that it used
to be the case that, when a man was buried, all his possessions,
including his dependants and animals, were placed on his funeral pyre.
There is occasional archaeological evidence to support this, at least in
part. In the King's Barrow, an Iron Age chariot-burial in east Yorkshire,
a Celt was interred with his dismantled vehicle and accompanied by the
horse team itself.[50] At Soissons, two cart-burials appear to have been
accompanied by entire funeral cortèges, comprising the complete bodies
of horses, bulls, goats, sheep, pigs and dogs (figure 5.8).[51] Annie Grant
points to a comparative sepulchral ritual which took place in the Kerma

Figure 5.8 The funeral cortège of animals found accompanying the Iron Age chariot-burial at Soissons, France. Paul Jenkins, after Meniel.

culture of prehistoric Nubia, at around 2500 BC.[52] Here animals were central to funerary ritual and entire, sacrificed animals – mainly sheep – were placed in the tombs, together with joints of mutton, thus differentiating between food for a feast or for the dead man and offerings to the gods.

Generally speaking, the animal remains which occur in graves are there for one of a distinct set of reasons. First, they may reflect funerary feasting, in honour of the dead and the gods associated with death. Second, parts of animals appear in graves as food-offerings, accompanying the dead to the Otherworld, either as sustenance, to keep him going on his long journey, or perhaps as payment to the underworld powers, a kind of entrance-fee for admittance to the Otherworld. A third group of animal remains consists of ornaments where, for instance, animal teeth may be perforated to form part of a collar or necklace. The appearance of just one bone of an animal may be present to symbolize the whole animal: such may be the case with the phalange of an aurochs at Mont Troté or the talus of an ox at Rouliers. Finally, some animals, like dogs or horses, may be present in the grave to accompany their master to the afterlife.

It is frequently difficult to make a distinction between food-offerings to the dead and remains of ritual feasting. Many Iron Age chariot- or cart-burials contain one or more joints of pork which show no signs of having been eaten. In the fifth to third centuries BC, Gaulish warriors were sometimes interred in rectangular graves with cuts of meat which were usually positioned at either end of the tomb.[53] In comparison with remains of funerary banquets, the food-offerings themselves often seem rather modest; good cuts of meat were not all that common. Other offerings to the dead, such as pottery, seem often to have been more important than actual food-offerings. Sometimes there is evidence that particular species, ages and cuts of meat were necessary to a specific rite in a certain community. Thus, cemeteries in the Ardennes, such as Mont Troté and Rouliers, contain food-offerings for the deceased which consist mainly of young animals.[54] Sometimes indifferent cuts of meat, like spinal columns, might be offered together with one good portion, perhaps an upper leg. Some offerings consist of a single piece of meat, others several pieces or articulated limbs. At the cemetery of Epiais-Rhus in the Paris Basin, changes in the traditions of food-offerings may be observed through time. In the free Gaulish period, pigs were favoured, but in Gallo-Roman graves, domestic fowls were more popular. At Tartigny (Oise) there were different combinations of animals in each of the five graves,[55] but the youth of animals such as pigs is a consistent factor in their choice. Sometimes the bodies of the animal offerings appear to have been treated in a curious way: at both Mont Troté and Rouliers in the Ardennes, pigs were interred with three out of four feet missing.[56] The absence of feet and lower limbs in some graves suggests that animals were flayed, the extremities being removed with the skin.

The main activity associated with animal ritual in Gaulish graves seems to have been linked with funerary feasting. There was butchery and cooking at Mont Troté and at Rouliers.[57] Pork and lamb were offered to both the dead and the bereaved at the ritual banquet. The food refuse from many cemeteries paints a picture of perhaps ostentatious ceremonies where vast quantities of young, succulent pigs and lambs were consumed and the bones tossed with apparent abandon into the grave.[58] Burials of the later Iron Age in the Champagne region contain remains of both ritual meals and food-offerings: complete skeletons are rarer than single bones or articulated limbs, and wild animals are very seldom attested.[59]

The so-called 'symbolic' remains of animals in graves are interesting: at Tartigny, one grave contained a hare, a one-year-old dog and the mandible of a horse 8 years old. This could be interpreted as a hunter's grave (with prey and hunting-animals represented), and it is espcially interesting that the jaw alone could represent the entire horse.[60] What happened to the rest we can only speculate: perhaps the animal was eaten. Likewise, the digit of an ox or the tooth of a bear might represent, symbolically, the whole beast (see chapter 3). Other symbolism may be present in the graves: the Romano-British cemetery at Skeleton Green (Herts.) was in use in the late first century to early second century AD. The burials here were cremations and they were accompanied by animal remains. Whilst the deposits could simply reflect food-offerings, there is something curious about their organization within the cemetery, in that – as we have seen – male animals were associated specifically with the burials of men and birds with women, whilst sheep accompanied both sexes.[61] This kind of evidence leads us to believe that there may sometimes have been elaborate and symbolic ritual whose meaning it is difficult for a modern enquirer to comprehend.

Sanctuaries

Animals were central to Celtic religion because of their importance in daily living. Sacred animals are dominant in Celtic imagery (see chapters 6, 8), and this preoccupation with the animal world is mirrored by sacrifices and rituals in holy places, in the sanctuaries where the Celts communed with the supernatural world. Shrines are especially good sites for learning about man–animal relationships. As is the case with sepulchral remains, animal deposits in shrines consist of both creatures which were consumed and those which were not. The former were once again apparently the remnants of ritual feasting, a time for conviviality between gods and humans. The latter were left for the inhabitants of the spirit-world to enjoy.

Many animal bones in sanctuaries bear signs of butchery and culinary preparation by the individuals worshipping there. Gaulish shrines such as Mirebeau (Côte d'Or), Ribemont sur Ancre (Somme) and Digeon (Somme) all contain such evidence. Species of beast, age, and cut of meat were all important. At Digeon, meaty limb-joints were particularly favoured and here, unlike most shrines, wild species are well represented. At Mirebeau, abundant ritual feasting is reflected by the carpet of bones, pots and jewellery on the floor of the shrine. At Gournay (Oise) only young pigs and lambs were eaten. Here, as elsewhere, the animals chosen for ritual consumption were apparently despatched outside the holy place and certain portions of meat only brought into the sanctuary. At Gournay, only the shoulders and long-bones of lambs are present. This may be reflective of elaborate rites associated with the killing of sacred animals, involving a number of different processes. Perhaps one part of the process was a sacrifice performed in a sacred enclosure, some pieces being eaten and the uneaten portions used in other rituals which do not manifest themselves archaeologically. A second series of rites may have included the consumption of portions which had already been butchered prior to being brought into the sanctuary specifically for a feast in the sacred space.[62] One interesting point about the preparation of meat for feasting is that, as seems to have been the case with graves, fire was used only sparingly; there are calcined bones, for instance, at Mirebeau (possibly the remains of a holocaust) but this is relatively uncommon.

The Celtic sanctuary at Gournay is of particular interest in terms of the different rituals represented by the animal deposits on the site. Here, the beasts whose bones were found in the shrine were treated in two entirely different ways: humans devoured the choicest portions of young, succulent pigs and lambs, while the gods seem to have been allotted tough, elderly meat that no human would have wished to eat. This apparently offhand attitude on the part of worshippers may in fact reflect instead a profound belief-system. The uneaten animals were mature horses and cattle. The horses were buried, unbutchered, in the ditch surrounding the sacred site, associated with offerings of weapons; the cattle were over 10 years old and had been used for work as traction animals before being sacrificed, left to decompose in a large pit within the sanctuary, and then reinterred in a series of ritual acts at the entrance to the shrine.[63] The ditch around the holy place at Gournay received both the bones of uneaten cattle and horses and the remains of ritual feasting on pigs and lambs, but the different species occupied discrete areas of the ditch,[64] perhaps because the elderly sacrificed and unconsumed beasts had a greater sanctity than the rubbish of the sacred

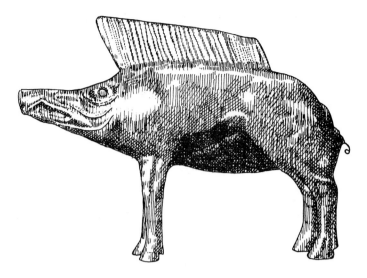

Figure 5.9 Late Iron Age bronze boar figurine, Neuvy-en-Sullias, Loiret, France. Height: 68cm. Paul Jenkins.

banquet (which none the less had sufficient sanctity to be buried within the consecrated space). Another Gaulish sanctuary where certain animals were not eaten but offered to the gods was Ribemont (Somme), which contained an extraordinary structure or ossuary built almost entirely of human long-bones but with several horse long-bones included as well.[65] In the cases where animals were offered, unconsumed, to the supernatural powers, the inference is that they were buried as gifts to the gods of fertility and the chthonic regions, who received the nourishment from the rotting carcasses, just as occurred in the pits outside shrines (see pp. 100–5).

In Britain, several shrines are associated with animal burials, often in pits. This occurred, for instance, at South Cadbury (Som.), West Uley (Glos.) and Hayling Island (Hants).[66] At Uley, the choice of goats and fowl (both relatively uncommon in Romano-Celtic Britain) may reflect a particular cult, that of Mercury, whose images have been found at the site[67] and whose emblems were the goat or ram and the cockerel. At Cambridge, a curious sunken shrine dating to the late second or early third century AD revealed evidence of elaborate animal ritual, involving burials of a complete horse, a bull and hunting-dogs, all carefully arranged.[68] Animals in shrines are discussed in more detail in the consideration of individual species which follows.

ANIMALS REPRESENTED IN RITUAL

Dogs

Dogs played an important part in the ritual activities of sanctuaries. The sacred site of Gournay was the scene of complex ritual involving dogs during the later Iron Age. Pieces of fifteen dogs were found, consisting especially of jaw-bones, implying that there were specific rites associated with heads or skulls. Certainly the bones present seem to have been carefully selected, and there is a marked absence of trunks, ribs and vertebrae.[69] At Ribemont, pieces of dog were deposited in the ditch surrounding the sanctuary.

Dogs were eaten as food in settlements, but there is only limited evidence for their consumption in shrines. However, butchery did take place at Gournay and Ribemont, which suggests that dogs were occasionally consumed as part of the ritual feasting. At Ribemont, one dog had its skull split open to extract the brain and tongue, just like the pigs found on Iron Age habitation sites.[70]

Dogs seem to have a particular association with sacred sites which have an aquatic connection. As early as the Bronze Age in Britain, dogs may have been sacrificed at the watery sites of Caldicot (Gwent) and Flag Fen (Cambs.).[71] This water association continues through time: Ivy Chimneys, Witham (Essex), was a religious site in the Iron Age, and was associated with a sacred pond.[72] The ditch contained skeletons of domestic animals and a row of dog teeth 'set as though in a necklace'. In the Romano-Celtic period, there is abundant evidence for the link between dogs and water: the Upchurch Marshes (Kent) received a deposit of seven puppies, one accompanying an adult bitch, buried in urns.[73] The

Figure 5.10 Bronze dog from the Romano-Celtic sanctuary at Estrées Saint-Denis, France. Paul Jenkins.

skulls of five dogs were deposited in a well at Caerwent (Gwent);[74] at Muntham Court (Sussex), several dogs were cast into a deep well near a circular shrine; the small Romano-British site at Staines, associated with a bridge, had a well in which sixteen dogs had been deposited, presumably as a ritual act.[75]

The repeated association between dogs and water may suggest a chthonic aspect to dog symbolism. That these animals may have been perceived as underworld creatures is supported by other contexts in which dogs were sacrificed, namely pits and graves. The deposition of a dog in a pit (figure 5.7) is not a dissimilar practice to its placement in a deep well: the relationship with underground forces is a feature of in both contexts. Dogs were often associated with pits in Iron Age and Romano-Celtic Europe. British ritual shafts also contained dog remains, especially the skulls,[76] repeating the evidence from Gournay and Caerwent. In the disused grain-storage pits of southern Britain, complete or partial bodies of dogs – with no evidence for their consumption – were interred together, sometimes with great care and within a complex context. The primary phase of occupation at Danebury, before 500 BC, when the settlement was first defended, is represented by a series of pits dug outside the line of the later defences. One of these was about 2 metres deep and in it were placed the bodies of two dogs, together with a selection of twenty other bones which represent a carefully chosen range of both wild and domestic species. After the animals had been positioned, chalk blocks were laid over the bodies and then a huge timber structure was erected over the middle of the whole deposit.[77] This must reflect an elaborate ritual, perhaps to do with the appeasement of the chthonic forces on whose ground the settlement was built. Multiple pit-burials sometimes include dogs accompanied by other beasts: at Twywell, two pigs and a dog were buried together. Interestingly, there is a recurrent association between dogs and horses, arguably the closest animal companions of man. At Blewburton a horse, a dog and a man were interred in the same pit, as a synchronous ritual act.[78] Horses and dogs occur together repeatedly enough for their association to be considered statistically significant at Danebury (figure 5.7), even though both dogs and horses were comparatively rare in the overall faunal assemblage.[79] The link between horses and dogs seems to have been very strong: at the sunken shrine in Cambridge (p.110), a horse and dogs were found buried together,[80] and at Ivy Chimneys, dog teeth were buried in the vicinity of the body of a horse.[81] Elsewhere in Britain the implied chthonic association continues to manifest itself: thus, two dogs were interred in a wooden box, together with pottery dating to the second century AD at the Elephant and Castle in South London.[82] In Continental Europe, too, the link between dogs and pits is demonstrated by the entire skeletons deposited in deep shafts at such locations as Saint Bernard, Bordeaux and Saintes in Aquitaine, and at Allonnes in the north of France. Dogs played a prominent role, too, in the ritual activities centred on the pits at Bliesbruck (Moselle), in which many parts of dogs were deposited.[83]

Celtic graves bear ample evidence of dog ritual: sometimes there is an indication that the animals were food-offerings, sometimes that they were sacrificed uneaten, in different ceremonies. In general, dogs appear far more frequently in the cemeteries of the later Iron Age. A dog formed part of a rather grisly ceremony at Tartigny (Oise): he was probably sacrificed at the death of his master. The man was interred with a hare, the jaw of a horse, and a young dog whose bones bore traces of cutting: the animal had apparently been skinned, and there were marks on the bones around the stomach which are indicative of the creature's evisceration;[84] whether dead or alive when he was subjected to this brutal ritual is not known. Other evidence of dogs accompanying humans to the afterlife occurs at the Iron Age cemetery of Acy 'La Croisette', in Champagne, where three small dogs were interred with their master.[85] But at Epiais-Rhus, dogs were food-offerings and pieces of dog, including isolated legs, represented gifts of meat for the journey of the deceased or a fee for his passage to the next world. The same cemetery produced evidence that some dogs were burnt, maybe sacrificed to the gods of death.[86]

Horses

In the sixth century BC, a cave at Býčiskála, at the eastern edge of Celtic Europe, in Czechoslovakia, was the focus of an elaborate ritual which involved the interment of forty women, possibly the result of human sacrifice, and the ritual killing of two horses which had been quartered, together with other offerings of humans, animals and grain. In a cauldron was a human skull, and another skull had been fashioned into a drinking-cup.[87]

Two Gaulish sanctuaries, Gournay-sur-Aronde (Oise) and Ribemont-sur-Ancre (Somme), display very distinctive rituals associated with horses, whose bones were used for religious purposes. At Gournay, seven mature horses were buried in the surrounding ditch.[88] The skeletons had been exposed and allowed to decompose sufficiently for manipulation of the bones to be possible; then the remains were regrouped in discrete anatomical collections and buried in isolated parts of the ditch. The fact that the horses were deposited in association with numerous weapons (many of which had been ritually bent or broken) may reflect a rite related to war (see chapter 4). We may recall the vow of the Cimbri at the Battle of Orange in 105 BC to dedicate all the spoil, sacrificed enemies, horses and weapons to the gods.[89] The evidence of

Figure 5.11 Horse skull placed as a ritual deposit in a disused Iron Age grain-storage pit, Danebury, Hampshire. By courtesy of the Danebury Trust.

very curious ritual behaviour can be seen at Ribemont, where a kind of bone-house was constructed: this consisted of a structure built from human limbs and those of horses, which had been carefully selected so as to be the correct length for symmetry and stability. The horses had been allowed to decompose to liberate the long-bones. There were more than 2000 human long-bones in this 'ossuary', placed crisscross, to form a square, open on one side, and with a central post. The whole construction was encircled by weapons and shield-bosses. The horse bones came from about thirty adult animals, mostly over 4 years old. There were no signs that butchery had taken place. Indeed, the humans and horses who formed the construction seem to have been treated without differentiation.[90] But in some sanctuaries, horses were apparently eaten in ritual feasts, as indeed were dogs, as we have seen.

Ritual in holy places associated with sacrificed or dedicated horses manifests itself all over the Celtic world: in the late Iron Age *oppidum* of Liptovska Mara (Czechoslovakia) a cult area was centred round a large pit containing the remains of burnt animals including horses and dogs.[91] At the other side of the Celtic world, one of the 'shrines' at the great hillfort of South Cadbury (Som.) was associated with pits containing horse and cattle skulls which had been carefully buried the right way up.[92] In Romano-Celtic Britain, horses were buried under the threshold of a third-century AD basilical shrine, at Bourton Grounds (Bucks.), perhaps as foundation-offerings.

Horses played a part in sepulchral ritual: two Iron Age vehicle-burials at Soissons (figure 5.8) were accompanied by horses, bulls, goats, sheep, pigs and dogs, all interred complete.[93] In Britain, the corpse in the chariot-burial at the King's Barrow in north-east England was interred not only with his dismantled chariot but his horse team as well,[94] although the animals were generally represented symbolically by bridle-bits or other harness. If the dead had been warriors, then the deliberate loss of valuable war-horses must reflect the very high status of their owners. But sometimes a single bone of a horse was placed in a grave as a symbolic, token presence: thus one horse tooth was included in the assemblage at Rouliers in the Ardennes, and at Epiais-Rhus;[95] and similarly at Tartigny, we have seen that a mandible alone represented an 8-year-old horse.[96] The two Ardennes cemeteries of Mont Troté and Rouliers each contained horses; these were young animals which had just achieved maturity,[97] in contrast to the much older animal represented at Tartigny.

Ritual pits, especially in Britain, demonstrate the importance of horses in sacrificial ritual, though there are Continental parallels, as in the pits at Saintes which contained the complete bodies of horses.[98] In the British pits, as is the case with dogs, particular attention was paid to the head (figure 5.11): skulls of horses were found ritually placed in pits at Newstead in southern Scotland.[99] The horses buried in the storage pits of southern England show no evidence that they were butchered, although horses were eaten on settlement sites. It is important to recognize that horses are overrepresented as 'special deposits' in storage pits, compared to the general animal populations on the sites containing these pits. Horses were buried either alone as entire carcasses, as partial skeletons, or as part of multiple animal deposits. A horse was interred in a pit at Tollard Royal (Wilts.);[100] and a horse, a dog and man together at Blewburton.[101] Dogs and horses appear together at Danebury again and again, an occurrence which must reflect a specific cult-practice, perhaps associated with hunting.[102] The skulls of horses at Danebury, which form the main evidence for horses here, were often deliberately placed at the very edge of the pit bottom, under the overhang of the lip, which is the same position as human bodies and skulls occupy. Horse-gear is also present as pit-offerings,[103] perhaps symbolically representative of the horse itself.

The horse ritual at Danebury is varied and interesting: in one pit, where a horse and a dog were interred together, one front and one hind leg of the horse were removed from their proper positions and the head of the horse was placed behind the torso, next to the dog. In another Danebury pit, the articulated head, neck and chest of a horse were placed in the hole after it had been partially filled with rubbish. The pelvis and sacrum were carefully and deliberately positioned over the vertebrae; the rest of the skeleton is missing. Two large nodules of flint were carefully placed inside the chest cavity, and Annie Grant suggests that the horse may have been cut open and eviscerated before its interment. The complete carcase of a young pig was placed against the horse, and a second one on the other side of the pit. In the same layer within the pit were burnt flints, chalk blocks, slingstones, sherds of pottery and a broken whetstone, which had been placed against the jaw of the horse.[104] This must reflect a complex ritual which we can have no means of reconstructing from the evidence at our disposal. All that can be said is that the horse seems to have been the centre of the cult practice represented by this particular pit.

Grant[105] argues that it could have been because horses did not contribute greatly to the economic base of such sites as Danebury that they were deliberately chosen for sacrificial ritual. Horses are expensive to feed and their most important quality is their speed, though they could be used as light draught animals. They were not a major food source. Her contention, therefore, is that surplus horses were available for sacrifice and that this may be why horses, like dogs, are overrepresented in cult contexts. But there are some problems with this argument. Elsewhere, Grant suggests that horses were not actually bred at Danebury but were probably rounded up from feral herds when required. If this were so, then there would be less likelihood of there being surplus animals around because only the ones that were needed would have had to be kept and fed as domestic beasts. The other problem is a religious one. If the whole idea of sacrifice is that it does represent a genuine secular loss to a community, is it not unduly cynical to introduce an argument based upon expediency as an answer to the problem of overrepresentation of horses in pits?

Pigs

Pork was an important source of food for the Celts (chapter 2) and, because of this, there is abundant evidence for the sacrifice of pigs to the gods. Pig rituals fall into two groups: the first where the animal was slaughtered but not eaten and was buried as a gift to the supernatural powers; the second where pigs were butchered and the pork either was placed as a food-offering to the dead or was consumed in a ritual feast.

Both types of pig remains occur in Celtic graves. In Gaulish cemeteries there is considerable evidence that pigs were favoured above other meat. There are also indications that certain cuts of pork were chosen for particular graves or cemeteries. Most distinctive of all is that in very many sepulchral contexts, age was an important factor and that the

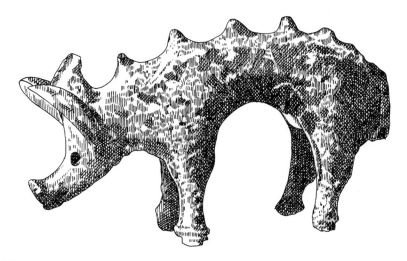

Figure 5.12 Late Iron Age bronze boar or pig figurine, Hounslow, Middlesex.
Paul Jenkins.

choice was for young animals, between birth and 2 years old. So in many instances, the optimum time to slaughter for meat (at the achievement of maturity) was ignored and a deliberate choice was made to kill the sacrificial pigs before this time.

The Iron Age cemetery of Tartigny contained five graves, each with a different selection of animal deposits. Pigs were the most frequent here, and definite evidence for food preparation and feasting was present: often the carcases had been split in two. There was evidence of a systematic method of ritual deposition: legs were without their extremities; spinal columns were most common; and the heads had been split to extract brain and tongue. Each grave possessed different deposits: in one there were only fragments of vertebra; in another, a 7-month-old piglet had been skinned and split in two; in a third grave, twelve fragments of spinal columns belonging to five individuals had been buried, together with part of a sow.[106]

In the cemeteries of the Ardennes region, pigs were a central feature of the funerary ritual, both as offerings to the dead and the gods and as part of the funerary banquet. The meat-offerings to the dead at Acy-Romance were once again from young animals. The same age preference was observed at Rouliers and Mont Troté. Here there were many juveniles but, interestingly, no boars. Both these cemeteries showed evidence of a curious rite, in which pigs were buried each with only one foot attached. At Rouliers, there is a suggestion that pigs accompanied the male burials, sheep the females.[107]

Other Gaulish cemeteries displayed similar emphasis on pig ritual:

117

changes through time, between the third century BC and the Romano-Celtic period, are discernible at Epiais-Rhus, and pork seems to have supplanted other meat as ritual offerings in later periods. Sometimes pigs are represented by just one bone, reflecting the offering of a single joint of pork to the dead: but heads, ribs and vertebrae were split to extract nourishment and are evocative of meals taken at the grave side. Filleting and food preparation took place at the cemetery of Allonville (Somme), where mandibles and bits of split skull were buried after a ritual banquet.[108]

Uneaten joints, offerings to the dead or to the gods, could be represented in graves either as single, modest pieces of meat or as partial, articulated skeletons, the latter indicating that the portions were deposited relatively fresh.[109] Joints of pork were placed near the heads of corpses in graves of people buried in Dorset in the late Iron Age,[110] as if in readiness for consumption by the deceased. Many chariot-burials, both in the Marne area of eastern France, like La Gorge Meillet, or in Britain, as at Garton Slack, contained pork joints.[111] One Yorkshire woman was buried clasping part of a pig in her arms. But the cart-burials at Soissons contained entire pigs, horses and other domestic animals who, uneaten, accompanied their lord to the Otherworld, to continue their service to him there.

Apart from graves, there is substantial evidence that pigs were sacrificed, sometimes consumed in ritual feasts where the spirits and humans were linked in convivial ceremonies. Pork was the favourite meat in most Gaulish sanctuaries: again, as with graves, the preference was for the young animal. Thus at Gournay[112] young pigs and lambs were butchered, cooked and devoured; at Mirebeau pigs and cattle were killed young; and at Ribemont at the beginning of maturity (at about 2 years old or slightly younger). At this shrine, the males were slaughtered at an earlier age than the sows, who were mostly 3 or more years of age at death. Choice of cut was equally significant in the sanctuaries: at Ribemont, people preferred the meat of the spine, chest and head; at Digeon the succulent upper limb portions were selected.[113]

British sanctuaries show some evidence for pig sacrifice: the late Iron Age shrine at Hayling Island (Hants) yielded large quantities of pig and sheep bones in the faunal assemblage.[114] One of the alleged late Iron Age shrines at South Cadbury (Som.) is associated with an avenue of burials of young pigs, calves and lambs.[115] The Romano-Celtic temple at Hockwold (Norfolk) had been built with the four columns of the *cella* (inner sanctum) resting in pits each containing pig and bird bones.[116] The inference is that these animal remains formed part of a foundation ritual, in which appeasement-offerings were made to the local gods where the shrine was built. The burial of a young boar at Chelmsford may similarly have been a foundation-offering.[117]

Pigs form a significant proportion of the animals buried as deposits in Celtic pits. The offerings at Argentomagus consisted mainly of pig; and a complete young pig was interred in a pit at Chartres.[118] 'Special deposits' in British pits also contain pigs, which may be partial, complete or multiple. The body of a pig deliberately covered with lumps of chalk was found at Chinnor (Oxon.).[119] Two pigs and a dog come from a pit at Twywell (Northants); at Winklebury (Hants) a pig and a raven were interred together; at Danebury, a pig and two calves were together in one pit, while in another were deposited two pigs and a horse.[120] At Danebury, pigs seem to have been especially important during the middle period of occupation (400–200 BC), whilst elsewhere[121] pig bones are particularly common in pits belonging to the Roman period.

Why were pigs so important in sacrificial ritual? One answer is that these animals were a favourite source of food for the Celts: thus it would be a genuine act of propitiation to share with the gods something valued in economic terms. Secondly, there may have been some fertility symbolism specifically associated with pigs. Farrowing sows produce large litters, which perhaps gave rise to imagery of general fecundity and prosperity. Pigs certainly are linked with fertility in some cultures: among some Nuba peoples of the Sudan[122] the bones of pigs protect granaries, and it is considered wise to keep the skulls of slaughtered pigs in the belief that this will ensure a continuing supply of these animals. In a Tosari burial at Jebel Kawerma, a human body was interred wrapped in a pigskin. This may have been a regenerative rite, to ensure the rebirth of the dead individual in the spirit world.

Cattle

Herds of cattle were a measure of wealth and a symbol of prosperity in Celtic society, and were crucial to the Celtic economy for food, draught, milk and leather. Like pigs, cattle played an important role in pits, graves and sanctuaries, as food-offerings, as a component in the ritual feast, or as uneaten offerings to the gods. Indeed, long before the Celtic period in Britain, as early as the Neolithic and Bronze Ages, the occurrence of cattle as deposits in major symbolic monuments suggests that they were of great importance in prehistoric ritual.[123]

One of the most important cult sites, in terms of its cattle ritual, was the sanctuary of Gournay-sur-Aronde, where a number of elderly cattle – mainly male and with a high proportion of bulls – were sacrificed. Age and masculinity seem to have been important. The animals present are not representative of a normal population. They were mostly more than 7 years old when sacrificed and thirteen were veterans of more than 12 years. The cattle had not been specially bred for sacrifice but had been used as draught animals first of all. The beasts were probably led into

Figure 5.13 First-century BC/first-century AD iron firedog, with terminals in the form of bulls' or horses' heads, Capel Garmon, Gwynedd. By courtesy of the National Museum of Wales.

the sanctified area and were despatched in front of a series of sacred pits: of these nine were grouped in sets of three and surrounded a larger oval pit. Each animal was led to the pit and then killed according to a precise ritual formula, in which a sharp blow was given by an axe to the nape of the neck, causing instant death. Since the head would need to be lowered in order to deliver such a blow, the animal had probably been offered food and was eating at the time of its death. There may have been an element of the animal's somehow seeming to consent to its death, by its acceptance of food. This form of killing was the result of particular choice: the more normal method of slaughter would be by cutting the animal's throat. The carcase of the ox or bull was then dragged into the great central grave-pit and allowed to decompose for about six months. In the surrounding pits, weapons were temporarily interred. Once the corpse was sufficiently rotted for the joints to be parted, the carcase was pulled out of the pit and the empty hole cleaned: tiny tell-tale bones have been found, attesting to the former presence of the cattle in this grave-pit. The main part of each animal (especially the head, neck, shoulders, spine and pelvis) remained within the sanctuary, while the rest of the body was taken away, perhaps for some other ritual purpose. What happened next to the carcases within the sanctuary formed a complicated and fascinating series of religious acts. The skulls were separated from the rest of the bodies: at some time after death the lower jaws were removed and the heads given a sword-thrust to slice off the muzzle. These skulls were re-exposed and stored, whilst the pelvis, neck, shoulder and spine of the cattle were carefully deposited in ordered heaps on either side of the sanctuary entrance. Successive acts each consisted of the placement of the bones of about ten animals. This behaviour was repeated at regular intervals of about ten years. The skulls were added after each deposition and were placed between each main layer. About 3,000 bones flanked the entrance, and there was sometimes synchronization of deposition, pairs of animals placed one on each side. In addition, more than 2,000 weapons from the nine interior pits were placed in the ditches with the bones, suggested as being consistent with the repeated dismantling of trophies which were previously displayed on the palisade or portico.[124]

Brunaux interprets the treatment of the cattle at Gournay as being associated with a chthonic ritual, in which the animals rotted and 'fed' the earth into which the decomposing flesh and blood soaked. The ten central pits were dug in the mid-third century BC, but in the late third or early second century the nine grouped pits served as foundations for the first temple, a building whose primary purpose was to protect the great oval decomposition-pit in which the animals rotted. This decomposition process may have been the most important of the rituals which took place at Gournay. The cattle may have been especially selected, perhaps because of appearance, temperament or even longevity. Their age and their use as working animals could mean that they were spoils of war, a factor which would have contributed greatly to their cult status. The piling up of cattle and weapons beside the sanctuary entrance was a religious act designed to guard the most vulnerable part of the temple boundary, where sacred and profane space was not physically delimited.

Other Gaulish and British sanctuaries show evidence of ritual involving cattle: at Digeon (Somme) oxen formed important offerings: and at Mirebeau (Côte d'Or), young cattle (between 2 and 4 years old) were killed and eaten in cult banquets. Interestingly, the selection of parts of animals for burial at Gournay – namely heads, spines, pelvises – contrasts with that at Ribemont (Somme), where cattle are represented above all by their ribcages.[125] In Britain, several shrines show signs of cattle sacrifice and ritual: outside a rectangular shrine at South Cadbury Castle, an adult cow was buried; another small sanctuary at the site was associated with six pits containing horse and cattle skulls. A third sacred building was approached by an avenue of pit-burials of young animals, including calves.[126] An Iron Age structure at Uley (Glos.), a possible precursor of the later Roman shrine, is associated with the deposit of iron spears and the articulated limb of a cow.[127] Ox or cow burials were present at a number of Romano-British sanctuaries, notably at Brigstock (Northants), Caerwent (Gwent), Muntham Court (Sussex) and Verulamium (Herts.). A complete bull was interred along with other beasts at the subterranean Cambridge shrine.[128]

Celtic graves have yielded evidence of cattle, either as food for the dead, offerings to the gods or meat for the funeral feast, though they were not as popular as either pig or sheep. We have to be careful in making such assumptions from the faunal evidence, however, since a cow or ox will, of course, yield much greater supplies of meat than either a pig or a sheep. Young animals accompanied burials in the early La Tène cemetery of Acy-Romance (Ardennes). Young cattle were again present at Mont Troté and Rouliers in the same region.[129] Sometimes entire animals were sacrificed when a person died: this happened, for instance at Soissons, a cart-burial accompanied by a cortège of animals including bulls; and another vehicle-burial at Châlon-sur-Marne included oxen.[130] By contrast, a single bone might be symbolically placed in a tomb as a token of a whole carcase, as at Rouliers. In the cemeteries of Champagne, cattle were more popular in the earlier Iron Age than in later periods. Here, a deliberate selection of portions was made, favouring the meaty limbs, thighs and shoulders.[131]

British burials, too, included cattle as grave-goods: the animal remains at the early Romano-British cemetery of Skeleton Green included cattle, the males seemingly deliberately chosen to accompany male humans.[132] In Dorset, late Iron Age bodies were buried with a joint of beef by the head, presumably as a food-offering for the dead or the gods of the underworld.[133]

Ritual pits, too, bear evidence of cattle-sacrifice and interment and here it was upon the skulls that the ritual appears to have been focused. Cattle are one of the main species represented in the corn-storage pits of southern England.[134] They appear at Danebury, particularly in the earlier phases, pre-400 BC.[135] Ritual pit-deposits of cattle occur widely in Celtic Europe: thus they were the species particularly favoured in the pits of the sacred site at Bliesbruck, where they are present usually as articulated bones, especially the vertebrae.[136] The mid- to late first-century BC cult site of Liptovska Mara in eastern Europe was centred on a large pit containing burnt animals, including cattle.[137]

It is clear that since cattle were so crucial to the rural Celtic economy – not simply for meat but for so many other products and for draught – they formed a significant component in sacrifice, gifts to the supernatural powers of commodities of great value to a community. We can have little perception of the precise rituals involved or of the belief-systems sur-

Figure 5.14 Bronze brooch in the form of a ram, fifth century BC, Aignay-le-Duc, Côte d'Or, France. Length: 3.7cm. Paul Jenkins.

rounding them. Classical writers are very silent on details of animal sacrifice, but we do have Pliny's comment[138] on Druidical sacrifice of two white bulls, on the occasion of the sacred rite of mistletoe-cutting, where the parasitic growth was severed from the holy oak with a 'golden' sickle and caught in a white cloak. The colours required for both animals and cloak may have been associated with the milky appearance of the mistletoe berries. Mistletoe, with its winter growth on an apparently dead host and the resemblance of its fruit to drops of milk, was a powerful symbolic promoter of fertility when prepared as a drink within a religious context. It may well be that the two bulls were sacrificed, like those at Gournay, to the chthonic gods, to replenish the fecundity of the earth.

Sheep

Less common than pigs, sheep none the less feature in the meat-offerings and ritual banquets of Celtic shrines and graves. Sheep seem to have been treated similarly to pigs, in that again the preference was for young beasts. Lambs of 3 or 4 months old were favoured at Gournay, but only the shoulder and leg portions were brought into the sanctuary and consumed. At Mirebeau, sheep were slaughtered at 2 years old, as they attained adulthood: this would be the optimum time for killing, in that the animal was at maximum size but young enough for its meat to be tender, so here, the succulence of the meat was a prime consideration.[139] Species preference sometimes manifests itself in sacred places: lambs for consumption were preferred above all at Gournay, whilst the preference was for pigs at Ribemont. At Hayling Island, both pig and sheep are especially well represented in the faunal assemblage of the late Iron Age shrine.[140]

The animal remains in graves often exhibit a predilection for both pork and lamb. In the Ardennes cemeteries of Rouliers and Mont Troté, both species played an important role as food-offerings: at Rouliers, the sheep seem particularly to have been associated with female tombs, pigs with the male burials. Once again, there was a preference, in sepulchral contexts, for young animals: the dead liked their meat tender. There is evidence for the lesser status of sheep over pigs in Gaulish graves, for instance, at Tartigny[141] and at Allonville, where in one tomb one sheep is accompanied by six pigs.[142]

Both British and Continental pits contained sheep as votive offerings to the underground or chthonic forces: at Allonnes, whole sheep were buried in ritual pits.[143] Skulls of sheep were cast into British wells in both the Iron Age and Romano-Celtic periods.[144] As 'special deposits' in corn storage pits, sheep are generally underrepresented compared to the general population. At Danebury, sheep were the main domestic species in the economy of the community, but relatively few have been found in the context of ritual pits at the site. A complete sheepskin with its lower limbs still attached, found in one Danebury pit, represents a considerable economic sacrifice to the owner. In one of the multiple animal burials at Danebury, two sheep and a domestic cat were interred together.[145] The scarcity of sheep in cult deposits at Danebury could mean one of several things: either sheep were economically too valuable to be 'wasted' in a sacrifice; or, because in secular life sheep were only eaten after they had been fully utilized for wool and milk (see chapter 2), the ritual reflected everyday life; or it may be that mutton was not particularly liked at all.

As far as the evidence allows us to judge, sheep were of secondary significance as cult-offerings compared to their crucial importance in the economy. They are consistently present in sanctuaries, tombs and other ritual contexts, but in terms of real numbers they take second place to pigs and sometimes to cattle as well. The reason for this may be a religious one or it may derive from economic considerations such as were suggested above in respect of Danebury.

Other animals

Bones of wild and domestic animals of species other than those already discussed turn up only sporadically in ritual contexts. Goats do not appear to have been common, although there is a problem here, in that it is often impossible to distinguish goats from sheep in faunal assemblages. But goats were buried entire as part of the funeral cortège at Soissons;[146] and there is some evidence for ritual goat-burials at Danebury (figure 5.2). Goats were prominent in the cult deposits at Uley, where they may have been associated with the cult of Mercury. More rare still are cats: again they appear at Danebury, in company with two sheep.[147] Two young wildcats were buried in a ritual pit at

Bliesbruck (Moselle), victims of an infection which evidently resulted in tooth loss and therefore starvation.[148]

Deer, bear, fox and hare are among the wild animals which were occasionally sacrificed and their bodies used for ritual purposes. The creatures of the wild were rarely eaten (see chapter 3). Two teeth of a young bear were buried in the Celtic cemetery of Mont Troté: the youth of the creature reflects the general preference at the site.[149] A young hare was buried entire, together with a young dog, in the tomb of a man, perhaps a hunter, at Tartigny.[130] The great ritual enclosure at Aulnay-aux-Planches (Marne) may have been used from the tenth to the sixth centuries BC. Here were sacrificed a dog, a fox and a young bear.[151] Fox and deer are relatively common among the wild creatures represented in ritual contexts, and on occasions they were apparently despatched together: thus at Winklebury, a red deer and twelve foxes were interred in an Iron Age pit deposit.[152] Deer and fox were prominent in the ritual assemblage of the Digeon (Somme) shrine, a sanctuary distinctive in its bias towards wild species.[153] Deer are perhaps the most common wild and hunted creature represented in British ritual pits.[154] At Ashill (Norfolk) boar tusks and antlers were buried in a well with more than a hundred pots;[155] and a pit at Wasperton in Warwickshire contained two sets of antlers arranged to form a square enclosing a hearth.[156]

Perhaps oddest of all creatures to be found in ritual contexts are frogs and toads: a chariot-burial at Châlon-sur-Marne contained a hundred frogs placed in a pot;[157] and a ritual pit in Aquitaine[158] contained toad bones. The amphibious nature of these beasts may have endowed them with a special symbolism associated with life and death.

Birds

The ability to fly endowed birds with great symbolic meaning for the Celts (see chapters 7, 8). It may have been, at least in part, for this reason that bird bones appear in ritual contexts. Birds may have been perceived as spirits or perhaps the souls of the dead. Among the Borneo tribe of the Iban, birds are regarded as a link between the living and the ancestral spirits, since they share the celestial domain of the spirits.[159]

Apart from a general symbolism, different birds played differing roles in sacrifice and ritual. In late Iron Age and Romano-Celtic contexts, domestic fowl and geese were present. Interestingly, Caesar comments[160] that neither geese nor chickens were eaten by the Britons, but both certainly appear as food-offerings in Gaulish graves[161] and indeed chickens do occur in late Iron Age domestic refuse on British sites.[162] Chickens in graves show signs of having been prepared as food, the heads and legs missing or the heads split in two.[163] Geese and chickens repeatedly occur together, as in Grave 3 at Tartigny.[164] The same association appears in sanctuaries such as Mirebeau, where geese, chickens and other species of bird are recorded. Very occasionally, in the Romano-Celtic phase, it is possible to link a bird species with a particular cult or deity. At the Romano-British shrine of Uley (Glos.), the animal bones reflect the deliberate selection of goats and chickens as offerings.[165] The temple was dedicated to Mercury, whose particular animal companions included the goat and the cock. Geese, too, may be linked with particular aspects of the supernatural. Geese are found in Celtic warriors' graves, probably on account of their appropriately alert, watchful and aggressive temperament. Interestingly, the goose is specifically associated with the Celtic Mars in the Romano-Celtic period.[166]

Although birds are not particularly common as sacrificial offerings in sanctuaries, there is occasional evidence of an incredible variety of species: at Mirebeau, chickens, ravens, geese, ducks and pigeons are recorded; there is a similar assemblage at Ribemont, but here the local thrushes and blackbirds were also sacrificed.[167] Sometimes birds were buried as foundation-offerings, to propitiate the spirits of the land on which sacred structures were erected: this happened at Hockwold in Norfolk, where birds were buried at the base of each pit containing the supports for the *cella* of the temple.[168]

Ravens seem to have been particularly singled out for ritual: they were associated especially with disused storage pits, where they are over-represented in relation to the normal bird population.[169] At the Iron Age hillfort of Winklebury, a pit contained a pig burial with a spread-eagled raven at the bottom.[170] A great many ravens occur in the Danebury pits, where they must have formed a special focus of ritual.[171] Carrion-birds occur also in Romano-British ritual pits or wells. Perhaps most curious of all is the dry well associated with the Romano-Celtic temple at Jordan Hill in Dorset, which was filled with pairs of tiles (sixteen in all), inside each of which were a coin and the skeleton of a raven.[172] Ravens may have been associated with pits and wells because of a perceived chthonic symbolism: ritual shafts penetrate deep underground, forming a line of communication between the living and the dead, the earth and the underworld powers. Ravens and crows, with their black plumage and their habit of feeding off dead things, were clearly seen as messengers from the Otherworld. Certainly in early Irish mythology (chapter 7) the goddesses of battle and destruction frequently appeared as ravens.

A curious event recorded by Strabo refers to birds which he describes as crows but which may, in fact, have been magpies. According to the Greek geographer, a kind of trial took place at a harbour called Two Crows, in which there lived two crows whose wings were partly white. People in dispute would come to this harbour, place a piece of wood in a high place and put barley cakes there. The birds would fly up, eat some of the cakes and scatter the rest: the man whose cakes were scattered won his case.[173] The white wings and the fact that the birds were always seen as a pair suggests that they were probably magpies.

It is undeniable that animals played a crucial role in early Celtic ritual. The faunal evidence on archaeological sites is strong and unequivocal. Iconography (chapter 8) and the vernacular sources (chapter 7) support the argument that animals were central to Celtic religious beliefs. The superstitions surrounding animals, some of which survive even today, may have their roots in early rituals and beliefs. The luck or ill-luck associated with magpies, the lucky black cat, the death-hound (Arthur Conan Doyle's *Hound of the Baskervilles*) may all have their roots in the Celtic past. Sir Walter Scott records a delightful story in his journal for November 1827:

> Clanronald told us, as an instance of Highland credulity, that a set of his Highland kinsmen, Borradale and others, believing that the fabulous Water Cow inhabited a small lake near his house, resolved to drag the monster into day. With this in view they bivouacked by the side of the lake, in which they placed, by way of night-bait, two small anchors, such as belong to boats, each baited with the carcase of a dog slain for the purpose. They expected the Water Cow would gorge on this bait, and were prepared to drag her ashore the next morning, when, to their confusion of face, the baits were found untouched. It is something too late in the day for setting baits for Water Cows.[174]

127

6

THE ARTIST'S MENAGERIE

During the pre-Roman Celtic Iron Age, the fascination, respect and admiration for the animal world manifested itself time and time again in the incorporation of animal designs in art, particularly metalwork. Animals were represented in their own right, for example as figurines, but more often zoomorphic forms were selected to form the interwoven parts of what were essentially abstract designs. The whole period, from about 700 BC to the first century AD, was a dynamic one, as far as art was concerned. Indeed, it is possible to observe a developing and ever-changing tradition which made greater or lesser use of the animal form. In the earliest, Hallstatt, phase of the Iron Age, the decorative iconography reflects the customs and traditions of the time. This was an aristocratic, horse-riding society and thus horses (figures 3.9, 4.3) and horsemen were common subjects for art. Cattle figures, too (figure 2.1), reflect a herding society, where these animals were symbols and manifestations of wealth. The development of art in the early La Tène Iron Age saw a number of foreign influences at work – from Italy, Greece and further east, perhaps as far as Scythia and beyond. Animal designs are of particular importance, but those represented were not only the homely domestic or hunted creatures by which people were surrounded in their everyday lives. In addition, there are lions, griffins, sphinxes and other exotic or fantastic creatures in the iconography of European metalwork. During the fourth to third centuries BC, art veered more towards 'vegetal' or floreate designs, and animal motifs were, temporarily, of less significance. But in the later third to second centuries BC themes based on beasts reasserted themselves, as decoration on weapons, as mounts for vessels, as harness ornaments, as jewellery designs, and as figurines. By the very late Iron Age, when Roman influences became ever more apparent, things changed again: animals were once more prominent in iconography, with bulls, boars, deer and wolves as particularly favourite subjects. Horses were featured, above all, on coins. In Continental Europe, the vigour of Celtic art diminished in the first century BC, and with it the predilection for

Figure 6.1 Bronze chariot-fitting decorated with long-necked birds, probably swans, late fourth century BC, Waldalgesheim, Germany. Height: 7.6cm. Paul Jenkins.

zoomorphic imagery. By contrast, in Britain and Ireland, Celtic society remained alive for much longer and, consequently, Insular art continued to develop and blossom into the first century AD and, in Ireland, for even longer.[1]

This chapter depends very much on its illustrations, and it is impossible to describe the role played by animals in Iron Age art without constant reference to them. What I intend to do is to introduce the different kinds of object which were decorated by Celtic artists with zoomorphic themes and designs. Two artistic features stand out very clearly: one is the merging of realism and abstraction, so that the animal form is often distorted and manipulated into a flowing design. This is sometimes so successful that it may be necessary to study an object very carefully in order to perceive the animal theme at all. This ambiguity in design can be seen perhaps at its finest in the first-century BC or AD

129

Figure 6.2 Crescentic bronze plaque with central roundel decorated with triskele, the arms terminating in birds' heads, first century BC, Llyn Cerrig Bach, Anglesey. By courtesy of the National Museum of Wales.

crescentic plaque (figure 6.2) from Llyn Cerrig Bach on Anglesey, where each element in a whirling triskele motif is a bird's head with a beak and large circular eye. There is an Irish horse-bit which is decorated with the heads of birds and humans:[2] the central ring of the bit has ducks' heads at each side, but if the object is turned upside-down, these become, instead, a human face. So there is a sense in which the art may represent different things to different people and the way an observer 'reads' the art will reflect the message conveyed. The second feature of this 'animalizing' art is the manner in which human and animal forms may become mixed. Thus one often finds a human face or head but with the ears of an animal: a fifth to fourth century BC bronze sword-hilt from Herzogenburg, Austria, is ornamented with a human face with large, hare-like ears (figure 6.3). Bronze harness-mounts of the same date from Hořovičky in Czechoslovakia are decorated with human heads bearing horns.[3] So the Celtic artist was taking zoomorphic subjects but adapting them and subordinating them to his art: the art itself takes precedence and the

130

Figure 6.3 Bronze sword-hilt in the form of composite creature, with hare's ears
and with arms terminating in birds' heads, fifth century BC, from a grave at
Herzogenburg, Austria. Height of face: 1.1cm. Paul Jenkins.

incorporation of animal designs is a means to the end of producing
pleasing art-forms. None the less, there is plenty of evidence that
animals were studied and their forms and temperaments understood.
Though an animal may be stylized, simplified or turned into something
odd, the essential nature of a given beast was comprehended and
somehow managed to manifest itself within the designs. A superb
example of this is the horse-mask found at Melsonby (Yorks.) but almost
certainly originally from the great stronghold of the Brigantes at
Stanwick (figure 4.14). Here, the long, horse-shaped mask is marked
with only a few simple lines to indicate what it is intended to represent,
but the 'essence' of the animal is there.[4]

ANIMAL DESIGNS ON WAR-GEAR

A distinctive group of decorated objects consists of items which were
concerned with warfare, with horse-riding, chariotry or combat itself. In
addition, there are objects which are not themselves part of battle regalia
but which depict warriors. One group comprises actual weapons or
armour which bear animal iconography in some form. The reasons for
such a choice of decoration may be varied: pure design may be one, but
there may also be magico-religious connotations in some instances,
where the presence of the animal image itself brings luck, good fortune,
protection and victory to the individual carrying an animal-ornamented
sword or helmet into battle.

Swords or their scabbards were favourite subjects for zoomorphic
decoration, which could be stamped or incised on the metal. A scabbard
of fifth to fourth century BC date found in a grave at Hallstatt[5] is
ornamented with realistic figures of soldiers and horses, whose riders
wear helmets, trousers and tunics and carry spears (figure 4.2). The

131

horses themselves have haunch-spirals, an artistic device frequently employed in the treatment of animal joints and sometimes considered as being of Scythian origin. By the third century BC, zoomorphic themes were common decoration on sword scabbards. Often these take the form of birds: depictions of birds' heads adorn scabbards coming from as far apart as Cernon-sur-Coole (Marne) (figure 6.4) and Drňa in Czechoslovakia; a British scabbard from the river Witham (Lincs.) is similarly decorated.[6] A grave in the cemetery at Obermenzing, Bavaria, contained the burial of a man accompanied by a sword decorated with birds' heads which spring from foliate designs (figure 6.5). Despite the presence of the sword, the owner was not a warrior but a surgeon, buried with a trephining or trepanning saw (used in operations to relieve pressure on the brain) and a probe.[7] The burial of a weapon with his body may mark his high status in society. A sword found at the site of La Tène itself was ornamented with three deer, tendrils of foliage hanging from their mouths, as if caught by the artist in the act of grazing. Sword-stamps in the form of boars are common occurrences, and this may well be because the boar was perceived as the spirit of aggression and invincibility.

Shields and helmets, too, carry animal designs, perhaps for apotropaic purposes. The shield from the river Witham (figure 4.18) originally bore the image of an etiolated boar on its outer surface, perhaps to protect its owner from harm. Boars were acknowledged as ferocious and

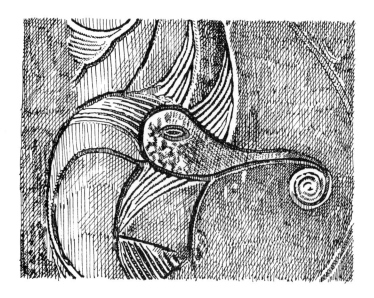

Figure 6.4 Detail of iron scabbard decorated with birds' heads, third century BC, Cernon-sur-Coole, Marne, France. Width of scabbard: 5.2cm. Paul Jenkins.

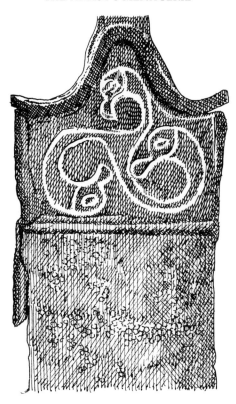

Figure 6.5 Top of iron scabbard decorated with triple bird design, *c*.200 BC, Obermenzing, Germany. Width *c*.4.8cm. Paul Jenkins.

were often depicted as symbols of war (chapter 4); thus they were frequently present as helmet crests (see pp. 134, 152) as well as on swords and shields. Bird motifs, similar to those adorning swords, appear on the bronze bosses of two shields from the Thames at Wandsworth. Interestingly, the early Ulster Cycle saga, the 'Táin Bó Cuailnge', describes a warrior who carries a shield bearing animal designs: 'he carried a hero's shield graven with animals.'[8] The zoomorphic iconography on helmets appears either engraved on the cheek-pieces or as free-standing statuettes worn as crests. An animal which is probably best interpreted as a wolf appears on the cheek-flap of a helmet from Novo Mesto in Yugoslavia, and two other helmets from this area bear crane motifs in the same position.[9] The most fascinating animal-adorned helmet is the Romanian one at Ciumeşti (see pp. 87–8), dating probably to the third or second century BC (figure 4.17). This is the one with the large figure of a raven crouched on the top, with hinged wings which flapped up and down when its wearer moved at speed. Whilst the iconography of the other helmets is probably present as a magical protection device, this latter represents pure aggression, designed to terrify the opponent facing the raven-bearer. It is almost certain that the raven was a Celtic battle emblem, an image of a black bird of destruction, just as it was in the early Irish written tradition (chapter 7). We know of other helmet-crests bearing animal motifs: the classical author Diodorus Siculus[10] alludes to the practice among the Celts of attaching projecting animal figures to helmets. Boar and bird crests are depicted on coinage, and on the Gundestrup Cauldron[11] armed horsemen are clearly shown with boars and birds attached to the tops of their helmets (figure 4.5). Perhaps, indeed, such helmets were normally worn by cavalrymen, although one of the foot-soldiers on the Gundestrup scene wears a boar-crest. The little bronze figurine of a bristling boar at Hounslow in Middlesex (figure 5.12) looks like a freestanding statuette but it was probably a helmet crest. Horns, too, adorned helmets: Diodorus mentions this, and there is the superb example of a late Iron Age horned parade helmet from the Thames at Waterloo Bridge in London (figure 4.16). Helmets carved on the first century AD arch at Orange in southern Gaul (figure 6.6) are also decorated with bulls' horns.[12]

Other accoutrements of war were adorned with animal motifs: the carnyx was a long-tubed Celtic battle-trumpet, which made a fearful braying sound;[13] its mouth was in the form of an open, snarling boar's head. Carnyxes are depicted on the battle scene of the Gundestrup

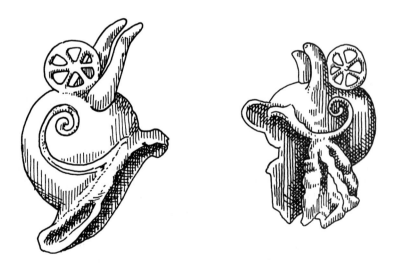

Figure 6.6 Bull-horned helmets carved on a Roman triumphal arch at Orange, France, early first century AD. Paul Jenkins, after Ross.

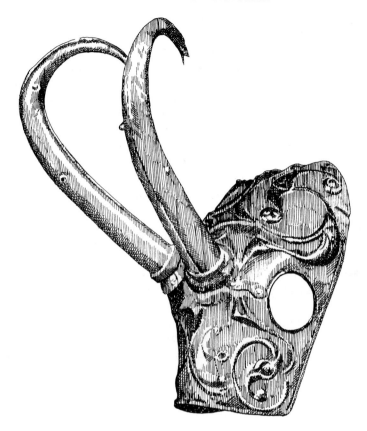

Figure 6.7 Bronze horned pony-cap, second century BC, Torrs Farm, Kelton,
Scotland. Paul Jenkins.

Cauldron, carried by infantrymen (figure 4.5). The mouth of a bronze
trumpet from Deskford, Grampian (Scotland), has been described on
p. 91 (figure 4.20). Dating to the first century AD, it has a movable jaw, a
vibrating wooden tongue and a pig's palate inside the mouth.[14] Like the
Ciumeşti helmet, this implement was designed to be frighteningly realistic and to unnerve the enemy with its shrieking roar. Perhaps most
curious of all objects connected with war and having artistic ornamen-
tation is the 'pony-cap' or chamfrein from Torrs in Scotland: this is a
metal mask into which two curving horns were later added (figure 6.7).
The cap itself carries ornament in the form of stylized birds, and originally the horns themselves terminated in cast bronze birds' head.
Professor Martyn Jope has suggested[15] that the Torrs mask was worn
not by a horse for protection in battle but by a human, presumably in
some kind of shamanistic ritual. Professor Jope points to the 'hobby-

135

horse' figure on the Aylesford Bucket, which is not a real horse because the legs bend the wrong way and are clearly those of two men in a horse-costume, perhaps performing in some religious 'pantomime'.

Horse harness was sometimes decorated with zoomorphic designs. Two back-to-back bulls' heads with knobbed horns adorn the bronze rein-ring at Manching (figure 2.4). The pair of first century AD splay-legged bull figures with curled-up tails from the Bulbury (Dorset) hillfort (figure 7.13) were perhaps fittings for a chariot or cart: the curved tails are so designed as to function as rein-guides, and each leg is pierced for attachment to wood.[16]

Depictions of warriors on horseback frequently decorate Celtic metal-work: this is particularly apparent in the Hallstatt Iron Age, where cavalry riding ithyphallic horses adorn such sheet-bronze objects as the bucket-lid at Kleinklein in Austria (figure 4.3). A brooch from Numantia in Spain is in the form of a mounted warrior (figure 4.7), a severed head beneath the horse's chin.[17] The little figure of a rider in sheet-bronze from a chariot-grave at Kärlich in Germany was probably applied to a vessel or fitting. There are horsemen images on one of the plates of the Gundestrup Cauldron, and they are frequent on coins.[18]

EATING AND DRINKING

The objects which were made for the preparation and consumption of food and drink frequently bear zoomorphic imagery, and there may well have been specific symbolism associated with such images. An early La Tène example is the pair of drinking-horns from the rich tumulus grave of Kleinaspergle, probably made in the fifth century BC, which terminate in rams' heads. The artists have used these animal heads to indulge their creative fantasies, and have departed from realism in the lines delineat-ing the faces.[19] Bronze vessels for mixing wine and flagons for pouring it bear images of the birds and animals familiar to people in daily life. A gold bowl from Altstetten, Zürich, is decorated with images of deer, and the sun and moon;[20] a bronze bowl from a burial at Hallstatt[21] has a handle in the form of an enchanting group of a cow followed by her calf (figure 2.21). This kind of iconography may have been chosen because of the importance of cattle as units of wealth and currency in a society which relied on its herds for its economic prosperity. Cattle quite often appear as handles for vessels: an example is the realistic bull at Macon in Burgundy. Many Hallstatt vessels were adorned with friezes of horses or horsemen, water-birds and suns (figure 6.8): the Kleinklein bucket-lid (figure 4.3) possesses all these motifs; and there is a close parallel between this iconography and that of an early sixth-century BC belt-plate at Kaltbrunn in Germany, which is decorated with rows of ducks, horses and solar motifs. Water-birds are popular images on repoussé-

Figure 6.8 Sheet-bronze vessel-stand decorated in repoussé with solar symbols and water-birds, Hallstatt Iron Age, Hallstatt cemetery, Hallstatt, Austria. Height: 32cm. Paul Jenkins.

ornamented vessels, and reflect an earlier Urnfield tradition.[22] Their meaning is obscure, but in Bronze Age iconography, they are frequently associated with sun symbols and sometimes form the prow and stern of solar boats. It may be that the water-bird, with its ability both to swim and fly, is an emblem of the two elements of air and water. Late Iron Age bronze vessels sometimes have spouts or handles in the form of animal heads: a bowl of the first century AD from Łeg Piekarski in Poland has a spout in the form of a boar; and another bowl from the river

Shannon at Keshcarrigan bears the head of a duck as its handle.[23] Sometimes creatures that existed only in the imagination were depicted. Flagons or jugs from graves possess handles or lids decorated with beasts that sometimes take weird and wonderful forms: the fourth-century BC princess's grave at Reinheim contained a flagon with a lid bearing the cast figure of an imaginary animal; a similar vessel comes from the chariot-burial of a lady at Waldalgesheim, and here the animal figure standing on the lid is a human-headed horse (these fabulous creatures of the Celtic imagination recur later on Iron Age coins). Two superb late fifth-century or early fourth-century BC bronze flagons from Basse-Yutz (Moselle) (figure 6.9) bear images of dogs on the handles and lids and, swimming along the spouts, are small ducks, 'the simple expression of a neatly observed bit of nature'.[24] These vessels are Celtic

Figure 6.9 Bronze wine flagon decorated with wolf or dog and birds, fifth to fourth century BC, Basse-Yutz, Moselle, France. Paul Jenkins.

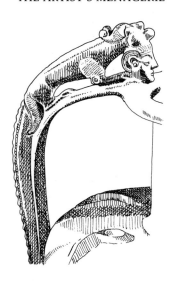

Figure 6.10 Detail of bronze flagon depicting human-headed animal, fifth century BC, from a grave at the Dürrnberg, Hallein, Austria. Paul Jenkins.

imitations of Italic beaked flagons, made in a Rhenish workshop. The flagon from a grave at the Dürrnberg (Austria), again of fifth-century date, has a human-headed beast as its handle (figure 6.10), and on the rim is a curious creature resembling an ant-eater with a long, trunk-like nose; both animals are decorated with shoulder-spirals.[25] Objects interpreted as flagon-mounts from such sites as the third century BC Czechoslovakian cemetery of Maloměřice (figure 6.11) are themselves fashioned in the form of beasts and birds: one mount consists of a complex and twisted design centred on an ox's head with great horns; another from the same site takes the form of a bird of prey.

Vessels ornamented with zoomorphic motifs may take the form not just of bronze containers but also of clay pots or wooden buckets with metal fittings. A number of bronze mounts for late Iron Age buckets are in the form of bulls' heads: those from Dinorben and Welshpool in Wales (figure 7.14) and Ham Hill (Som.), are good examples of a common type of escutcheon. The mount from Boughton Aluph (Kent) is in the form of a human head but with jutting bulls' horns.[26] Pots used for holding liquid or for cooking food bear animal imagery, often in the form of a frieze around the belly of the vessel. Among the earliest of these are the pots from the seventh-century barrow-group at Sopron in Hungary, which depict scenes from everyday life, including horse-riding (figure 4.10), cattle-herding, cart-pulling and hunting.[27] A pot at Radovesiče in Czechoslovakia had been placed in a hut (perhaps a shrine) in about 400 BC: on the vessel was a frieze of swans, picked out in

139

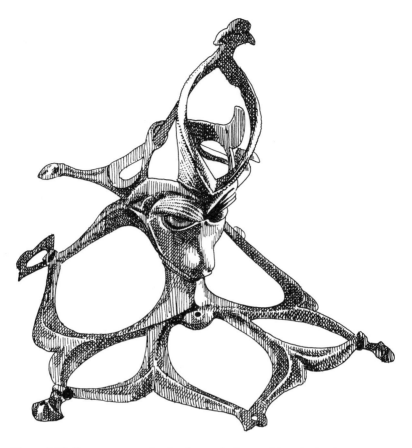

Figure 6.11 Bronze mount in the form of a horned head, third century BC, Maloměřice, Czechoslovakia. Height: 18cm. Paul Jenkins.

red paint (figure 7.7). Vincent Megaw[28] has suggested that the birds may represent migrating wild swans and that there could be a link between these images and the swans which played such an important role in later Celtic myth (chapter 7). A beautiful long-necked fourth-century BC bottle or flask has engraved ornament on the shoulder, consisting of a range of wild creatures: three hinds, a stag, a hare pursued by a hunting-dog and two boars. The pot comes from a Bavarian cemetery of fifty barrows at Matzhausen (figure 3.3), found in a tomb with a family group of a man, a woman and a child.[29] Another grave, at Lábatlan, Hungary (figure 3.5), contained a pot with incised and stamped ornament in the form of a graceful, long-bodied deer being attacked by a wolf or dog which sinks its teeth into the neck of its victim. The hide of both animals is represented by circular stamps. The vessel dates to the third or second century BC.[30] In the late Iron Age, pots continued to be decorated with animal friezes: the painted pot from Roanne (Haute-Marne) is an example (figure 1.1).

Apart from containers, representations of animal ornament appear on other paraphernalia associated with the consumption of food. The flesh-fork from Dunaverney, Co. Antrim in Northern Ireland (figure 2.25) is a rare example of an implement which must have been used to spear boiling meat from a cauldron once it had cooked over the fire. Here, a positive decision was made to decorate a utilitarian object with animal images: all along the length of the fork are freestanding figures of swans and cygnets,[31] echoing the water-bird themes of earlier metalwork in Europe. The other important items associated with feasting are iron firedogs, which are frequently ornamented with bull-head terminals. The most spectacular of these is the Capel Garmon firedog from North Wales (figure 5.13), with its magnificent horns and elaborate and fanciful manes. The Capel Garmon find[32] was clearly a very precious object: indeed, recent experiments suggest that the complete process of manufacture could have taken as long as three man-years. The firedog was found deliberately buried in a peat-bog lying on its side with a large stone at each end. It was probably a votive gift to the spirit of the sacred pool in which it was deposited. The artist made no attempt to create a realistic image of a bull's head: instead he fashioned a strange, hybrid creature with the horns of a bull but with mane and facial details more suggestive of a horse. Jean-Louis Brunaux[33] has put forward a convincing argument for there being a direct association between the imagery of firedogs, with their bulls' or rams' head, and the sacrificial feast in which oxen or sheep were consumed. The function of these firedogs was probably to contain fires,[34] rather than for spit-roasting, as has been argued in the past, but even so, their link with feasting is not negated. The recent 'Celts in Wales' exhibition at the National Museum of Wales[35] had an impressive reconstruction of a Celtic round house, inside which was a cauldron suspended over a fire, which was guarded by a pair of replicas of the Capel Garmon firedog.

ANIMALS IN PERSONAL ADORNMENT

Jewellery is particularly interesting because it seems likely that certain motifs combined a decorative function with magical or symbolic properties. This is especially true of the zoomorphic iconography which is often incorporated into jewellery design.

Many Iron Age Celtic brooches, which had a genuine function in fastening clothes as well as an ornamental purpose, are in the form of beasts (figure 6.12), which are unrealistic and in some manner fantastic, often being part-man, part-monster or made up of composite animals.

Figure 6.12 Detail of bronze, coral-inlaid brooch, with terminal in the form of a cat's head, mid-fourth century BC, Chýnovsky Háj, Czechoslovakia. Length of brooch: 7cm. Paul Jenkins.

This weird supernatural element may well point to the perception of magical, amuletic properties. Most of the surviving brooches come from burials and a very large number consist of bird forms. One very interesting, coral-inlaid brooch from the Reinheim princess's grave is in the form of a hen,[36] a newcomer to temperate Europe in Hallstatt times and thought to have been imported from India. Remains of domestic chickens have been found at the Hallstatt stronghold of the Heuneberg in Germany.

Neckrings or torcs, symbols of status and high rank, were worn by the higher echelons of society in life and in death. The animal iconography which is sometimes present may reflect this high status, in addition to possessing magico-divine symbolism. The sixth-century Hallstatt prince buried in a rich wagon-grave at Hochdorf, Germany was interred with a gold neckring decorated with rows of tiny horsemen, as if evoking the dead man's own knightly rank. The bull-head terminals on a late second-century BC silver torc at Trichtingen near Stuttgart (figure 6.13) may again reflect the status and wealth of a nobleman, perhaps the owner of great herds. It is notable that the bulls on the torc are themselves adorned with torcs.[37] An early La Tène lady, cremated along with her chariot at Besseringen in Germany, was buried wearing a magnificent gold neck-ornament (figure 6.14) in which two wedge-tailed eagles

142

are depicted as part of the design. The motifs on some arm- and neckrings are sufficiently complicated to suggest the representation of a myth or sacred story: both the gold neckring and an armlet from the grave of the high-born woman at Reinheim bear similar iconography, which includes females whose heads are surmounted by those of a bird of prey with large round eyes and hooked beak (figure 7.17).[38] This theme is reminiscent of the Irish myth of the raven-goddesses, the Badbh and the Morrigan, who possessed the ability to change at will from human to bird form. Other possible mythology may be observed in the gold neckrings at Erstfeld in Switzerland: one scene depicts a bull or ox being threatened by a bird with enormous talons.[39]

One persistent theme, which can be traced right back to the Urnfield Bronze Age (from around 1300 BC), is that of the sun-wheel and water-bird. We have seen this combined iconography on the vessels, and it is particularly prominent on jewellery. A group of La Tène bronze torcs (figure 6.15) from the Marne region – Catalauni, Pogny and Somme-Taube – consists of plain metal rings with a single group of images comprising a four-spoked wheel flanked by two ducks.[40] Pendants, of Hallstatt and later date, carry similar imagery: those from Charroux and Hauterive in France consists of small sun-wheels apparently in boats with a swan or duck at each end.[41] These date to the earliest Iron Age, as does the complex pendant at Forêt de Moidons (Jura), which is made up of rings, sun symbols and ducks.[42] The most attractive ornament of this

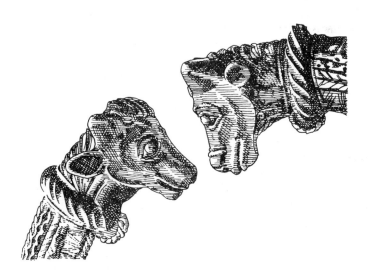

Figure 6.13 Terminals of silver torc decorated with bull's heads, second century BC, Trichtingen, Germany. Length of heads: *c.*6cm. Paul Jenkins.

143

Figure 6.14 Detail of gold neckring decorated with a pair of eagles, fifth century BC, Besseringen, Germany. Width of detail: *c.*4cm. Paul Jenkins.

group comes from a grave at Nemejiče in Czechoslovakia, which is in the form of a bronze chain and a miniature wheel, with water-birds perched at the hub and rim, beaks down, as if eating or drinking from a bird-table (figure 7.5).[43] There could be religious symbolism here, or the

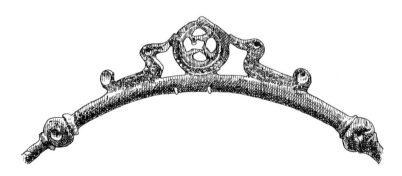

Figure 6.15 Iron Age bronze torc decorated with wheel and water-birds, Marne, France. Paul Jenkins.

144

scene may simply represent a charming vignette from life, the capture in art of a subject witnessed by the artist.

ANIMALS AND CULT ART

There are a few objects in Iron Age art which are of outstanding significance in terms of an association between animal iconography and religion. One group consists of cult cauldrons, great vessels which were undoubtedly of ritual rather than of secular use. These cauldrons are from Denmark, but the imagery owes a great deal to Celtic traditions. The huge Rynkeby Cauldron is decorated with the image of a human head flanked by two bull-heads; an inner plate depicts two wild animals, one on either side of a triskele.[44] The Brå Cauldron is fitted with suspension-rings ornamented with birds' heads; the handle-mounts are in the form of bulls (figure 2.6).[45] But the most spectacular animal-decorated cauldron is that from Gundestrup, a large, silver, once-gilded, vessel whose inner and outer plates, decorated by many different artists, are covered with repoussé iconography of gods, plants and beasts of all kinds, both real species and ones which owed their form to the imagination of their creators (figure 6.16).[46] The cauldron was probably made sometime between the second and first centuries BC: its iconography shows mainly Celtic influence, but the most likely place of manufacture is eastern Europe – Romania, Hungary or Bulgaria. The 'Gundestrup Zoo' which adorns the five inner plates is fascinating in its variety and in the clear importance of zoomorphic imagery. Stags, bulls, gods and boars are among the temperate European species represented, but there are also elephants flanking the figure of a goddess;[47] leopards accompany the Celtic sky-god;[48] and a trio of winged griffins gambol beneath him (figure 6.17). Many of these exotic creatures are related to the fantastic beasts belonging to the repertoire of silversmiths living in the Lower Danube. Bulls figure very prominently: on one plate are three identical bulls each threatened by a hunter with a sword and a hound above and beneath each bull (figure 5.3).[49] The baseplate of the cauldron features an enormous dying bull, perhaps a wild aurochs, which sinks to its knees before the onslaught of a hunter and his dogs (figure 5.1). The killing of the bull seems to be important, perhaps as an act of sacrifice or as a representation of a myth of death and re-creation, similar to that of the Persian Mithras, who slew the divine bull so that the earth would be nourished by its blood. The bull imagery is very persistent on this cult vessel: the sky-god with his solar wheel is attended by a small human figure who wears a bull-horned helmet with knobs on the end of the horns. These knob-horns recur elsewhere in bull images, for example on the firedog at Barton, Cambridgeshire (figure 2.23); the figurine from Weltenburg near the *oppidum* of Michelsberg in Bavaria;

and on the bull-heads on the bronze rein-ring at Manching (figure 2.4). Megaw has suggested that the knobs on bull-horns may be associated with stock management and the use of knobs in farming.[50] But, to my mind, this is unlikely, especially in view of the horns on the Gundestrup figure. In any case, there is no evidence for the use of such knobs in Celtic husbandry. I think that such horn terminals are more likely to relate to some form of symbolism, perhaps related to some 'defunctionalizing' device, introducing non-realism to the image in order to render it appropriate as a sacred motif.[51]

Some of the zoomorphic imagery at Gundestrup has very definite divine associations, which may be linked with the unequivocal religious iconography of Romano-Celtic Europe. Such is the monstrous ram-headed serpent, which appears on more than thirty monuments or figurines in Gaul and Britain. This hybrid creature, which combined the

Figure 6.16 Gilt silver cauldron decorated in repousseé with mythological scenes, second to first century BC, Gundestrup, Jutland, Denmark. Diameter: 69cm. Paul Jenkins.

146

Figure 6.17 Inner plate from Gundestrup Cauldron, depicting wheel-god, a being with a bull-horned helmet, ram-horned snake, leopards and winged mythical creatures. Paul Jenkins.

fertility symbolism of the ram with the chthonic and regenerative imagery of the snake (see chapter 8), occurs three times on the Cauldron, once on the same panel as the wheel-god, a second time in company with the stag-god Cernunnos. The latter association is particularly significant, since it is with Cernunnos that this idiosyncratic beast appears on the monuments of Romano-Celtic Gaul.[52] Cernunnos is the stag-antlered god, lord of animals, nature and abundance. At Gundestrup, he sits cross-legged, wearing tall antlers on his head, wearing one torc and holding a second (again a recurrent and distinctive feature of his symbolism in Gaul), and grasping a ram-horned serpent in his left hand (figure 6.18). Beside him and facing him is his stag, who has identical antlers; the close affinity between god and animal is very clearly reflected, and the stag may even be Cernunnos in non-human form. With the god also are two bulls, a wolf, two lions, a boar and a dolphin ridden by a boy. This early image of Cernunnos can be related to another depiction, far away from Denmark, at Camonica Valley in north Italy, where a rock carving dating to the fourth century BC depicts a standing antlered anthropomorphic figure, with two torcs and a horned serpent (see chapter 8). The third depiction of the ram-horned snake at Gundestrup appears on the Celtic army scene depicted on one of the plates (figure 4.5).[53] This comprises a curious set of images which includes a great tree or branch set horizontally along the plate, apparently supported by the tips of six spears carried by marching infantrymen beneath it. Above the tree, at the top of the plate, ride four cavalrymen led by the horned serpent. Behind the horsemen stands a god, apparently dipping a human sacrificial victim into a vat, perhaps to bless the battle about to take place. The zoomorphic imagery of this plate is intense: in addition

147

Figure 6.18 Inner plate from Gundestrup Cauldron, depicting the antlered Cernunnos as Lord of the Animals. Height of plate: 20cm. Paul Jenkins.

to the snake and the cavalry horses, one of the horsemen wears a horned helmet, a second has one with a boar-crest and yet another sports a bird perched on his helmeted head. The last infantryman below the tree carries what appears to be a sword, rather than a spear like his companions, and he alone of the foot-soldiers has a boar-crested helmet, while the others are bareheaded. Facing the first foot-soldier is a leaping dog, and behind the soldiers march three more infantrymen bearing open-mouthed boar-headed carnyxes.

Whilst it is the five inner plates on which the greatest variety of divine and zoomorphic imagery is to be found, the seven outer panels of the cauldron are not devoid of animal iconography. These outer plates possess figural decoration very different from the narrative, mythological scenes of the inner panels. Each bears a depiction of a human bust, four male bearded heads and three female. The male figures[54] each have large heads and diminutive upthrust arms: clasped in the hands of two of them are images of animals, which must be meant to represent effigies, perhaps of wood, rather than living (or dead) beasts (figure 6.19). One of the figures holds two antlered stags, the other a pair of curious seahorse-like creatures, with horses' manes and front legs but with wings on their backs, long tails and no hind legs. Beneath the god's shoulders are two small 'acrobats' with a long, two-headed boar or dog stretched between them. A third 'male' panel shows a god holding two small human effigies by one arm each and these humans in turn brandish smaller boar-figures, balanced on their hands; a dog and a winged horse prance beneath the humans. The effigies held by these male figures are strongly reminiscent of the cult imagery of the *Viereckschanzen* of Fellbach-Schmiden near Stuttgart (figure 2.13).[55] This consisted of a square ritual enclosure surrounding a sacred well, from which came oak carvings of animals, including a stag. There are carved hands holding the creatures, as if they were once grasped in precisely the same manner as portrayed on the cauldron. According to dendro-chronological evidence, the oak from which the Fellbach Schmiden figures were made was felled in 123 BC. The three 'female' panels carry less zoomorphic symbolism but some is present:[56] on one, the goddess is accompanied by a small man, embracing or wrestling with a large animal, perhaps a cheetah.[57] On a second 'female' plate, another god-dess has one arm upheld, a tiny bird perched on her thumb. Above are two eagles (recalling the two on the Besseringen neckring); beneath her breast is a small dog or boar lying on its back as if in play.

It is quite clear that the Gundestrup Cauldron depicts some kind of complicated mythological narrative, perhaps an epic of creation or an account of the activities of a Celtic pantheon. We will never fully understand it; all we can do is to examine links between its iconography and the Celtic imagery known from other sources, and to note the sheer abundance of animals, a veritable zoo (or safari park) reflecting so many species both familiar and strange to the Celtic world.

A completely different but equally important piece of zoomorphic imagery which dates to the early Iron Age is the Strettweg cult wagon from Austria, made in about the seventh century BC. It comes from the

Figure 6.19 Outer plate of Gundestrup Cauldron, depicting a god holding animal effigies. Paul Jenkins.

burial of a man who was cremated and his remains interred with an axe, a spear and three horse-bits, beneath a mound. He was a warrior of note, a knight, and the presence of this unique wagon-model must imply his high status. The central figure on the wheeled platform is a goddess, bearing a shallow dish above her head. Before and behind her are two groups, each consisting of two women with a large-antlered stag between them whose antlers they hold, and behind them are a man and a woman, she with earrings, he with an axe and an erect phallus. Flanking these humans and stags are pairs of mounted warriors with spears, shields and pointed helmets (frontispiece).[58] The wagon frame bears pairs of bulls' heads at both front and rear. The Strettweg group appears to represent some kind of cult, perhaps involving a ritual hunt or sacrifice of a stag to the goddess, who possibly raises a dish full of its blood in acceptance of the offering. The dead chieftain in whose grave the cult wagon was placed may even have taken part in such rituals himself: he may be depicted as one of the axemen or a horseman; he was, after all, sent to the Otherworld with an axe and horse-trappings.

SCULPTURE AND FIGURINES

Few figural sculptures of La Tène date survive, even if they ever existed in quantity at the time, and there are even fewer animal representations among them. The southern Gaulish group of early sanctuary carvings, some of them dating as far back as the sixth century BC, have zoomorphic themes: horses are especially prominent. At Mouriès, schematized engraved images of horses and horsemen predominate, and one beast has three horns.[59] From the shrine of Roquepertuse, not far away, came a frieze of four horse-heads in profile, and a carved goose perched on top of a lintel guards the temple.[60] The sanctuary at Nages had a lintel carved with trotting horses alternating with severed heads (figure 4.6),[61] and a helmeted stone bust of a warrior is incised with a group of horses beneath his neck.[62] This group of shrines was probably associated with the worship of a war-god; they contained figures of warriors and have revealed evidence for a ritual which involved head-hunting and the offering of the heads of their enemies killed in battle as votive gifts to the gods.

The 'Tarasque' of Noves in southern Gaul (figure 6.20) is a large stone figure of a lion or wolf, with great teeth and long curved claws: it slavers over a dismembered human limb which hangs from its jaws and beneath each front paw is grasped a severed human head. It dates to the third or second century BC.[63] Very similar, though cruder, is the monster from Linsdorf, Alsace.[64] Both these figures appear to represent the triumph of death over human life, death being perceived as a ravening wild beast. The allegory may have been influenced by traditions of the

Figure 6.20 The 'Tarasque of Noves', a limestone figure of a wolf or lion devouring a human arm, and with its claws resting on human heads, third century BC, Noves, Provence. Height: 1.12m. Paul Jenkins.

Mediterranean world, where lions and sphinxes decorate tombstones, to remind humankind of the victory of death.

The rock art of Camonica Valley is relevant to a consideration of pre-Roman zoomorphic sculpture. This north Italian valley near Brescia had a long tradition of carving on the sloping rocks from the Neolithic until the later first century BC. In both Bronze and Iron Ages, the wild animals which the Camonicans hunted, especially stags, were depicted on the rocks (see chapter 3). In addition to hunt scenes, which portray not only the victims but also the horses and hounds of the hunters, there are agricultural scenes of ploughing, using oxen for traction. Birds, too, are frequently represented: they may have had an oracular function, for they are sometimes placed before a person, as if communicating with him, or are associated with shrines.[65] This rock art gives us a glimpse of the way of life of one Celtic community, which depicted its daily activities and its religious life, almost as a kind of iconographic commentary on life, death and its perceptions of the supernatural world.

Figurines of many different animals date from the pre-Roman Iron

151

Age and these may have played a secular or religious role. The creatures represented were those which reflected man's natural association with the animal world. Of the wild animals, deer and boars were the most commonly depicted: bronze deer, like that from Rákos Csongrád in Hungary (figure 3.1), were common in eastern Celtic lands, from the third century BC.[66] A small stag made in about 100 BC was found at Saalfelden near Salzburg.[67] A bronze group of hunters, a stag and a boar come from Balzars in Liechtenstein.[68] Made in the third century BC, the stag's antlers are enlarged and exaggerated, just like those on the deer at Strettweg, as if the artist felt it important to stress this essential 'stag-ness'. The Balzars boar is similarly treated, with the dorsal bristles erect and emphasized, presumably to call attention to the ferocity of the beast at bay.

Boar figurines are relatively common from the middle to later Iron Age. Some of them may be helmet crests or standard-fittings rather than statuettes *per se*:[69] this is probably true of one of the three little first-century BC boars from Hounslow, which quite clearly once stood on a convex base, probably a helmet. In general, Iron Age boar figurines display this characteristic dorsal crest, which is sometimes developed by the bronzesmith into a glorious scroll design. This happens, for instance, at Lunçani in Romania[70] (figure 2.22) and Báta in Hungary.[71] Thus, not only is the natural aggression of the animal captured but the feature of erect dorsal bristles is utilized by the craftsman in order to display his artistic expertise. But despite their stylization, all the boars display the essential elements of a beast which was fierce, aggressive and dominant, a clear image of combat. Whilst the small figures are often fittings, this cannot be true of the great bronze boar-figures found at Neuvy-en-Sullias (Loiret) (figure 5.9),[72] one of which is virtually life-sized. These, together with a magnificent stag and horse, date to the very end of the pre-Roman Iron Age, when they were probably buried in a secret hoard to prevent them from being looted by the Roman conquerors.

Of domestic animals, bulls are most commonly represented as figurines. Horses occur in the earlier Iron Age; the little bronze from a chariot-grave at Freisen in Germany is an example (figure 2.11).[73] But generally speaking, in the later Iron Age, horses were depicted mainly on coins rather than as statuettes (see pp. 156–8). But cattle, especially bulls, were popular. We have already seen that the bull-theme was chosen to decorate objects, like cauldrons, bowls and firedogs, which were concerned with food. The representation of bulls as figurines must reflect respect and veneration for these animals, which were so crucial to the maintenance of the herd and admired for their virility and spirit. Cattle were, of course, required for food, milk and hides (chapter 2) and oxen were essential for pulling the plough. Bulls were represented from the earliest Iron Age: often, the horns are selected by the artist for emphasis and exaggeration. A small bronze bull with huge upcurved horns, dating to the seventh century BC, was buried in a grave at Hallstatt.[74] Another, treated similarly and of sixth-century date comes from the curious site of Býčiskála in Czechoslovakia (figure 2.1),[75] where the bodies of many women and beasts (among them horses which had been quartered) may represent a ritual slaughter or sacrifice. Both these little bulls once again reflect the artist's genuine rapport with his subject, his understanding of it and his ability to combine art with naturalism. Later bull figures maintain this realism, but less schematically: the statuette from Weltenburg in Bavaria[76] dates to the second or first century BC, and is a faithful portrayal of the animal.

Dogs too were represented. In the Romano-Celtic period, the creatures were associated with a number of cults, notably those of Nodens and Nehalennia (chapter 8). But earlier, figurines of dogs were made to accompany the dead in their graves, much as real dogs were buried with their masters in Gaulish tombs (chapter 5). One curious and unique Iron Age statuette is made of blue glass banded in white and gold: it comes from a second-century BC warrior's grave at Wallertheim in Germany.[77]

HILL-FIGURES: THE UFFINGTON WHITE HORSE

There are about fourteen white horses in Wessex, of which only one has a genuine claim to antiquity. This is the White Horse of Uffington, which was carved high up on the chalk escarpment, immediately below the Iron Age hillfort of Uffington Castle (figure 6.21). The interesting point about the drawing of this horse is that it was not a simple graffito cut into natural chalk. Instead, a trench was deliberately dug into the

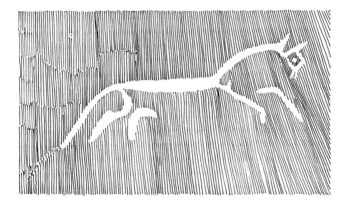

Figure 6.21 The White Horse at Uffington, first century BC, Uffington, Oxfordshire. Paul Jenkins.

lynchet (a deep accumulation of plough wash at the edge of a field) and this was filled with chalk. The image was therefore cut into an artificial trench especially prepared for it: the whole animal appears entirely in chalk rather than as an outline cut into turf, a startlingly clear sight from a long distance.

At present, the horse is abstract in design with a long, thin, sinuous body, disjointed legs and a bird-like, beaked face. Its style alone has led to its interpretation as a Celtic image belonging, perhaps, to the local tribe of the Atrebates. Similar treatment of horse images can be seen on Celtic coins and on a bronze Iron Age horse-model found at Silchester, the tribal capital of the Atrebates. But the present horse at Uffington is by no means identical to its original. It has to be remembered that it has undergone as much as 2,000 years (if it is indeed Celtic) of silting, erosion and scourings or cleanings. There is the danger, too, that it has been restored as a deliberate archaism: the 'beak', for instance, re-sembles Celtic images of horse-heads and there was a medieval tradition of depicting beaked animals: this occurs, for example, on a thirteenth-century jug in the British Museum.

If we envisage the Uffington White Horse as a landmark, it has to be appreciated that silting has caused the figure to tilt away from the viewer who is observing the horse from below. It was originally on much more of a slope and its body was thicker. The animal was sub-sequently much more of a landmark, more easily visible when it was originally carved than today. Indeed, the horse has seemingly 'crept up the hill'; this has given rise to a local legend that the horse has climbed the hill on his own. This weathering effect was appreciated in the eighteenth century: Francis Wise in 1738 wrote in a letter that the rains

> occasion the turf on the upper verge of his body . . . to crumble, and fall off into the white trench . . . which is the reason why the country people erroneously imagine that the horse . . . has shifted his quarters and is got higher upon the hill than formerly.

The Uffington White Horse has a long historical pedigree: the first accounts date back to the eleventh and twelfth centuries. White Horse Hill is mentioned in 1084, and there is another early reference in 1190. Thus the horse must have been a well-known landmark well before 1200. The earliest certain picture of the White Horse is on a Sheldon Tapestry map dating to the late sixteenth century in the Victoria and Albert Museum.

Numerous scourings of the White Horse have been recorded, from about 1650 to 1900. Traditionally, scourings took place every seven years. In the seventeenth century, Thomas Baskerville alluded to the obligation on local inhabitants 'to repair and cleanse this landmark, or else in time it may turn green like the rest of the hill, and be forgotten'.

He also suggested that the people working on the horse should enlarge the belly as it was too slender when seen from a long way off. In 1720, Thomas Cox wrote about the people around midsummer going to weed the horse to keep it in shape and colour. After the work was completed, there were feasting and jollification, ceremonials and festivals. Twenty years later, Francis Wise expressed his regret that the scouring had been left to the common people, who were not bothering to do it properly. There was an angry retort to this allegation by one William Asplin, who wrote a pamphlet called 'The Impertinence and Imposture of Modern Antiquaries Displayed'. In it, Asplin stated that the scourers were energetic enough with the mattocks and spades but were somewhat hurried to get their reward, 'a bellyful of ale'. Another comment some thirty years later in 1770 says that after the midsummer scouring, the people went off to different public houses to spend the evening in 'all sorts of rural diversions'. The scourings and associated festivities continued until after the Industrial Revolution and the introduction of the railways. Thomas Hughes, author of *Tom Brown's Schooldays*, wrote a treatise entitled 'The Scouring of the White Horse', which was a graphic description of the last great scouring in 1857.

Various festivals and legends surround the White Horse. We know of a late fertility festival of cheese-rolling down the steep slope where the horse is carved, into the field below. A tradition is that the White Horse was Saint George's mount: there is, of course, Dragon Hill nearby. Francis Wise records this in the eighteenth century. A supremely bad verse written by a shepherd on White Horse Hill in the early nineteenth century is worth recording:

> If it is true as I heard say
> King George did here the Dragon slay,
> And down below on yonder hill
> They buried him, as I heard tell.

But the strongest view is that the original Uffington White Horse was carved perhaps around 50 BC as the tribal emblem of the Atrebates and associated with the Iron Age hillfort of Uffington Castle on the hill above. There is evidence of Roman activity in the slighted (i.e. destroyed by enemy action) hillfort ditches, which may possibly have some religious significance. The question has to be asked whether the early date suggested for the carving can be substantiated on stylistic grounds alone. Recent work by the Oxford Archaeological Unit has thrown some valuable new light on the horse itself and its surroundings. First, the area is under pasture – rare in this region – and it is now known that it was under grass in antiquity too. This could be significant: the inference is that the area was perhaps deliberately kept clear of arable usage from very early and that the horse may also have thus been carved early.

Research is also being carried out on the construction of the image itself, partly to try and establish a chronological sequence, partly to attempt to substantiate or disprove that its present style was the original design. What has been discovered is that the horse is, in fact, a kind of equine layer-cake; at least four layers of chalk-filled trenches have been found. The horse was extensively restored after the Second World War and at this time, a trench adjacent to the 'beak' of the horse was excavated. The results showed two successive phases of beak, separated by hillwash and positioned some way above the chalk bedrock. The Oxford Unit has now reopened this trench and has revealed not two but four successive beaks, the earlier beaks larger than the present one. More investigations around and below the belly of the horse have proved that it was once thicker but that it always possessed this highly stylized shape. There is no evidence that it was once more naturalistic in form.

These new investigations have already demonstrated that the schematism in the design of the Uffington image is genuine, implying a Celtic origin for the horse. It has partially laid to rest controversy concerning the chronology in that, if the horse had been a more naturalistic, horse-like creature when it was first carved, then this would argue for a later date, perhaps within the Saxon period. A new optical dating technique developed by the Oxford Research Laboratory is currently being employed to try and date the silt deposits interstratified with the horse carvings. Preliminary results endorse the view that the horse is an authentic carving of the pagan Celtic period.

If it is Celtic, then the Uffington White Horse could be one of Britain's earliest pieces of monumental evidence for horse symbolism.[78]

ANIMALS ON COINS

By the second century BC the tradition of striking and using coinage had spread right through Celtic Europe, reaching its peak during the first century BC. The coins derived from Mediterranean prototypes but their iconography shows independence and individuality on the part of the Celtic die-cutters. The imagery on the reverse of many coins has zoomorphic themes; some of these depict manifestly religious subjects and it is possible, on occasions, to link coin iconography with other Celtic art. Indeed, animal types are far more numerous than human representations on the reverse of Celtic coins. The creatures depicted were 'as often as not fantastical beasts, composed of elements drawn from more than one animal, but in other cases plain, routine, representations of farmyard and forest animals'.[79]

Of the domestic animals, the horse is by far the most ubiquitous motif on coins. Often horsemen – or horsewomen – and charioteers, both male and female (figure 4.13), ride across the coins. Depictions of female chariot-drivers were especially favoured among the Redones and Turones of north-west Gaul.[80] Sometimes the soldier has a boar-headed carnyx or an animal crest on his helmet[81] reminiscent of the kind of zoomorphic imagery that has already been discussed. The horse itself clearly fascinated the Celts and their artists: the coin-designer had a wonderful time splitting up the body of the horse into complex patterns, whilst at the same time managing to retain the distinctive character and integrity of the animal. The horse on Celtic coins is frequently associated with solar symbolism (figure 6.22).[82] This image derived ultimately from gold staters of Philip II of Macedon (359–336 BC) which bore the head of Apollo on the obverse and the chariot of the sun-god on the reverse. Celtic moneyers adopted the horse-and-chariot theme and made it their own: often the vehicle is reduced to a single wheel, but the sun is frequently prominent, and chariot wheel and sun seem often to be interchangeable, the rayed solar disc appearing beneath the horse and a naturalistic wheel symbol in the celestial position above it. This sun–horse symbolism is something which may be traced far back into the Bronze Age in northern and central Europe. In the Romano-Celtic period, the solar horseman, a sun-shield in his hand, confronts the forces of evil on the Jupiter columns.[83] Curious things may happen to horses in coin imagery: fantasy is introduced in the triple-tailed creatures common to Britain and Gaul.[84] A silver coin from Bratislava (figure 4.9) depicts a prancing horse, with a triple phallus or triple teats.[85] Another way in which the horse is removed from the real world is by its endowment with a human head: this may mean that rider and horse are being fused and synthesized to achieve complete unity (figure 4.13).[86] Finally, it may be possible to establish a link between the horses on Celtic coins and the Romano-Celtic horse-goddess Epona. Certain coins in central Gaul show a mare accompanied by a foal. A gold stater issued by the tribe of the Aulerci Cenomani of western Gaul depicts a mare

Figure 6.22 Celtic coin decorated with horse and sun symbols, Midlands, England. By courtesy of the National Museum of Wales.

suckling a foal. This is reminiscent of Burgundian images of Epona, where the goddess rides a mare which suckles its young (figure 8.6).[87]

After horses, boars are the most common zoomorphic image on the coins. These may appear on the summit of battle-standards or in their own right. Distinctive in their artistic treatment are the raised and spiky dorsal bristles, portrayed in precisely the same manner as the figurines described above. On a coin at Maidstone in Kent, a boar and stag appear together, with greatly exaggerated spines and antlers respectively (figure 3.4).[88] Very frequently boars are associated, like the horse, with solar imagery, the sun motif being balanced either above the dorsal crest or beneath its feet.[89] Hilda Ellis Davidson suggests that the raised spines on the boar's back actually symbolize the rays of the sun.[90] There are a number of instances where boar images are in close association with those of humans. They may perch on top of human heads, and are not always there as helmet crests; an example is a coin from Esztergom in Hungary (figure 6.23). Among the Aulerci Eburovices are coins depicting a human head with a boar on its neck.[91] This iconography has been linked to that of a stone sculpture which may date to just before the Roman period (first century BC or AD), a representation of a god in human form, over whose torso strides a boar, bristles erect (chapter 8).

Figure 6.23 Silver coin depicting human head surmounted by boar, early first century BC, Esztergom, Komáron, Hungary. Diameter: 1.7cm. Paul Jenkins.

On Armorican coins,[92] a warrior may carry a severed head in one hand, a boar image in the other, as if to emphasize the war symbolism of the animal. Some Breton issues, notably of the Osismi, show curious imagery on the obverse, comprising a large central human head surrounded by smaller heads attached to it by chains, and with a boar perched on top of the main head. The reverse of one such coin[93] depicts a human-headed horse beneath which is a small boar. Again the boar may be present as a battle emblem, perhaps a helmet crest on the large severed head of the obverse, and a war motif on the reverse. Finally, some odd coins of the Bellovaci[94] are interesting since they form a link between coin art and cult imagery: these depict boars held up as effigies by humans, and are strongly suggestive both of the iconography of the Gundestrup Cauldron's outer plates and that of the Fellbach-Schmiden cult images.

Bulls occur frequently on coins, often associated with horses, and perhaps also celestial images: some bear lunar crescents between their horns. But many may simply be present because they were economically important to the Celtic peoples. In addition to bulls themselves, there are gods with bulls' horns, especially among the Danubian tribes.[95] Stags, however, are rare, though the Maidstone coin, alluded to in connection with boar images, bears a beautiful stag figure with enormous antlers. A unique coin, said to have been discovered at Petersfield (Hants)[96] bears an image of the stag-antlered anthropomorphic god Cernunnos (figure 8.20). The ram-horned serpent, ubiquitous companion of Cernunnos in Romano-Celtic Gaul, again appears on the coins. An Arvernian issue displays the image of a horse accompanied by a crane which seemingly attacks a ram-horned serpent threatening the underbelly or genitals of the horse.[97] This could represent a dualistic myth or allegory, in which the chthonic snake confronts the celestial forces represented by the solar horse. But in most iconography, the ram-horned snake is a beneficent beast, evocative of plenty and fertility, so it is probably not presented on the coin purely as a destructive element. It could be that what is represented is a dualistic scheme showing the interdependence of life and death, sky and underworld. It is worth remembering that the ram-horned serpent accompanies the sun-god on the Gundestrup Cauldron. In addition, a Romano-Celtic altar from Lypiatt in Gloucestershire (figure 8.19) combines the symbolism of the solar wheel with that of the horned snake.[98]

A group of Armorican coins contains some very curious zoomorphic symbolism: a wolf is depicted, apparently devouring the sun and moon; beneath his paws are an eagle and a snake. The wolf is huge in relation to the cosmic symbols he consumes. This, once again, could represent the dualistic, allegorical struggle between sky and chthonic forces, reinforced by the celestial eagle (Jupiter's bird) and the earth-bound serpent.

But Paul-Marie Duval[99] links this iconography with a Teutonic myth in which the death and resurrection of the world are symbolized by a ravening wolf swallowing the heavens and all life on earth, followed by the renewal and rebirth of the universe:

> Then shall happen what seems great tidings: the wolf shall swallow the sun: and this shall seem to men a great harm. Then the other wolf shall seize the moon, and he shall also work great ruin; the stars shall vanish from the heavens . . . and all the earth will tremble.[100]

Another related coin-type[101] depicts a wolf perched on a horse, itself a solar symbol. Here the same dualistic conflict may take place. The horse is protected by an apotropaic triskele symbol. Whatever the precise symbolism of the wolf, there is no doubt that it was held by the Celts in awe and respect as a formidable forest adversary of man and as a wild version of the dog.

Of the birds that appear on Celtic coins, most prominent are the marsh-birds, such as the crane, and the crow or raven. The obverse of the Maidstone coin (with its reverse images of stag and boar) shows two facing cranes (figure 7.9). The question is whether the symbols of obverse and reverse are related. In any case the die-cutter was evidently preoccupied with zoomorphic themes. On a coin of the Lemovices,[102] a crane perches on the back of a horse: we are reminded of the early Romano-Celtic imagery of Tarvostrigaranus, the Bull with Three Cranes, on a stone of the earlier first century AD from Paris (figure 8.11).[103] Horse and crane are again in company with one another, together with a horned serpent on the Arvernian coin examined earlier. The symbolism of the crane is unclear: there is sometimes a link with warfare, in that cranes occur on Roman military iconography, and Celtic shields depicted on the early first-century AD arch at Orange are decorated with crane motifs. We have seen, too, that crane-like birds are engraved on late Iron Age helmets (figure 7.8). Ross[104] alludes to the military associations of these wading-birds in the early vernacular sources, where (perhaps because of their harsh cry) they are linked with evil or unpleasant women. But the Greek farmer Hesiod, writing in the eighth century BC, has an interesting allusion to cranes as weather forecasters, thus relating these birds to agriculture:

> Take heed what time thou hearest the voice of the crane, who year by year, from out the clouds on high clangs shrilly. For her voice bringeth out the sign for ploughing and the time of winter's rain, and bites the heart of him that hath no ox.[105]

Finally we must look at the role of the raven in coin iconography. In both British and Gaulish coinage[106] there occurs the curious image of a horse on whose back is an enormous carrion-bird, sometimes with a small cake or pellet in its beak. Its talons dig into the back of its mount and the reins are apparently held by nothing except the bird itself. The scene must surely reflect a Celtic myth: the bird is huge in relation to the horse, a device which supports the interpretation of the bird as a supernatural being. The pellet in the beak is a detail which recurs on other bird iconography: the late Iron Age raven figurine from the hillfort at Milber Down in Devon bears this cake, as do the two raven-statuettes from the Romano-Celtic hoard of religious bronzes from Felmingham Hall, Norfolk.[107] The imagery of these coins is idiosyncratic and it is tempting to link it with an important early Irish myth concerning the war-goddess Badbh Catha (Battle Crow), who wreaked havoc on the battlefield, unmanning armies by her appearance among them as a huge raven, gloating over the bloodshed.

The imagery of the coins really sums up the entire theme of this chapter: in pre-Roman Celtic art, we are introduced to a bewildering tapestry of interwoven subjects and symbols associated with animals. Vincent Megaw was right in his allusion to a 'Celtic zoo'.[108]

7

ANIMALS IN THE EARLIEST CELTIC STORIES

The earliest vernacular writings from Ireland and Wales provide a wealth of mythology and tradition relating to animals, endorsing the Celtic attitude to the animal world that is implied by other evidence. These oral traditions were compiled in written form in the early Christian period. The Irish material began first to be preserved in writing in the sixth century AD, but only a very few fragments of manuscripts survive from a period earlier than 1100. Much of the early Insular material was compiled by Christian redactors, monks who worked in Irish monasteries during the twelfth century. But some of the stories – the Ulster Cycle is a prime example – undoubtedly include much that relates to pre-Christian pagan traditions.

For Ireland, the prose tales which are of greatest interest to us consist of three groups, of which one, the Mythological Cycle, includes the *Book of Invasions* (the *Leabhar Gabhála*). The *Book of Invasions* records the activities of the Tuatha Dé Danann, a divine race of beings who inhabited the island before being driven underground to create an Otherworld kingdom by the next invaders of Ireland, the Gaels (or Celts). The second important cycle is the Fionn Cycle, which relates the story of the hero Finn. This is especially interesting because there is a close association between Finn and the natural world. The third Insular collection is the Ulster Cycle, of which the most influential group of tales is the 'Táin Bó Cuailnge', the Cattle Raid of Cooley. This group contains the stories of the conflict between Ulster and Connacht, symbolized by the fight between their two great bulls, the exploits of the young superhuman hero Cú Chulainn and of other individuals of supernatural status.

For Wales, the most relevant written Celtic material consists of the *Four Branches of the Mabinogi*, the 'Tale of Culhwch and Olwen', and related stories, such as 'Peredur' and the 'Dream of Rhonabwy'. The Four Branches are four separate but related stories: the tales of Pwyll, Rhiannon and Pryderi, and Pwyll's sojourn in Annwn (the Welsh underworld); Branwen and Bendigeidfran, children of Llŷr and the great battle between Britain and Ireland; Manawydan and the journey of

Figure 7.1 'Celtic Cranes', a drawing by Jen Delyth.

Pryderi, Rhiannon and himself into England; and Math, lord of Gwynedd, which includes the story of Gwydion, Lleu Llaw Gyffes and the treacherous Blodeuwedd, the lady conjured out of flowers. The 'Tale of Culhwch and Olwen' is a quest tale, in which Culhwch desires to wed Olwen, but is forbidden to do so by her father until he has performed a series of near-impossible tasks. The Culhwch and Olwen story is one of the earliest in the Welsh tradition, belonging perhaps to the tenth century in its original form. The *Mabinogi* was probably compiled in the eleventh century from material which is probably some centuries older.[1]

The vernacular legends tell stories of gods and heroes, the supernatural world, battles, quests and romances. And interwoven with these heroic stories are special, supernatural animals. There are many tales of enchanted beasts, with superhuman wisdom or the ability to communicate with both gods and humans. A strong thread running through the early written tradition is the concept of skin-turning, shape-changing or metamorphosis from human to animal form. This is a phenomenon which is paralleled in the Norse myths: an example is the god Loki, who shifts shape to a number of different forms at different times. Magic beasts continually interrelate with human heroes, sometimes luring them to the Otherworld; and some creatures, especially pigs, are self-regenerating, being constantly killed, eaten and reborn, in order to provide ever-replenishing supplies for the Otherworld Feast.

163

Sometimes, the beasts described are exotic species which would not actually have existed in the Celtic world. Thus, we hear of the lion smote by Peredur, in a Welsh tale of that name, associated with the *Mabinogi;*[2] and another lion appears in deadly combat with a huge snake, witnessed by Owein, in 'The Lady of the Fountain', another early Welsh story. Animals were important in Irish divination, according to the Insular literature. The ninth-century AD glossator Cormac comments on a divination rite known as Himbas Forosnai, whereby the future was foretold by chewing the flesh of pigs, dogs or cats.[3]

It is clear from the stories that animals played a large role in the Celtic consciousness, a role in which beasts were respected and not held in low esteem, the chattels of humans. They were herded, hunted and consumed, but at the same time they were perceived as being of crucial importance and possessed high rank by being closely associated with the supernatural world.

HUNTING AND WILD ANIMALS

There is a strong hint in the vernacular literature of a close correlation between hunter/hunted and the divine world. Hunted animals were sometimes perceived as messengers of the Otherworld powers, the means of bringing living humans, either directly or indirectly, to the underworld. The hunted creature itself may be enchanted or possess magical qualities: it may be a transformed human or a god in zoomorphic form.

Tales of the hunt involve, above all, the wild pig or boar and the stag. In Insular tradition, the hero Finn and his war-band, the Fianna, repeatedly pursue magic stags or boars in the hunt. These beasts lead the hunters to secluded places where they encounter supernatural beings, and undergo strange, sometimes perilous, experiences.[4] There is a great deal of hunting mythology in Welsh literature: in the First Branch of the *Mabinogi,* a hunted stag is the means by which the hero Pwyll, lord of Arberth, encounters Arawn, ruler of the underworld Annwn. The stag itself is not of supernatural origin but it forms the link between the worlds of humans and the gods. Pwyll goes hunting with his pack of hounds; he encounters another pack of strange dogs which are killing a stag. Pwyll sets his own dogs at the stag and claims it as his own kill. Unknown to him, the other dogs belong to Arawn and the two hunters meet in anger. It is clear from the description of Arawn's dogs that they are Otherworld creatures, for they are shining white with red ears. Animals coloured like this are always from the underworld and we encounter similar creatures in the Insular tradition. Although Pwyll and Arawn meet in inauspicious circumstances, the encounter is important and possibly predetermined, since Arawn

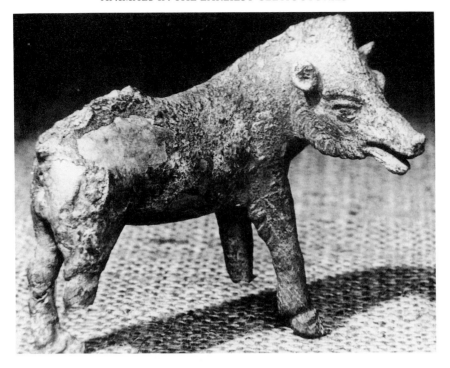

Figure 7.2 Late Iron Age bronze boar from a chieftain's grave at Lexden, Colchester, Essex. Miranda Green.

needs a mortal hero to fight for him against Hafgan, a rival Otherworld king.[5]

Hunting mythology recurs elsewhere in the *Mabinogi*: the Third Branch tells the story of the enchantment of Dyfed, over which a spell has been cast by an unknown agency, causing the disappearance of nearly every living being in the land. The two heroes of the tale are Manawydan, brother of the great Bendigeidfran and probably himself a divinity, and Pryderi, the son of Pwyll and lord of Dyfed. After the enchantment of their land, the two heroes make their living by hunting; their dogs disturb a boar, which is clearly of supernatural origin, for it is enormous and shining white. This boar lures the dogs into a deserted fort in which there is a magic golden bowl. Pryderi follows the dogs, touches the bowl and is stuck fast to it; when his wife Rhiannon goes in search of him, the same fate befalls her.[6] So once again, the animal is the means by which the supernatural powers make themselves known to humans.

The whole of the early Welsh story, the 'Tale of Culhwch and Olwen', is constructed around a great hunt, part of a complicated quest story in which Culhwch is given a series of Herculean labours to perform by the giant Ysbaddaden before he can win the hand of Olwen, the daughter of the giant. The quarry of this great hunt is one Twrch Trwyth, an enchanted boar who was once a king. To help in the task of obtaining the shears, comb and razor from between Twrch Trwyth's ears, Culhwch enlists the aid of Arthur and of the divine hunter Mabon, son of Modron. Twrch Trwyth and his followers (all similarly enchanted pigs) lead the heroes all over South Wales, Ireland and Cornwall before he is finally brought to ground.[7]

The hunt as a way of life is strongly emphasized in these tales. Thus in the Third Branch of the *Mabinogi*, Manawydan says that since he has lost his hunting-dogs (lured away by the magic boar) he can win no livelihood. In another early Welsh tale, the 'Dream of Rhonabwy', we are introduced to a board game played by Arthur and Owein ap Urien. The game is called *gwyddbwyll*, which closely resembles chess but in it the pieces consist of a king pursued by huntsmen.[8] In the 'Lady of the Fountain', Owein witnesses a battle between a snake and a white lion: he kills the serpent but takes the lion with him as a hunting companion.[9] The implication of all the stories is that hunting is closely associated with the supernatural world and not simply a profane, secular activity. Hunting may have been largely restricted to heroes or the aristocracy, and could well have been subject to strict rules and taboos. If hunting was 'special' in some way – and this is implied by literary references to it – then this may account for the negative evidence of the archaeological record (see chapter 3), in which the scarcity of wild animal bones on Iron Age sites suggests that hunted wild animals were not a significant factor among food animals, even though hunting undoubtedly took place for reasons other than the provision of food.

Stags

In addition to their role as the quarry of hunters in the Irish and Welsh literature, stags receive a great deal of attention in the vernacular tradition. They are associated with wild nature and with the forest, with speed and strength and sometimes with wisdom. The 'Tale of Culhwch and Olwen' describes a supernatural stag which can communicate with one of Arthur's men and helps in the quest for Mabon. In the *Mabinogi*, a stag is the agent through which Pwyll and Arawn meet.[10] The Irish band of warriors, the Fianna, are presented as being closely linked with the natural world, for which the deer may be used as a symbol. In the Fionn Cycle, Finn's wife Sava is part-deer, part-woman: the first time Finn meets her, she is in the shape of a fawn, having been transformed thus by the magic of the Black Druid. Her son, Oisin, is perceived as having an affinity with deer and is sometimes described as half-fawn, half-child:

Figure 7.3 Stone relief of Gaulish hammer-god with dog, Nîmes, France.

his name means 'Little Deer'.[11] In another story of Finn, a lady from the *sídh* (or Otherworld dwelling-place) of the Irish god Donn mac Midir is sent in the shape of a fawn to lure Finn to Donn's domain. In a second version of that tale, it is the god Donn himself who turns into a stag by his own magic, in order to entice the hero to the underworld. In one story about the Irish underworld god Donn, which is concerned with jealousy and revenge, we hear of the *sídh* of one Cliodh, whose queen turns a hundred girls from the *sídh* into deer, in a fit of jealous rage. Donn acts as their guardian but the queen next changes him into a stag. The hero Finn hunts the deer and both stag-god and enchanted hinds are killed.[12] Thus in both the Welsh and Irish traditions the stag is bound up with the notion that gods needed living humans to come to their realms and employed stags as intermediaries. The whole concept that living men were required by the gods seems to be based on the idea

167

Figure 7.4 Late Iron Age bronze figurine of a stag, Milber Down, Devon. Miranda Green.

that in the shadowy lands of the dead, the strength of a living, full-blooded hero is needed to fulfil a particular purpose: in the case of Pwyll, Arawn required him to kill Hafgan; it was apparently impossible for Arawn to accomplish this himself.

Stags are associated with the divine world in other ways: we know of an Irish goddess Flidhais, deity of forests and wild things, who kept herds of deer as if they were cattle.[13] Stags were often associated with shape-changing: we have seen this already with Finn. It occurs again, for instance, in 'Math', the Fourth Branch of the *Mabinogi*, where Math, lord of Gwynedd, punishes his nephews Gwydion and Gilfaethwy for their trickery. The penance imposed on the brothers is that, for a year each, they are changed into three different pairs of animals, one of which consists of a stag and a hind.[14] In the 'Tale of Culhwch and Olwen', various magic animals are consulted, including a supernatural stag, the Stag of Rhedynfre, who is able to speak to Arthur's man Gwrhyr Interpreter of Tongues.[15] In Irish mythology, the war/mother-goddess, the Morrigan, is able to change shape from human to stag form. In the Irish 'Colloquy of the Ancients', a three-antlered stag is mentioned,[16] a magical creature whose antlers are increased to the sacred power of three, presumably to enhance his symbolism as a potent supernatural being.

Boars and pigs

It is impossible, in the literature, to separate wild and thus hunted pigs/boars from domestic pigs, since the two are usually not distinguished in the legends. What is clear from the writings of Wales and Ireland is that pigs were crucially important both in terms of food and religion and often the two are very closely interlinked. Like stags, fierce wild boars of supernatural size and strange appearance occur as enchanted, Otherworld creatures, sometimes luring humans to the realms of the gods. Mention has already been made of the great white Welsh boar encountered by Pryderi and Manawydan in the *Mabinogi*, and the enchanted Twrch Trwyth in the 'Tale of Culhwch and Olwen'. Another magical boar in the same story is Ysgithyrwyn Chief Boar, whose tusk the giant Ysbaddaden demands of Culhwch in order to shave himself with it.[17] One of Twrch Trwyth's seven follower-pigs is Grugyn Silver-Bristle, who speaks with Gwrhyr, Arthur's man who is able to communicate in any language, whether that of human or of beast.[18] The interesting thing about the 'Tale of Culhwch and Olwen' is the amount of boar symbolism in the story. This comes sharply into focus with the recognition that Culhwch himself has pig associations and, according to some scholars, is actually a personified pig.[19] 'Culhwch' means 'pig-run' and the story is that his pregnant mother was badly frightened by pigs, gave birth to Culhwch at the sight of them and abandoned him. He was found and reared by the swineherd, and given his pig-name because of the circumstances of his birth.[20] Elsewhere in the Welsh tradition, enchanted, transmogrified pigs are encountered. One of the three punishments inflicted by Math on Gwydion and his brother consists of their transformation into a boar and a sow: they produce a piglet whom Math metamorphoses by magic into a human boy, but he retains his pig-name 'Hychdwn' (*hwch* means 'pig').[21]

There is a great deal of pig lore in the Welsh tradition. When Pwyll, lord of Arberth, has killed Hafgan on behalf of Arawn, king of Annwn, Arawn in gratitude sends Pwyll, and later his son Pryderi, a number of gifts, the most valuable of which were herds of pigs, *hobeu*, the first introduction of the pig to Wales (according to the literature). This gift is the reason for the conflict between North and South Wales chronicled in the Fourth Branch of the *Mabinogi*: Math and Gwydion want to obtain these animals for Gwynedd and so make war on Pryderi of Dyfed, who owns the only pigs in Britain. In the story, Gwydion goes to Pryderi and asks for some of the pigs: Pryderi replies that he is under a bond or covenant with his country not to give away or sell any pigs until they have bred twice their number. Gwydion replies that Pryderi need not break his bond, if he will accept a better gift in exchange for the pigs.

Pryderi agrees and receives from Gwydion a magnificent present of twelve stallions and twelve greyhounds decked with gold. But Gwydion and his followers make haste to depart with the pigs, since he has conjured up the stallions and hounds by magic, and the spell will last only the one day. Battle is joined on discovery of Gwynedd's treachery, and Pryderi is slain.[22] The pigs can be seen to represent an extra-ordinarily valuable asset for the Celts of the Welsh literature, made especially significant by their origins as a supernatural gift from the Otherworld.

Another special pig in Wales is again associated with the Gwynedd magician Gwydion. In the tale of Lleu Llaw Gyffes, a swineherd tells Gwydion how his sow goes out each morning and he can never keep track of where she goes. Gwydion tracks the sow and finds her feeding in the valley now called Nantlleu, under the oak-tree where the stricken Lleu Llaw Gyffes is perched as an eagle. The sow is clearly a super-natural pig, whose role is to lead Gwydion to Lleu and thus effect the transformation of Lleu by Gwydion back into a human being (see pp. 172–3).[23] One of the early Welsh Triads, 'The Three Powerful Swineherds of Britain', describes another magical or supernatural sow, called Henwen (the Old White), who gives birth to a number of very curious offspring including a wolf-cub, an eagle, a bee, a kitten and a grain of wheat.[24]

Boars and pigs are equally prominent in Insular tradition. As in the Welsh stories, these creatures may be fierce, shape-shifters and associated with the Otherworld. Their role in secular, ritual and underworld feasting is particularly prominent. In Irish mythology, there was a series of *bruidhne* or hostels which belonged to gods of the Otherworld. Each *bruiden* would host feasts which featured great cauldrons which were continually replenished, especially with pork. Pigs were killed and boiled or roasted every day, but were constantly reborn to be killed again.[25] The *sídh* or fairy mound of the Dagdha, the Irish father-god, has three trees which perpetually bear fruit (indicative of immortality), an inexhaustible supply of drink and a pig that is always alive, no matter how many times it is killed and consumed.[26] The Irish sea-god Manannán possessed magic swine who reappeared after having been eaten. The imagery is very similar to the New Testament story of the loaves and fishes. There are a number of Ulster tales concerning pigs and the feast. In the story of Mac Da Thó's pig, Mac Da Thó, king of Leinster, acts as host of the feast to the enemy companies of Ulster and Connacht, and provides a huge pig over whose best portions rival champions squabble. A similar situation occurs at the 'Feast of Bricriu' (a divine mischief-maker), where there is again a quarrel over the hero's joint of pork. In both these stories, the enormous size of the pig indicates that it is the Otherworld Feast which is described, though

170

classical writers such as Diodorus Siculus[27] also record this champions' dispute in secular contexts. The pig is inextricably linked with this supernatural banquet: indeed, the divine lord of the Otherworld was perceived in the form of a man with a pig slung over his shoulder. In the story of 'Da Derga's Hostel', the doomed King Conaire, on his way to his pre-ordained death, meets this Otherworld deity: he is grotesque, with one arm, one leg and one eye (this last feature is a magic sign, as is the case with Odin in Norse myth). He carries an iron fork and, on his back, a roasted pig which – horrifically – is still squealing.[28]

Pigs and boars are thus associated with Irish feasting and the Otherworld. Pleasant though this image is, it has overtones of death which lead to another aspect of the pig in Insular tradition, as a destructive, death-dealing creature. The Welsh Twrch Trwyth has his Irish counterpart in Orc Triath, a huge, destructive animal who is described in the *Book of Invasions*. In the Insular tale of the Battle of Magh Mucrime, numberless pigs issue from the mouth of the underworld, the Cave of Cruachan: these are magical pigs of death, who can be neither counted nor destroyed.[29] In the Fionn Cycle of tales, a huge boar named Formael kills fifty soldiers and fifty great hounds in a single day: Formael is terrible to behold – enormous, blue-black, with stiff bristles and such a sharp, spiky dorsal ridge that each spine can impale an apple. (In the National Museum of Wales's coin collection is a Celtic Iron Age coin depicting a boar on whose erect spines are impaled circular objects which could be fruit.) Formael's supernatural status is confirmed by his huge jutting teeth and by his lack of either ears or testicles.[30] The link between the boar of destruction and the Otherworld Feast is epitomized by the boar hunted by the hero Finn. The screech it lets out when Finn corners it summons a huge peasant who picks up the boar and carries it off over his shoulder (evoking an image precisely similar to that of the lord of the underworld feast). The great churl leads the Fianna into his *sídh* by chanting a spell over them. The pig itself is transformed by the peasant into a young man, his own son.[31] Another enchanted and destructive pig is the boar of Boann Ghulban, who also appears in the Fionn Cycle. This creature is used by Finn to rid himself of his rival for the beautiful Gráinne. Finn induces Diarmaid to hunt the boar (knowing it will be the cause of his death). The story varies in its conclusion: in one version, Diarmaid is slain by the boar; in the second, he overcomes the beast but is killed by the poisoned bristle of the dead animal. The tale has a twist in that the boar is in fact Diarmaid's enchanted foster-brother.[32]

Birds

In Welsh and Irish early literary tradition, birds feature as enchanted, metamorphosed creatures, with magical and supernatural qualities. It is

Figure 7.5 Iron Age bronze chain and pendant in the form of a wheel and birds from a grave at Nemejiče, Czechoslovakia. Paul Jenkins.

probably above all because of their power of flight that birds were endowed with particular symbolism, but colour, the ability to swim, voice and character were all factors in defining the specific roles of birds in the British and Insular stories. The main species of bird which appear are the raven, the swan, the crane and the eagle. Eagles feature particularly in the Welsh sagas: in the Triad called 'The Three Powerful Swineherds of Britain', the notable sow Henwen gives birth to some curious offspring including an eagle.[33] In the 'Tale of Culhwch and Olwen', the Eagle of Gwernabwy is described as one of the oldest animals on earth. This creature is one of the beasts whom Culhwch and Arthur consult in their search for the divine hunter Mabon and to whom Gwrhyr is able to speak.[34]

The most important eagle story is to be found in 'Math', the Fourth Branch of the *Mabinogi*. Lleu Llaw Gyffes (the Bright One of the Skilful Hand), son of Arianrhod, has a curse put on him by his mother, that he will never have an earthly wife. The magician Gwydion intervenes and together with Math, his uncle, conjures for Lleu a woman of flowers, Blodeuwedd. But she is unfaithful and conspires with her lover Gronw to murder Lleu. Since Lleu is a supernatural being, he can only be killed

172

in a certain position. Blodeuwedd tricks her husband into simulating the manner in which he may be slain; Gronw is waiting for this and runs him through with his spear. As Lleu feels the mortal blow, he gives a great cry and turns into an eagle, which flies up into an oak-tree. There follows a gruesome image in which the eagle sits in its tree, shaking its feathers and raining down a shower of rotting flesh and maggots onto the ground beneath. Gwydion traces the transformed Lleu by following a certain sow who goes to the tree to feed on the maggots and tissue. The magician then entices the eagle down from the oak with a song or spell, strikes the bird with his magic wand and Lleu returns to human shape, albeit as a shrunken man of skin and bone. As punishment, Blodeuwedd is transformed into an owl, cursed and shunned as the enemy of all other birds and compelled never to show her face by day.[35] The character of Lleu is interesting. His name, Bright One, may refer to his nature as a sun-god of light. Certainly, the bird of the Romano-Celtic sky-god was the eagle and Jupiter's sacred tree was the oak. So we may be seeing here a genuine link between the symbolism of the European sky-god, which is evidenced archaeologically, and the western post-Roman literary tradition. In addition, the cult of the sky-god involved dualism, a positive and negative, light and dark, conflict and interdependence, which may also be reflected in the symbolism of the eagle and the owl (birds of day and night) in the *Mabinogi* legend.

Figure 7.6 Bronze cauldron-mount in the form of an owl, third century BC, Brå, Jutland, Denmark. Paul Jenkins.

Swans

Water-birds, and swans in particular, feature in the Insular legends, generally as metamorphosed women, and very frequently they are described as being linked to each other by gold or silver chains. In the tale of the 'Dream of Oenghus', the young god of love dreams of a girl whom he has never seen and with whom he falls in love. He eventually finds out her name and discovers that she dwells at a lake where, along with 150 companions, she is transformed every alternate year to the form of a swan. The girl's name is Caer Ibormeith (Yew Berry) and, significantly, her transformation occurs at the great winter festival of Samhain, which marked the Celtic new year, a time when the barriers between the natural and the supernatural worlds were temporarily dissolved. The image of the chained swans occurs here: when Oenghus finds Caer's lake, he sees the 150 young women, each pair linked by a silver chain. Caer is the tallest and she wears a chain of gold, signifying her special status. Oenghus asks Caer's father, Ethal Anbual, for his daughter's hand but he will not countenance the match, and Oenghus learns that the only way he can take Caer is at Samhain, when she has changed into her swan shape. He goes to the lake, changes himself also into a swan, and the two fly to Oenghus's dwelling at Brugh na Bóinne, first circling the lake three times, lulling everyone to sleep for three days and three nights with their enchanting song. The chains and the meta-morphosis indicate that Caer is a superhuman being, as indeed is Oenghus himself.[36]

The Ulster demi-god Cú Chulainn is repeatedly associated with Otherworld swans. A flock of splendid but destructive birds appears at the time of Cú Chulainn's conception, laying waste the area around the royal palace of Emhain Macha. The timing of the episode suggests a profound link between swans and the life of the hero, and indeed the birds recur throughout Cú Chulainn's adulthood. In one story, he is associated with a flock of swans; significantly, as with Oenghus, this happens at the festival of Samhain: the hero fastens a flock of swans to his chariot when it is stuck in a marsh.[37] In another tale, a girl called Derbforgaill falls in love with Cú Chulainn and she and her maidservant pursue him, having first taken the form of two swans. As with Oenghus's birds, the pair are joined by a chain, this time of gold. Cú Chulainn aims his sling at one of the two birds: she is struck by the stone and falls to the ground badly wounded, returning to the human form of Derbforgaill as she hits the ground, the blow apparently acting as the catalyst which has effected the transformation. Cú Chulainn sucks the stone from the wound but, in doing so, tastes her blood. He is thus debarred from mating with her because of a taboo.

One of the most poignant early Irish stories concerns the children of

Figure 7.7 Pottery dish ornamented with red-painted swans, *c.*400BC, Radovesiče, Czechoslovakia. Diameter of dish: 28cm. Miranda Green.

Lir, a sea-god. Lir marries one Eve, the eldest of the three foster-daughters of Bov, king of the divine race of the Tuatha Dé Danann. Lir and Eve produce four children, two sets of twins (a girl and a boy in each pair). Eve dies giving birth to the younger twins, and Lir then marries her sister Eva. The twins are adored by their father, but Eva soon develops a maniacal jealousy of the children and plots their downfall. She entices the four to a lake, named Lake Derravaragh, in the centre of Ireland where, with the aid of a druidical wand, she turns them into swans. The full curse is that they remain in bird form for a total of 900 years, though they retain the power of human speech. Eva proclaims that the curse will not be lifted until the swan-children hear the bell which is the voice of Christianity in Ireland and until a prince from the north marries a princess of the south. The four bewitched children remain human in all but shape, and they possess the power of incredibly sweet singing, which makes all who hear it happy and which attracts many other birds to their lake. By the end of the 900 years, St Patrick had arrived in Ireland to spread the Christian message. One of Patrick's followers, Kernoc, builds a church on Inish Gloria, where the enchanted swans dwell. They hear the church bell and come to Kernoc, who takes care of them. Soon afterwards, the other part of the prophecy comes to pass and Decca, daughter of Finnin, king of Munster, weds Largnen of Connacht. The curse is over, the swans are released from their bird form but, alas, they are humans 900 years old and they instantly die of old age. Kernoc buries them together, raising an earth mound over them and marking their graves with a tombstone with their names in ogam (an ancient Celtic linear script).[38]

Cranes

In Insular mythology, whilst swans are generally portrayed as beautiful, sweet-voiced birds, often associated with comely young women, cranes are conversely depicted as unpleasant and mean, though again linked closely with females. In the *Book of Leinster*, the divine Midhir, a god of the Tuatha Dé Danann, possesses three cranes which guard his *sídh*, Brí Leith, from intruders. But these birds possess the additional reputation of unmanning warriors, robbing them of their will to fight. So the cranes are essentially birds of ill omen, to be feared and avoided. This bad-luck image may be linked with the taboo on eating crane flesh in early Ireland, which was noted by Giraldus Cambrensis in his *Expugnatio Hibernica*.[39] The identification of cranes with unpleasant women may have been due to the harsh and raucous screech of the birds which could have been perceived as similar to the hectoring speech of a scold. The Irish sea-god Manannán possessed a 'crane-bag' full of treasures, the skin of a crane who was once a woman transformed as a result of her jealous nature. The Irish hero Finn is also connected with cranes in at least two stories. In one tale, 'Cailleach an Teampuill' ('The Hag of the Temple'), Finn is associated with cranes of death: here the hag's four sons are in the form of cranes who can only become human if the blood of an enchanted bull is sprinkled over them.[40] The association between bulls and cranes is interesting because of certain Romano-Celtic iconography (chapter 8) which consists of images of bulls with cranes on their backs. In another tale, the crane appears in a pleasanter light: as a child, Finn is saved from falling to his death over a cliff by his grandmother, who metamorphoses to the form of a crane and breaks his fall.[41] Like the swan, certain characteristics of the crane lend themselves to a particular image and mythology. The swan is associated with grace, beauty and youth, but the crane is identified with parsimony, harshness, death and old age. In both cases, particular heroes are perceived to have an affinity with the birds and their destiny is inextricably bound up with them: for Cú Chulainn it is the swan; for Finn, the crane.

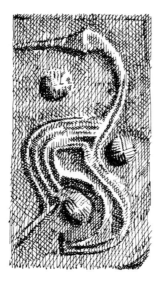

Figure 7.8 Cheek-piece from first-century BC helmet with crane design, Šmarjeta, Yugoslavia.

Figure 7.9 Celtic coin depicting two cranes, Maidstone, Kent. By courtesy of the National Museum of Wales.

Ravens

The major characteristic of ravens in the early literature is of evil, death and destruction. In addition, a strong image repeated in many of the stories is that of ravens as prophets, foretelling the future – which was itself usually linked with death. The concept of ravens as birds of omen is interesting; indeed, they were used by Irish Druids in augury (predicting the future by studying the flight of birds).[42] In the Insular tradition, their prophecy is generally associated with the disastrous outcome of battles. The connection between ravens and oracular utterances may have arisen because of the harsh but distinctive 'voice' of the raven, which may have been perceived as resembling human speech. Usually the gift of prophecy is sinister, but in the case of the Irish hero-god Lugh, ravens warn him of the approach of his enemies, the Fomorians, and thus influence the result of the second Battle of Magh Tuiredh. Indeed, some authorities identify Lugh as a raven-god.[43] In one Irish poem, 'The Hawk of Achill', this association is very clear.[44]

The relationship between battles, prophecy and ravens occurs above all in connection with a group of Irish war-goddesses who sometimes assume the form of ravens or crows. The Badbh and the Morrigan both possess the ability to appear as one or three entities and to transmogrify into raven form. Their most unpleasant habit is to appear on the battlefield, as prophets of doom and disaster, causing fear and havoc among the warriors and gloating over the bloodshed. One of these raven-deities, the Morrigán, advises the Dagdha on the outcome of battles before they take place.[45] Badbh Catha (Battle Crow) gloats over the destroyed soldiers at the battles between Ulster and Connacht.

The Ulster hero Cú Chulainn is as closely linked with ravens as he is with swans: in general, ravens reflect the malevolence of the underworld.[46] The Morrigan alights on Cú Chulainn's shoulder at his death, to symbolize the passing of his spirit. Two magic ravens act as oracles in the tale of the 'Wasting Sickness of Cú Chulainn'. On one occasion, the young warrior uses his sling to destroy a large flock of Otherworld ravens who are swimming in the sea and whose evil nature is made clear. Cú Chulainn performs a curious ritual with the last bird he kills, beheading it and bathing his hands in its blood, before setting its head on a rock.[47] This image of carrion-birds emerging from the underworld to do evil on earth recurs elsewhere. In the first Battle of Magh Tuiredh, between the Tuatha Dé Danann and their enemies the Fir Bholg, the Irish high king Eochaid has a vision or dream which he asks his Druid to interpret for him. In this dream he sees a huge flock of birds emerging from the depths of the ocean, alighting all over Ireland, wreaking havoc and destruction among the people. Similarly, in the story of a hero named Caoilte, he and his followers journey to an Otherworld *sídh* for Caoilte to be healed. The divine *sídh*-dwellers tell him that, before they will cure him, he must rid them of a terrible scourge, three ravens that appear every Samhain (the 1st of November festival) and carry off three boy-children from the *sídh*. Caoilte kills all three ravens which scream horribly as they die.[48] The triple form of these creatures suggests that they are in fact the triple raven-goddesses, the Morrigan or the Badbh.

Their habit of eating carrion, black colouring and cruel character make ravens natural symbols of death. But white ravens also appear in the stories. The Irish god Midhir has two white ravens which fly out of his *sídh* when it is dug up by the king Eochaid.[49] Perhaps they represent the souls of the divine occupants of the mound. Ravens with white feathers were considered to be birds of good omen. Interestingly, the Greek geographer Strabo alludes to white-feathered ravens being used in the settling of disputes: the man whose barley cakes were scattered by the birds won his case.[50] It is possible that the white-feathered birds were

Figure 7.10 Stone relief of god with fruit, ravens and dog, Romano-Celtic, Moux, Burgundy. Width: 27cm. Miranda Green.

179

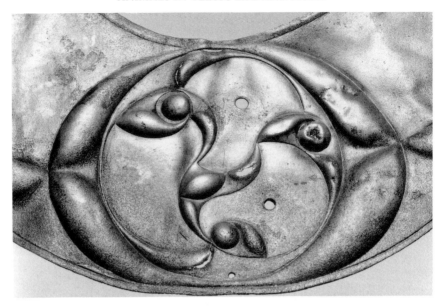

Figure 7.11 Triskele with birds' heads, on a first-century BC bronze plaque at Llyn Cerrig Bach, Anglesey.

not in fact ravens but magpies, also members of the crow family. If that is so, then it is interesting that their good-luck symbolism, still part of today's superstition, should have such antiquity. Ravens occur, though less frequently, in the Welsh myths. The Second Branch of the *Mabinogi* revolves around the superhuman hero Brân (Bendigeidfran – Blessed Brân, whose name means 'Crow'). In the 'Dream of Rhonabwy', Owein has an army of ravens who possess magical powers of recovery after injury. The birds are harassed by Arthur's warriors and, even when they are grievously wounded, they are instantly healed and turn on their aggressors, routing them in their turn.[51] The Welsh tale of 'Peredur' is interesting because the raven symbolism there precisely parallels that of the Irish story of Deirdre. Peredur sees a raven eating a duck in the snow: he likens the colours of the scene – white, red and black – to the colouring of his beloved, with her white skin, red cheeks and black hair.[52] In the story of Deirdre, she witnesses her foster-father Conchobar skinning a calf in the snow and a raven drinking the blood. She prophesies that the man she loves will have hair as black as the raven, skin as white as the snow and cheeks as red as the blood.[53]

Of all the individual bird species in the written mythology, the raven is perhaps the most complex and interesting. It has a close affinity with the supernatural world and indeed can be a form of female divinity. The overwhelming image of the raven is that associated with the evil aspect of the Otherworld. It issues from the nether regions as a harbinger of doom and death. It appears to armies, reminding them that in war no one wins except death itself. The raven is an oracle, but again most of its portents are negative and fear-inducing. The blackness, the cruel, tearing beak, glittering, pitiless eyes, and its predilection for dead flesh endowed the raven with this dark, sinister imagery. Only occasionally is the raven projected in a more positive light, as friend to man, appearing to warn and to protect.

Birds as magical creatures

Particular species of bird were perceived as symbolic and representative of certain qualities or features possessed by – say – ravens, cranes or swans. But birds in general also played a role in the early Celtic literature, probably because of their powers of flight and their ability to sing. Birds could be seen as messengers from the supernatural world and as mediators between god and humans. In the Irish Happy Otherworld, magical birds lulled sick or wounded men to sleep and healed them with their sweet music.[54] The Insular goddess Clíodna possessed birds who dwelt on two Otherworld islands in the sea. They are described as being similar to blackbirds but larger, red in colour, with green heads: they laid eggs of blue and crimson. If humans ate these eggs, they themselves began to grow feathers, but when they washed their bodies, the feathers fell off. Other birds, eating huge purple berries in a forest, had white bodies, purple heads and golden beaks.[55] The description of Clíodna's birds makes it quite clear that they are unearthly, belonging to the divine world: they are of no known species and their colouring is exotic. These Irish birds have their counterpart in early Welsh tradition. In 'Branwen', the Second Branch of the *Mabinogi*, the hero Bendigeidfran prophesies that after his followers have beheaded him (at his own behest), they will dwell seven years in Harlech and the Birds of Rhiannon will sing to them from over the sea.[56] The three birds of Rhiannon reappear in the 'Tale of Culhwch and Olwen,'[57] where they are described as having power in their song to wake the dead and lull the living to sleep. There is another bird episode in 'Branwen'. In the story, Branwen is persecuted at the court of her husband Matholwch, king of Ireland. He has cut off all her means of communication to mainland Britain, but Branwen overcomes this problem by training a starling to fly over the sea to her brother Bendigeidfran, with a message begging him for help. This triggers the great war between the Britons and the Irish.[58]

Figure 7.12 Romano-Celtic clay figurine of a cockerel, Nijmegen, Netherlands.
Paul Jenkins.

Snakes

Before leaving the creatures of the wild, we need to look at the role of
serpents in the early myths. These reptiles possessed a complex symbolism in the Romano-Celtic world (chapter 8), evoking images of
water, fertility, death and regeneration. All these concepts emanated
from qualities or properties perceived in the physical appearance or the
behaviour of snakes. Their rippling, sinuous movements and long
winding bodies endowed them with river imagery; their shape, large
numbers of young and the male's double penis evoked fertility symbolism. The association between snakes and renewal or healing came
about because of their habit of sloughing their skin several times a year,
apparently being reborn. The chthonic or death symbolism is self-
evident: snakes are carnivorous and their method of poisoning their
victims well-known. In addition, they are generally earthbound, and
can emerge from narrow crevices, seemingly from deep below the
earth.

The superhuman Ulster hero Conall Cernach had an affinity with
snakes: there is a story in the 'Táin Bó Fraich' of an enormous serpent
which guards a fort containing treasure. Conall is induced to attack the
stronghold but the creature, far from opposing him, instead dives into
his waist-belt. When the fort has been overcome, Conall releases the
reptile and both are unharmed by the encounter.[59] Another treasure-
guarding snake is recorded in Pembrokeshire by Giraldus Cambrensis:
he describes a well containing a precious torc or neckring which is
protected by a snake who bites potential thieves.[60] Interestingly, this
story has its counterpart in Norse myth, where supernatural snakes
protect treasure: one such animal was Fafnir, a serpent killed by Sigurd
the Volsung in order to get at the guarded treasure.[61] War, evil and
destruction are associated with snakes in a number of Irish stories. The

hero Finn kills a series of fantastic snakes, including a gigantic water-snake, that are threatening the land.[62] In another Insular tale, the war-goddess the Morrigan produces a son named Meiche, who carries within him the seeds of Ireland's destruction. He is slain by the divine physician Dian Cécht, and the boy's heart is found to contain three serpents: it was believed that if the creatures had been allowed to grow to maturity inside Meiche's body, they would eventually have wiped out all animal life from the face of Ireland.[63]

THE DOMESTIC ANIMALS: CATTLE, DOGS AND HORSES

Cows and bulls

Early Irish society was underpinned by cattle-owning (and cattle-raiding). This is clear from much of the literature. The greatest bull-story symbolizes the importance of this animal and of cattle in general to the fertility and florescence of Ireland as a whole. This is the 'Táin Bó Cuailnge' or 'Cattle Raid of Cooley', which chronicles the conflict be-tween two supernatural bulls, the Findbennach, or White-Horned of Connacht in the south and the Donn or Brown of Cuailnge in Ulster.[64] The fight between these two giant beasts symbolizes the antagonism and longstanding hatred between Queen Medb of Connacht and King Conchobar of Ulster. The story begins with domestic jealousy: in bed one night, Medb and her consort Ailill each boast of their possessions. It appears that they are equally rich in all things except that Ailill possesses a magnificent white-horned bull. Medb hears of the equally splendid Donn of Ulster and tries in vain to acquire him. Then she declares war on Ulster, to obtain the animal by force. The war culminates in a combat between the two bulls themselves, which rages over days and nights and ranges over much of the land. Finally, the Ulster bull prevails and slays Ailill's Findbennach, but dies of the effort. This symbolizes the Pyrrhic victory of Ulster over Connacht.

What is most interesting about the two bulls is that they are not only supernaturally large, but they possess human levels of understanding and intelligence. Cormac, son of Conchobar and prince of Ulster, upbraids the Donn for flagging and slipping back under the onslaught of his opponent. The Donn comprehends and responds by summoning all his strength to make a greater effort.[65] The reason for the human spirit of the two animals is that they are in fact enchanted creatures, metamor-phosed from human shape. The Ulster hero Ferghus describes how they are skin-changers who were originally divine herdsmen in human form, named Rucht and Rucne. They underwent a series of transformations, being at one time ravens, then stags, champions, water-beasts, demons and water-worms. Ross[66] suggests that the two bulls may originally

183

have been bull-lords, guardians and promoters of the fertility of the herd.

An important early Irish ritual recorded in the literature is the *tarbh-fhess*, which means 'bull feast' or 'bull sleep'. The *tarbhfhess* was a method of selecting a king by means of divination, associated particularly with the rulership of the royal seat of Tara (Co. Meath). In the ritual, a bull was killed and a man, chosen as the medium, ate his fill of the flesh and drank the broth in which the meat had been cooked. Then he slept and a truth-spell was chanted over him by four Druids. In his sleep, the man then dreamed and saw a vision of the rightful king-elect.[67]

Bulls and cows are the subject of many other Insular myths and stories. The war-goddess the Morrigan turns a girl named Odras into a pool of water because her cow has been mated by Odras's bull. This punishment was presumably in revenge for the insult done to a goddess in mating her supernatural beast with an earthly creature. The Morrigan herself may have a particular affinity with cattle: when she appears as a young girl to Cú Chulainn and he spurns her, she unmans him by changing into different forms, including that of a hornless red heifer. The colouring may signify the Otherworld association evidenced elsewhere in instances of supernatural cows which are white with red ears, or in the hounds of the Welsh underworld god Arawn which are also white and red-eared. The Irish Iuchna had three of these cows, on whose heads reposed three men transformed into birds.[68] This image immediately calls to mind the iconography of Tarvostrigaranus, the Bull with Three Cranes perched on his back and head (figure 8.11), depicted in Gallo-Roman sculpture (chapter 8). The abundance of cow imagery reinforces the dependence of Ireland upon cattle. The goddess Brigid

Figure 7.13 Bronze bull-mount from a cart or chariot, first century BC, Bulbury, Dorset. Length: 6.4cm. Paul Jenkins.

IN.

Figure 7.14 Bronze bull-head mounts, first century BC/first century AD:
(a) Welshpool, Powys; (b) Dinorben, Gwynedd. By courtesy of the National
Museum of Wales.

was reared on the milk of an Otherworld cow. Boann, a goddess of
Ireland and the personification of the river Boyne, is called She of the
White Cow. In a story of the conflict between the Tuatha Dé Danann
(the divine race of Ireland) and the Fomorians, chronicled in the *Book of
Invasions*, the oppressive king Bres demands an impossible tribute from
every Irish household, consisting of milk from a huge number of identi-
cally coloured cows. The divine Lugh solves the problem by conjuring a
herd of cows by magic; then Nechtan, king of Ireland, dyes all the cows
brown.[69]

Dogs

Since Stone Age times dogs have occupied a particular place among
animals in their peculiarly close relationship to man, sharing his hearth
at night and guarding his household, working with him during the day
as sheepdogs or hunters. Dogs have a close symbiotic relationship with
humans, a relationship that is reflected in the early literature. In the

Third Branch of the *Mabinogi*, Manawydan laments the loss of his dogs, and comments that without them he cannot hunt and his livelihood is destroyed.[70] Dogs were often highly prized: in 'Math', Gwydion's gift to Pryderi in exchange for Dyfed's precious pigs includes twelve grey-hounds;[71] and greyhounds are among the presents given to Pwyll by Arawn of Annwn, in the First Branch.

Dogs are very closely associated with the supernatural: archaeological evidence for dog ritual in pagan Celtic Europe suggests that they pos-sessed an underworld role (see chapters 5, 8). In 'Pwyll', Arawn, king of the underworld, has a pack of shining white, red-eared dogs,[72] their colouring proclaiming their Otherworld origins. The Cwn Annwn or Hounds of Annwn were death omens, described in an early Welsh poem as small, speckled and greyish-red, chained and led by a black, horned figure. These were ghost dogs which appeared only at night to foretell death, sent from Annwn to seek out corpses and human souls.[73] Both Welsh and Irish sources describe dogs with supernatural powers, some of them larger than life-sized. Mac Da Thó, king of Leinster, but in reality an Otherworld deity, possesses a large hound, coveted by Conchobar of Ulster and by the people of Connacht, Ulster's deadly enemies. Mac Da Thó invites heroes of both sides to a feast in which an enormous pig is slaughtered, and there follows the inevitable squabble over who should be allotted the champion's portion of pork. Fighting breaks out and the King of Leinster released his hound to see which side it will favour: it chooses the Ulstermen. The superhuman status of Mac Da Thó is indicated by the huge size of both his dog and his pig.[74]

In the Welsh 'Tale of Culhwch and Olwen', Culhwch's quest for the hand of Olwen is associated with a number of tasks connected with supernatural dogs: one of his 'labours' is to seek the two whelps of a great bitch called Rhymni, who is in the shape of a she-wolf and extraordinarily swift:[75] Another hurdle Culhwch has to clear is that of obtaining the Whelp of Greid, of whom it is said that no leash can hold him but the leash of Cors Hundred Claws and the collar of Canhastyr Hundred Hands. The only huntsman capable of controlling the hound is the divine hunter Mabon.[76]

In early Ireland, the prefix 'Cú' (Hound of) was frequently used in the Celtic names of heroes, to denote warrior status. But the most famous so named – Cú Chulainn, the Hound of Culann – had a very special and close relationship with dogs. As a young boy, he is called Sétanta, but he kills the huge guard dog of Culann the smith and, as a penance, he takes the dog's place and also his name. This affinity with dogs recurs in the adult life of Cú Chulainn: he has a *geis* (a bond or taboo) on him that he must never eat hound-flesh. But he is offered dogmeat at a feast, and there is another *geis* on him never to refuse hospitality. He breaks the first rule and eats the meat; this act weakens the hero's supernatural strength and leads ultimately to his death. The episode is interesting, since it implies that dogmeat was a traditional food for the early Celts; this is borne out by the archaeology of Iron Age Europe, where dog remains are part of food refuse on settlement sites (chapter 2). But at the same time, dog ritual was very prominent in Britain and Gaul, and there is evidence that dogs fulfilled a special role in Celtic religion.

Horses

Like dogs, horses have – and had in antiquity – a special relationship with humankind. They were indispensable in battle, were used in hunting and were regarded as prestigious (chapter 4). In the First Branch of the *Mabinogi*, Pwyll and the underworld lord Hafgan fight on horseback. When Pwyll sees Rhiannon for the first time, they are both mounted, as are his followers.[77] Horses were important in Welsh gift-exchange; thus presents sent between Pwyll and Arawn consist of horses, greyhounds and hawks (all hunting-animals). In the Fourth Branch, Gwydion conjures up greyhounds and horses as presents for Pryderi of Dyfed in exchange for the pigs given to his kingdom by Arawn.[78] The high status of horses is demonstrated in the Second Branch, when Branwen's brother Efnisien mutilates the horses of her betrothed, Matholwch of Ireland, thus offering the Irish king an unforgivable insult and promoting the catastrophic hostility between Britain and Ireland.[79]

Giraldus Cambrensis[80] chronicles an ancient Irish tradition concerning the inauguration of kings in Ulster. A white mare is sacrificed and the meat cooked in a cauldron; the king-elect sits in the cooking-vessel, bathes in the juices, eats the flesh and drinks the broth. Before the mare is killed, however, the candidate imitates a stallion and pretends to mate with her.[81] This is highly symbolic: the mare appears here to represent the land of Ireland, whose fertility is assured by her union with the mortal king. The association between the mother-goddess and horses is present in the image of Macha, both a single and triple goddess, with strong equine affinities. In one of her three identities, Macha seems to be half-woman, half-horse: she is the divine bride of a human, the Ulster widower Crunnchu. At the great Ulster Assembly, Crunnchu brags that his wife can outrun any of the competitors in the horse-race; he is held to his word and he forces Macha to run against the king's horses, even though she is nine months pregnant at the time. She wins the race but dies in childbirth immediately afterwards, giving birth to twins and cursing the Ulstermen as she dies.[82]

The link between women and horses occurs in the *Mabinogi* where, in the First Branch, the story of Pwyll and Rhiannon is told. Pwyll first sees Rhiannon riding past him on a large, shining white horse: attracted by

Figure 7.15 'Celtic Horses', a drawing by Jen Delyth.

her, he follows but, though his steed is swift and she does not appear to be going very fast, he cannot catch up with her. Next day, the same thing happens and Pwyll sends his fastest horseman to intercept the lady, but in vain. In desperation, Pwyll calls to her to stop and she immediately halts.[83] It is clear from this and from the shining whiteness and great size of the horse that both Rhiannon and her mount are of supernatural origin. The horse symbolism continues: later in the story, Rhiannon is framed for the alleged murder of her 3-day-old son, and the penance prescribed by her husband is that she behaves like a horse, waiting by the gate of Llys Arberth and offering to carry visitors to the palace on her back, for seven years.[84] Many scholars have seen a close link between the Rhiannon of the Welsh legend and the Celtic horse-goddess Epona (figure 7.16), who is depicted in Romano-Celtic iconography seated side-saddle on a mare (chapter 8).

Certain superhuman individuals are portrayed as having a strong affinity with particular horses, with whom their lives and destiny are intricately bound. This is the case both with the Welsh hero Pryderi and the Ulster demigod Cú Chulainn. In the First Branch of the *Mabinogi*,

Rhiannon's son is stolen as a baby, believed to have been killed by his mother. The scene moves from Llys Arberth to the home of one Teyrnon Twryf Liant, lord of Gwent Is-Coed: he has a mare who foals every May eve but on each occasion the foal disappears. One such night, Teyrnon decides to keep watch in the stable: the mare produces the strongest and most beautiful foal he has ever seen, but straight away a giant claw comes through the stable window and grabs the foal. Teyrnon strikes off the claw with his sword; there is a terrible scream and Teyrnon rushes outside, but the darkness is so profound that he can see nothing. On re-entering the stable, he sees a tiny baby lying on the threshold, wrapped in a silken shawl. He and his wife foster the child, who grows up far

Figure 7.16 Stone carving of Epona, Meursault, Burgundy. Paul Jenkins.

faster than a normal human infant: when he is 3 years old, he is considered sufficiently old and responsible to be given the foal as a present. The little boy turns out to be the image of Pwyll, and Teyrnon, knowing the story of the royal loss, realizes that this must be the missing prince. The royal family is reunited amid much rejoicing and the boy is named Pryderi.[85] Thus the early life of the young lord is intimately related to that of Teyrnon's foal, born at almost exactly the same time. The horse symbolism of the boy's mother Rhiannon must also be remembered.

The story of Pryderi and the foal has its Insular parallel in the life of Cú Chulainn. He is born at the same time as twin foals, and they become his two great war-horses, the Black of Saingliu and the Grey of Macha.[86] The Grey is clairvoyante and weeps tears of blood immediately prior to her master's death.[87] It is significant that Cú Chulainn's horse is named . after the great mother-goddess Macha, herself a horse-deity.

Supernatural horses can play good or evil roles: in the 'Tale of Culhwch and Olwen', Culhwch has to obtain two miraculously swift horses, Gwyn Dun Mane of Gweddu and Du, the horse of Moro Oerfeddawg – the White and the Black[88] – to help him hunt the enchanted boar Twrch Trwyth. More sinisterly, red horses feature in the Irish myths as beasts of death: in the tale of 'Da Derga's Hostel', King Conaire travels to an underworld *bruiden* to meet his fate; on his way, he encounters three red horsemen, harbingers of death, messengers from the Otherworld, Da Derga's domain.[89] Red is the Irish colour of death: we have noted already the underworld hues of dogs and cattle who are white and red, and the hounds of Annwn who are speckled reddish-grey. In the tale 'The Death of Ferghus', there is a death-image of a horse emerging at a gallop from the sea: he is multicoloured, with green legs, a golden body and a crimson mane, a magic horse who carries men across the ocean to the Otherworld.[90]

ENCHANTMENT AND SHAPE-CHANGING

We have discussed the way in which certain kinds of animal were depicted and perceived in the early literature. But underpinning any analysis of the roles different beasts could play are two basic principles concerning animals in general. The first is the concept of the enchanted creature, which possesses qualities beyond its natural limits: the properties of human speech or wisdom, or the ability to communicate with the world of the supernatural. The second, related, idea is that of shape-changing, skin-turning or transmogrification, in which an animal has assumed a different form, either from another animal or from a human or divine being.

A good example of the enchanted beast is the Salmon of Wisdom, a

Figure 7.17 Detail of gold armring, in the form of a figure of a goddess surmounted by a bird of prey, fourth century BC, from the grave of a 'princess' at Reinheim, Germany. Paul Jenkins.

creature who appears in both Welsh and Irish myths. In the 'Tale of Culhwch and Olwen', he is known as the Salmon of Llyn Llyw, one of the oldest beings on earth. He is one of the group of creatures consulted by Culhwch and Arthur as to the whereabouts of Mabon, the divine hunter. The concept of the Salmon of Wisdom or Knowledge is further developed in an Insular legend concerning the hero Finn. In the story, Finn comes across the bard Finnegas, who has been fishing for the Salmon for seven years, in a pool. As Finn arrives, the bard catches the fish and gives it to Finn to cook, bidding him on no account to taste the fish. But Finn burns his thumb on the hot flesh and puts it in his mouth: he begins instantly to acquire knowledge; Finnegas then gives him the fish to eat and Finn becomes infinitely wise. The Salmon itself, we are told, acquired its omniscience by eating the nuts of the nine hazel trees growing beside a well at the bottom of the sea.[91] The implication must be that this wisdom comes from the chthonic, underworld regions.

We know of other enchanted beasts, which in some manner transcend their normal state. Magically swift horses, Gwyn and Du, are used by Culhwch to track down the skin-turned boar Twrch Trwyth. Gwyn

Dun-Mane is described as being 'as swift as the waves'. Wise and knowledgeable beasts help Culhwch in his quest: the Ouzel (a mythical bird) of Cilgwri; the Stag of Rhedynfre; the Owl of Cwm Cawlwyd; the Eagle of Gwernabwy and the Salmon of Llyn Llyw, all exceedingly old.[92] Some enchanted animals are destructive and dangerous to humans: in 'Peredur' a magic stag is incredibly fast and savage; it has a single sharp horn, kills all the other creatures it encounters and consumes all the foliage in the forest.[93] Exotic animals such as lions occur in 'Peredur' and in 'The Lady of the Fountain'. In the Irish 'Voyage of Teigue', an island is populated by sheep as big as horses: one flock consists of enormous rams, one of which possesses nine horns, is extremely aggressive and attacks men. It is so big that when Teigue kills it, thirty men are needed to carry the ram away.[94]

In many early Celtic stories, a peculiar rapport between men and animals is recorded. In the 'Táin', Queen Medb has a bird and a squirrel habitually perched on her shoulder, perhaps symbolizing her link with the land. We have already noted the affinity between Conall Cernach and the treasure-guarding serpent. In a Welsh legend Owein, keeper of the forest, has the power to summon all the denizens of the woodland, who pay homage to him. Similar incidents are found in early Irish Christian tradition, where many saints are recorded as having peculiar power over the animal world. An example is St Ciarán of Saighir, who tames a wild boar which then builds a monastic cell with its teeth. Both it and other wild creatures – a fox, badger, wolf and stag – relate to Ciarán as disciples to their master or as monks to an abbot.[95]

The most prominent aspect of the enchanted beast theme is metamorphosis or shape-shifting. Both the Welsh and Irish traditions are full of stories that illustrate it. It can occur in one of three ways: a god or superhuman individual changes from human to animal form or vice versa from choice; the shape-changing is imposed on one being by another, as a punishment or in revenge; or a creature may be transformed for a particular purpose.

If we look first at shape-shifting as punishment or revenge, we can see a recurrent pattern whereby heroes or gods deal with unacceptable behaviour by depriving the malefactor of human status and causing him or her to adopt an animal shape. In most instances, however, the metamorphosed creature retains all its human faculties, apart from its physical form. In the *Mabinogi* and the 'Tale of Culhwch and Olwen', the punishment theme is a recurrent one. In 'Math' (the Fourth Branch), Math, Lord of Gwynedd, punishes his nephews Gwydion and Gilfaethwy for their treachery by turning them into three pairs of different animals for three consecutive years. Each pair produces offspring, which are born in the forms of a fawn, a piglet and a wolf cub. Math changes each one into a human boy, but each retains his animal name, and is thus never entirely free of the zoomorphic association: the names are Hychdwn (*hwch* means 'pig'); Hyddwn (*hydd* means 'stag') and Bleiddwn (*bleidd* means 'wolf').[96] In the Culhwch quest tale, a central character is Twrch Trwyth, an enchanted boar accompanied by seven young pigs (once men), including one Grugyn Silver-Bristle. When asked by Arthur how they came to be in pig form, Twrch Trwyth replies that he was once a human king but that God had transformed him and his followers into pigs as a punishment for their evil ways. In the same story, Ysbaddaden Chief Giant, father of Culhwch's lover Olwen, recounts how two oxen, called Nyniaw and Peibiaw, which Culhwch must obtain for him, are humans transformed into cattle for their sins.[97] What is interesting in the Twrch Trwyth episode is that when Arthur's interpreter Gwrhyr addresses Twrch Trwyth, he goes to him not in human form but as a bird, as if communication were easier between beast and beast (even of different species) than between animal and human.

In Irish mythology, individuals were transformed from human to animal shape either in revenge for an alleged wrong or as a punishment for antisocial behaviour. Thus Fuamnach, the jealous wife of Midhir, turns Étain into a pool of water, whence she is transformed next into a worm and ultimately a purple fly.[98] In another jealous act, Lir's wife Eva turns her four stepchildren into swans for 900 years.[99] The Irish sea-god Manannán has a 'crane-bag' made from the skin of a crane who was once a woman, transformed because of her jealousy.[100] In some instances, transmogrification appears to have been imposed for no clear reason. Thus, the 'Táin Bó Cuailnge' has as central characters two bulls who were once herdsmen. They have gone through multiple changes, but they began as humans.[101] In the Fionn Cycle, the Black Druid turns Sava, Finn's future wife, into a fawn, for some purpose of his own, but not as a punishment, as far as we know. Perhaps transmogrification was a means of obtaining power over another being. There are other instances of coercive transformation where we are not sure of the reason for it. Thus, in a tale of Oenghus, the Irish god of love, his first love, Derbrenn, has six pigs who had been her foster-children before their shape-change.[102] We know of two transmogrified dogs, Bran and Scéolang who had been the human nephews of the hero Finn.[103] In another Finn story, we hear of the four sons of the Hag of the Temple who are in the form of cranes and can only be rescued from this state by magical blood.[104] Some individuals are transformed into animals not as a punishment for anything but in order to fulfil some particular purpose of the transformer. This is often associated with the Otherworld: Irish enchanted pigs or stags may be metamorphosed humans who, in their animal form, lure their hunters to the Otherworld or are the cause of their destruction. Thus Diarmaid's foster-brother, an enchanted boar, is

Figure 7.18 Stone relief of Cernunnos, with antlers and ram-horned serpents forming his legs, Cirencester, Gloucestershire. Betty Naggar.

the instrument of Diarmaid's death, used by the jealous Finn in order to rid himself of his rival for the affections of the beautiful Gráinne.[105] Elsewhere in the Fionn Cycle a deer, which is actually the god of the underworld in disguise, entices Finn the hunter to his *sídh* or Otherworld dwelling. In another tale about Finn, it is a metamorphosed boar who lures him to the underworld.[106]

Very often, transmogrification from human to animal form takes place by choice. Thus in 'Manawydan' (the Third Branch of the *Mabinogi*), the magician Llwyd sends his wife and her women as mice to eat Manawydan's corn, in revenge for a wrong done by Pwyll, former lord of Dyfed. The story chronicles the women's desire to become mice so that they can perform this deed of destruction. In another voluntary shape-shifting episode, Finn's grandmother changes herself into a crane so that she can take to the air and save her grandson from falling to his death over a cliff.[107] Sometimes gods or heroes choose to spend time in different animal guises: thus the Irish Fintan sojourns for long periods as a salmon, an eagle and a hawk.[108] In 'The Dream of Oenghus', the swan-girl Caer is carried off by Oenghus who himself adopts swan shape.[109] Midhir and Étain escape from her husband's court in the form of swans,[110] by means of the god Midhir's powerful magic. In one of the tales of Cú Chulainn, the young hero is wooed by Derbforgaill, who takes the form of a swan.[111]

The most dominant of the voluntary shape-changers are the Irish battle-goddesses, the Badbh and the Morrigan, who can skin-turn at will to raven form and by their horrific presence can wreak havoc among armies. In the story of an encounter between the Morrigan and Cú Chulainn, the goddess first appears to him as a beautiful young woman. It is the eve of battle and Cú Chulainn has more important things on his mind than amorous entanglements: he spurns her impatiently and, in her resentment, she attacks him first in the form of an eel, then a wolf and finally as a red heifer,[112] this last signifying her Otherworldly status. But it is usually in the form of a raven that she appears to the Irish heroes. The Badbh is another such goddess: as Badbh Catha, or Battle Crow, she shows herself to hapless men as a harbinger of doom. In 'Da Derga's Hostel', she appears ambivalently as a crow or black-clad, crow-like old hag, prophesying King Conaire's death.[113]

The reason why traditions developed whereby the world was inhabited by supernatural beasts and by beings transformed from human to animal form needs to be considered. One important point to realize is the apparent ease of interchange between anthropomorphic and zoomorphic perceptions: there was no rigid barrier in the Celtic mind between the human and animal form.[114] This must imply that animals were not considered to be significantly lower in status than humankind. In addition, the properties of animals – speed, sharp hearing, keen sight, the ability to fly – may have elevated them in Celtic eyes and have caused them to be perceived as in some ways superior to humans. We cannot know how and why beasts were given such importance in this earliest Celtic literature, but the attitude to the animal world which is projected in the vernacular stories reflects perceptions which are clearly presented in the iconographic evidence, and to which we turn in the next chapter.

Conchobar laid his hand upon his son, Finnchad Fer Benn, the Horned Man – so called because of the silver horns he wore . . . .

(The Táin)

8

GOD AND BEAST

Let them not sacrifice animals to devils.
(Pope Gregory in a letter to Mellitus, Abbot of Britain, AD 601)

The Celts were animists: they believed that all aspects of the natural world contained spirits, divine entities with which humans could establish a rapport: animals themselves thus possessed sanctity and symbolism. They were perceived as being at the same time similar to and very different from humans. Certain creatures were observed to have particular physical or mental qualities and characteristics, and distinctive patterns of behaviour. An animal, like a stag or horse, could be admired for its beauty, speed or virility. Dogs were seen to be keen-scented, useful in hunting, guarding and in healing themselves. Snakes are destructive, fertile and have the curious habit of sloughing their skin. Birds are keen-sighted and are able to fly, leaving behind the bonds of earth. Thus, admiration and acknowledgement of a beast's essential nature led easily to reverence of those qualities and abilities which humans either did not possess at all or possessed only partially.

Reverence of animals gave rise to a religion in which they were an integral part, playing an important role in cult and worship. The use of animals in sacrifice and other ritual has been discussed in chapter 5. Here, the sanctity of animals will be explored with reference to a complex religious iconography. Particular animals were sometimes represented as isolated images but the most striking symbolism consists of representations of animals either as companions to anthropomorphic divinities or where animals and human concepts became merged. The theme of this chapter is also closely interleaved with that of animals in pre-Roman Celtic art (chapter 6), which forms the backdrop to the religious imagery described here. This theme was only developed fully during the Romano-Celtic period, when the Celtic and Roman artistic traditions united to form a new, hybrid toreutic symbolism. The fusion of human and animal images is something which relates closely to the metamorphosis or transmogrification of human to animal and vice versa which is so vividly described in the vernacular literature of early Wales and Ireland (chapter 7).

When the Romans introduced their Mediterranean culture to the lands of Celtic Europe (in the mid-first century BC in most of Gaul and the mid-first century AD in Britain), they filled a number of lacunae in the indigenous tradition. One was the written expression of facts and thoughts. Another was the custom of representing the gods in human form, a comparative rarity before the Roman period. In lands such as Gaul and Britain, deities acquired names which have survived mainly through inscriptions. At the same time, images of gods and goddesses were set up in temples, public places and private homes, to honour the divinities represented and to communicate their power, by means of visual symbolism, to their human devotees.

From inscriptions and above all from iconography, it is possible for us to construct a picture of how the pagan Celts perceived their gods and the world of the supernatural, which they believed controlled all human affairs. What is of interest here is the manner in which animals were seen as a fundamental part of that other, non-human world.

The Roman and Greek deities were essentially humans writ large, suprahumans. Animals were represented with them in iconography, but were present in a clearly subordinate role. In classical religion, animals illustrated an aspect of either the god's mythology or his cult. To give an example, Mercury, the herald of the gods, is often depicted with a cockerel, which is the herald of the new day. Another emblem of Mercury is the tortoise, a motif which refers to a story in which Mercury (Hermes) invented the lyre using the shell of a tortoise. In neither instance does the animal possess any independent identity nor has it any real religious status. But in the pagan Celtic world, the iconography presents a far more complex tapestry of symbolism, in which beasts appear to play a much more prominent role. It could be argued that, because there are no written myths about the gods in this early period of Celtic history, it is impossible to judge whether or not an animal is present as a companion to a Celtic god because of its mythological role. This is a valid point, but it cannot be the whole story. In terms of the imagery itself, beasts are far more significant than in classical iconography. Whilst Mercury is identifiable with or without his zoomorphic attributes, a Celtic goddess like Epona depends upon her equine symbolism for her very identity. Moreover, the manner in which Celtic deities took on the characteristics – such as horns, antlers, hooves – of animals is something quite outside the Mediterranean tradition (with the exception of Pan) and must reflect something rather more fundamental in the perception of the position of the animal in relation to the god.

DOGS AND DEITIES: FROM NODENS TO NEHALENNIA

As scavengers and carrion-eaters, dogs came to be associated with death, in both the classical and Celtic religious traditions. Some of the

Figure 8.1 Romano-British bronze dog, Canterbury, Kent. Paul Jenkins.

ritual treatment of dogs (chapter 5) in Gaul and Britain may point to this aspect of their symbolism. The bodies of dogs have repeatedly been discovered, deliberately buried in deep pits and shafts, perhaps as offerings to the underworld. Dogs were used in the hunt (chapter 3) and this may have been the origin of their symbolic link with death. But three beneficial aspects of dog behaviour gave rise to a number of cults which first manifest themselves in Romano-Celtic cult iconography. These three characteristics are fidelity, the guarding instinct and the perceived ability of the dog to heal itself with its saliva.[1] The first two relate directly to the animal's relationship with people. The healing facility caused the dog to be adopted as an image by devotees of curative deities in order to render their imagery all the more potent and to remind worshippers of the efficacy of their cults.

Healers and hunters

The Burgundian tribe of the Aedui possessed a great many therapeutic sanctuaries, based upon the numerous mineral springs of the region. One of these was at Mavilly (Côte d'Or), an important shrine presided over by the Celtic version of Mars, a peaceful healer in Celtic contexts. The spring-water was apparently considered as helpful in the cure of eye disease, a scourge probably resulting from malnutrition among the Gauls and Britons. The god of Mavilly is depicted on several stone carvings: on one, he is accompanied by a dog and a raven and by a suffering pilgrim, his hands covering his eyes as if he is in great anguish.[2] The shrine of the healer Apollo Belenus at Sainte Sabine, also in Burgundy, yielded several small sculptures of babies, presumably offerings designed to stimulate a cure for afflicted infants: one of these images consists of a child strapped into a cot; it has a dog curled up on its legs.[3]

In Britain, one of the most important curative cult-establishments was situated at Lydney, overlooking the river Severn in Gloucestershire. We

198

know the name of the presiding deity from inscriptions: he was Nodens, a name which is philologically related to that of the Irish god of the Tuatha Dé Danann, Nuada Argat-lam (Nuada of the Silver Hand), who is described in the Mythological Cycle. The sanctuary at Lydney, built in the third century AD, was clearly supported by a wealthy and enthusiastic clientele: there were impressive buildings here, embellished with mosaics. They included a guest-house or hostel for pilgrims, a set of baths and a long structure which has been interpreted as a dormitory where visitors slept and encountered the healing-god in a vision. That the sanctuary was devoted to a curative cult is demonstrated by the presence of such objects as a votive model arm, dedicated to the god in the hope that the diseased limb would be replaced by a whole one. Interestingly, the model shows evidence of some kind of disease which deformed the fingers. The pilgrims who visited Nodens's shrine also suffered from eye afflictions: physicians specializing in eye problems stamped boxes of ointment with their mark, and some of their stamps have been discovered at Lydney.

The interest of Nodens's sanctuary for us is that, whilst no images of the god himself in anthropomorphic form have been found, no less than nine representations of dogs were present, indicating that this animal was sacred to Nodens. The canine images represent many different types but the most spectacular figure is the bronze statuette of a deer-hound (figure 8.2).[4] The presence of this hunting-dog is interesting, especially in view of the epigraphic evidence for Nodens, for his name is paired with either Mars (a well-known healer in the Celtic world) or Silvanus, who was the Roman god of wild nature and of the hunt. This apparently enigmatic link between hunting and healing may recur at Nettleton Shrub in Wiltshire, where a sanctuary, very possibly a curative establishment, was set up to Apollo Cunomaglus – a native Celtic soubriquet meaning 'Hound-Lord'.[5] The seeming dichotomy between the concepts of hunting and healing may be resolved by a close examination of the Divine Hunt, a theme which, in many cultures, including that described in early Insular legend, embodied ideas of regeneration and immortality by means of the pursuit and killing of prey, and of death. The shedding of blood, in order to give life and food, came to symbolize rebirth and healing/renewal.[6]

The link between healers, dogs and the cult of Silvanus is reflected in the iconography of the Gaulish hammer-god of Burgundy and the Lower Rhône Valley. In Provence, the hammer-god is often depicted with the leaf-crown and wolfskin cloak of a nature-god and on altars, for instance at Glanum, where hammers were engraved on altars dedicated to the local version of Silvanus.[7] Both in this region and further north in Burgundy, images of the hammer-god are distinctive in their inclusion of a dog, seated at its master's feet and often gazing up at him (figure

Figure 8.2 Bronze figure of a deer-hound from the third century AD shrine of the healer-god Nodens at Lydney, Gloucestershire.

7.3). On an altar at Nîmes, the dog is comparatively large, with long floppy ears, perhaps a hunting-dog;[8] but a relief of the same deity at Monceau near Autun depicts a small animal, a terrier perhaps, or even a lapdog.[9] The hammer-god's main function seems to have been the promotion of prosperity and abundance: in Burgundy, he was associated especially with wine and the grape harvest. The presence of the dog could indicate that there was a hunting aspect to his cult or it could simply be there as a faithful healer-guardian-companion. But in addition, there may be an association between the hammer-god and healing. A few examples among many will suffice to illustrate the point: an image of a drunken god wielding a hammer comes from a spring site at Cussy, and at Vertault the god of the spring is depicted with two acolytes, one of whom is flanked by hammers. The deities of several Burgundian thermal springs received stone hammers as votive offerings.[10]

Nehalennia and the goddesses

The tribe of the Morini lived in what is now the Netherlands, bordering the North Sea coast. They venerated a local Celtic goddess, Nehalennia, and set up two temples in her honour. She was a divinity of seafarers, and protected merchants and other travellers who regularly risked their lives and their merchandise in the perilous journey across the sea. Nehalennia's cult was a successful one: visitors came to worship from as far away as Besançon and Trier. And it was a wealthy cult: the two shrines to the goddess were embellished with numerous altars and images set up in supplication or in thanksgiving. Nehalennia's two sanctuaries, at Domburg on the island of Walcheren and at Colijnsplaat on the East Scheldte estuary, are both now submerged beneath the North Sea. However, many of her altars have been recovered, and these display a rich and complex iconography which throws some light on the nature and functions of the goddess. Nehalennia is generally depicted seated, with baskets of fruit as emblems of prosperity and often with marine symbols to signify her presidency over the sea. But most distinctive of all the motifs associated with this North Sea deity is the dog. On nearly every surviving stone – and there are more than a hundred – a large, benign, hound-like animal sits patiently by the goddess's feet, facing his mistress (figure 8.3). The dog is seated very close to Nehalennia: sometimes its nose touches her. Its whole mien is that of watchfulness and protection. It appears to be a symbol of the benevolent guardian, at one level of the goddess herself; at another its image is clearly that of a peaceful and friendly protector of humankind, just as Nehalennia is herself a protectress against the vicissitudes of sea travel. So here, the animal both reflects and reinforces the role of the anthropomorphic divinity. The image of the dog served as an immediate semiological message to Nehalennia's devotees, reminding them that worshippers at her shrines enjoyed her patronage and guardianship.[11]

Many Celtic goddesses, apart from Nehalennia, were depicted with dogs as companions throughout Romano-Celtic Europe: often these deities are of a general mother-goddess type, seated and nursing a small lapdog on their knees. At Trier, a goddess called Aveta was venerated with little clay images of a lady who carried fruit, or swaddled babies or lapdogs; this symbolism is repeated nearby at the rural sanctuary of Dhronecken. Other images in the area consist of clay figurines of a goddess bearing fertility emblems of corn or bread, and offering fruit to a small dog.[12] This divinity appears to have been local to the tribe of the Treveri, and all the associated symbols imply that here the dog was interchangeable with such fertility motifs as corn and babies, as if the animal itself represented fecundity and abundance. It is equally likely that the beast's role reflected a healing or regenerative aspect of the goddess's function.

Female deities accompanied by dogs are recurrent images in Luxembourg and among the Sequani and Ubii (around Windisch in Switzerland and Köln respectively). Even in Britain the goddess with a lapdog was worshipped, invoked by the offerings of small figurines at Canterbury and at Dawes Heath, Essex.[13] Other images of mother-goddesses are more like Nehalennia: stone carvings of a divinity with a large animal seated next to her.[14]

In Britain, depictions of the triple Mothers or *Deae Matres* include dog imagery: a lively relief from Cirencester (Glos.) portrays the Mothers

Figure 8.3 Stone relief of Nehalennia with her hound, Colijnsplaat, Netherlands.
By courtesy of the Rijksmuseum van Oudheden, Leiden, Netherlands.

Figure 8.4 Stone figure of a pilgrim carrying a pet dog, perhaps symbolic of a votive offering to Sequana, Fontes Sequanae, near Dijon. Paul Jenkins.

seated together on a bench, in a relaxed attitude, each accompanied by a small boy. The central goddess nurses a lapdog. On another sculpture, from London, the dog is present as the emblem of one goddess, the two others carrying bread and grapes and a human infant.[15] So again, as in the Treveran imagery, the symbolism of the dog is very closely allied to that of fertility and florescence. But perhaps it adds a new dimension to the cult, introducing an element of curative renewal. Since the Mothers did possess an Otherworld dimension,[16] it is possible that the dog is present to reflect that particular role, sharing its chthonic symbolism with that of the classical world. We have already seen that, in ritual, dogs may well have had an affinity with the underworld (chapter 5).

EPONA AND THE HORSE-DEITIES

Epona

The Celtic goddess Epona is specifically identified by her horse symbolism. Her name is etymologically related to a Celtic word for horse and she is defined iconographically by the presence of one or more horses:[17] the goddess is usually depicted either riding side-saddle on a mare or between two ponies or horses (figures 8.5, 8.6). Epigraphic dedications and images of Epona indicate her immense popularity within the Celtic world: she was first and foremost a Gaulish goddess, being venerated particularly in the east of Gaul and the Rhineland. But she was known also in Britain, perhaps having been introduced by travellers or by the army;[18] and she was worshipped as far east as Bulgaria. Epona's cult was practised by a wide range of people in Romano-Celtic society: she was a soldier's goddess, beloved especially by cavalrymen stationed along the Rhine frontier. But she was equally at home among the

Figure 8.5 Stone statuette of Epona, Alesia, Burgundy. Paul Jenkins.

Figure 8.6 Stone relief of Epona with foal, Brazey, Burgundy. Miranda Green.

peaceful communities of the Aedui and Lingones of Burgundy and among the romanized Treveri of the Moselle Valley.

Epona's horse gives her a composite yet cohesive identity. To soldiers, she was perhaps above all a protectress of both the cavalryman and his mount. It was natural for the horseman to worship a deity who would keep his horse from harm on the battlefield and thus keep the soldier, Celt or Roman, safe as well.[19] To the civilian population, Epona was primarily a kind of mother-goddess: her imagery frequently suggests fertility symbolism. These images are particularly powerful in Burgundy, where the goddess sits side-saddle on a mare beneath which is a suckling or sleeping foal (figure 8.6).[20] Sometimes Epona feeds the foal with corn or fruit: on a bronze statuette from Wiltshire, the goddess sits between two ponies who turn towards the corn held in a dish on her lap. It may be significant that the one pony is male and other female, a detail which enhances the fertility symbolism in Epona's imagery.[21]

Among the Burgundian Aedui, where the mare-and-foal image is such a strong tradition, it is probable that Epona was perceived especially as a divinity who presided over the craft of horse-breeding. Some iconography in this area depicts simply a mare and foal (figure 2.12): Epona herself is absent.[22] Aeduan cavalry were renowned and used by Julius Caesar in his Gallic campaigns (chapter 4), and their territory is good for horse-rearing. Indeed, it is in the land of the Aedui that the only known temple dedicated to Epona has been discovered, at Entrains-sur-Nohain (Nièvre).[23] Epona's imagery is full of symbolism of the earth's bounty, just like that of the Mothers: she frequently appears carrying baskets of fruit or loaves of bread.[24]

The fertility aspect of Epona's cult, indicated by her corn, fruit, bread and mare-with-foal, is endorsed by her overt link with the Celtic triple mother-goddesses: on a stone at Thil-Châtel in Burgundy, a dedication alludes to both Epona and the Mothers, and the horse-goddess herself is referred to in multiple form, echoing the plurality of the *Deae Matres*;[25] and at Hagondange (Moselle), Epona is actually depicted as a triple image,[26] a direct borrowing of the Mothers' iconography. Like the mother-goddesses, Epona was associated with the cults of healing springs, especially in Burgundy,[27] implying that her role was as wide as that of the Mothers themselves. She was associated also with death and regeneration beyond the grave: this is shown partly by the context of some of her images and partly by symbolic details. Depictions of the goddess have frequently been found in cemeteries: one of the most important of these is at La Horgne-au-Sablon which was used for burials of the people of Metz, capital of the Mediomatrici of eastern Gaul.[28] Here, several images of Epona were dedicated by relatives of the deceased, and one depicts the goddess on her mare, leading a mortal to the Otherworld. Some of Epona's attributes or emblems point to a dual level of symbolism: one is the key, which the goddess carries on carvings at Gannat (Allier) and Grand (Vosges).[29] At one level, this symbol may be interpreted as the key to the stable door, reflecting a straightforward horse association. But in wider perspective, the key may also symbolize the entrance to the afterlife, the Otherworld. Another dual motif is the *mappa*, a kind of napkin, held by Epona on a sculpture at Mussig-Vicenz near Strasbourg.[30] In a secular capacity, the *mappa* is closely linked with horses in that it was traditionally used as a signal for starting Roman horse-races.[31] But if we look behind this mundane symbolism, we can see a more profound meaning, perhaps suggestive of Epona's role as presider over the beginning of life, just as her key may be indicative of death and the afterlife.

Epona was a popular goddess precisely because of the complex nature of her cult. Her essential association with horses led to a series of extensions to that nuclear role, all of which remained sympathetic to the basic zoomorphic identity. The horse is absolutely crucial to Epona's definition: the equine symbolism gave rise to many different levels of meaning, with the result that Epona was worshipped not only as patroness of horses but also as a giver of life, health, fertility and plenty, and as a protectress of humans even beyond the grave.

The horseman cults

A cult of an equestrian warrior-god was important in both Gaul and Britain. On an Iron Age carving at Saint-Michel-de-Valbonne (Var) in southern Gaul is depicted the simply incised image of a horseman with a head of exaggerated size, riding over five severed human heads.[32] This may reflect the Celtic practice of decapitating enemies and collecting their heads as trophies, which is so graphically illustrated by classical commentators on the Celts, who describe the Gaulish cavalryman hanging these grisly spoils of war from his saddle.[33] A sculpture from the Provençal *oppidum* of Entremont depicts just such a horseman, with the severed head of his opponent, eyes closed in death, hanging from the neck harness of his horse.[34]

In Britain, a god perceived as a warrior on horseback was venerated particularly in the east of the country, among the Catuvellauni and Coritani. Brigstock (Northants) was the site of a series of shrines dedicated to a horseman-god depicted on small bronze figurines. Amongst the many eastern British horseman images, we should note the warrior, carved on a small stone, at Margidunum (Notts.), with his spear and shield (figure 4.8).[35] One named horseman was Mars Corotiacus, represented by the statuette of a warrior riding down a fallen enemy, at Martlesham in Suffolk.[36]

A powerful deity who was sometimes depicted on horseback was the sky-god.[37] He appears thus on the top of the 'Jupiter–giant columns', monuments that were set up especially in eastern Gaul and the Rhineland (figure 8.7). These columns represent trees: they are decorated with stylized bark and occasionally also with oak leaves and acorns, as at Hausen near Stuttgart.[38] Frequently the monuments are dedicated to Jupiter, the Roman sky-god, but the sculptured groups which surmount them represent a Celtic god. He is depicted galloping on a speeding horse, cloak flying, riding down a semi-human, semi-serpentine monster beneath his mount's front hooves. The god brandishes a thunderbolt and sometimes a solar wheel which he bears like a shield. The iconography appears to represent a dualistic cult, with the celestial horseman and the chthonic giant locked together in an interdependent relationship. Here, the never-ending opposition of life and death, light and dark, day and night, summer and winter, sky and underworld is enacted. There is little evidence of actual conflict – the sky-god carries no weapon – but the symbolism clearly reflects the dominance of the celestial world and the subjugation of the giant, whose face is frequently contorted with the agony of his equine burden.[39] In these images, the horse has a crucial role, firstly as the mount of the sky-god. But it has a deeper significance too: it is the horse which has physical contact with the chthonic being beneath its thrashing hooves, and it is the horse which, together with the god's shield-wheel, represents the solar nature of the cult. In Celtic religion, horses had a very close affinity with the sun.[40] Indeed, before the first millennium BC in temperate and northern Europe, the horse was a solar animal which was depicted in iconography pulling the sun's chariot across the sky. At Trundholm in Denmark, a community of worshippers in about 1300 BC dismantled and deliberately buried in a peat-bog a model wagon drawn by a slender figure of a horse and carrying a great gilded bronze sun-disc. The solar horse was equally important to the Celts: many coins depict a horse associated with sun symbols and the wheel of a chariot (figures 4.9, 6.22), the latter motif deriving from gold staters struck by Philip II of Macedon in the fourth century BC. Some derivatives of the equestrian sky-god support the interpretation of the horse as a solar animal: sometimes, as at Mouhet (Indre),[41] the horse itself is missing from the group but instead the giant kneels, crushed by the weight of the sun-wheel on his shoulders, as if the solar image were perceived as interchangeable with the horse. The beast was deemed an appropriate companion to the sun and sky-god: swift, beautiful and proud, invaluable in warfare and prestigious as a riding-animal, its high secular status was reflected in its importance as a means of transporting the lord of the heavens across his celestial domain.

Other gods possessed horses which were sacred to them, although the anthropomorphic images of these deities have not themselves survived. A magnificent bronze horse from Neuvy-en-Sullias (Loiret) (figure 4.4), dating to just before the Roman conquest (and thus at the interface of free Celtic and Romano-Celtic culture), bears a dedication to 'Rudiobus'.[42] Another bronze figurine, from Bolards in Burgundy (figure 8.8), consists of a horse inscribed to 'Segomo', a Celtic epithet meaning 'victorious'.[43] Mars Mullo, the surname meaning 'mule' was invoked at Rennes and Allonnes in north-west Gaul.[44] The healer-god Apollo in his Celtic guise was associated with horse imagery: thus at Sainte-Sabine in Burgundy Apollo Belenus was venerated in a shrine in which supplicants dedicated clay horse figurines to their patron god.[45] We know of Apollo Atepomarus, 'Great Horseman' at Mauvières (Indre).[46] Horses were given as votive offerings to other curative deities: at the healing shrine of Sequana at Fontes Sequanae near Dijon, pilgrims purchased wooden images of horses and dedicated them to the goddess;[47] the same practice occurred at the sanctuary of Forêt d'Halatte

Figure 8.7 Reconstructed Jupiter–giant column, Hausen-an-der-Zaber, near
Stuttgart, Germany. Württembergisches Landesmuseum, Stuttgart.

Figure 8.8 Bronze horse dedicated to the god Segomo, Bolards, Burgundy.
Paul Jenkins.

near Senlis (Oise), where simple stone horses were presented to a curative divinity whose name is unknown.[48]

The Celtic deities with whom horses were associated in epigraphy and iconography were those whose images were enhanced by the qualities which this animal possessed as a secular companion of humankind. The speed, courage, intelligence and fertility of horses were all admired by the Celts and they thus formed part of the symbolism of divinities to whom such qualities were also ascribed.

Figure 8.9 Romano-Celtic bronze horse figurine, Carrawburgh,
Northumberland. Miranda Green.

THE BIRD-LOVERS

In many cultures, past and present, special, supernatural powers have been attributed to birds, mainly because of their power of flight and their ability to leave the bounds of earth. This has led to a belief that birds in flight might represent the souls of the dead freed from the body. In addition, the nature and behaviour of certain birds gave them a particular symbolic significance. Thus in the Celtic world, ravens were considered to be representatives of death and destruction, because of their black plumage, their carrion habits and their cruelty to other birds: their collective term is 'an unkindness of ravens'. But ravens were also perceived to have prognosticatory powers and were thus associated with oracles: this may have arisen from their distinctive 'voices' and their ability to mimic human speech. Water-birds perhaps symbolized a link between the elements of air and water; doves peace and harmony because of their temperaments and so on.

The raven-deities

In Irish mythology, ravens were associated above all with the fearsome triple goddesses of war and destruction, the Morrigna (singular Morrigán) and the Badbh.[49] These Insular ravens represented the bloodshed of the battlefield and the pitiless destruction of man by man. That ravens were linked with warfare in Iron Age Europe is indicated by the presence of such objects as the helmet from Romania, with its movable raven crest (figure 4.17) (see chapters 4, 6).

In Romano-Celtic iconography, ravens were presented not as birds of destruction but as peaceful attributes of beneficent divinities. This may have been due partly to their supposed oracular powers, for which they were apparently used by Irish Druids in divination.[50] The Graeco-Roman Apollo was associated both with prophecy and with healing, and the occurrence of raven images at some of these Celtic therapeutic sanctuaries may derive from a similar association. The god who presided over the Burgundian healing spring shrine at Mavilly was depicted in company with a large raven[51] and a sick pilgrim who apparently suffered from an eye affliction. It is even possible that the raven's bright eyes represented clear vision. Many of the goddesses are portrayed with ravens as attributes: Nantosuelta is one of the few for whom we have a name. She appears on images at Sarrebourg near Metz and at Speier in Germany, accompanied by a raven.[52] Nantosuelta's name means 'Winding Stream', but this gives little clue as to her identity or function. She is normally depicted with her consort Sucellus, The Good Striker, a god whose main attribute was a long-shafted hammer or mallet. The couple seem to have been venerated as bringers of prosperity and domestic well-being: Nantosuelta's other motifs include a house symbol and a hive; Sucellus often carries a small pot or goblet, perhaps filled with wine. The goddess may have been perceived as a kind of mother-goddess, and it is interesting that in Luxembourg a distinctive type of goddess was worshipped, a deity whose image consisted of a lady seated within a house-shaped shrine and accompanied by a raven. Here again then, the house and bird symbols are associated.[53] It is well established that the Celtic mother-goddesses had an association with death and the Otherworld as well as with fertility and florescence. This is why small images of the Mothers are sometimes found in graves and at the bottom of wells.[54] So it may be that where ravens are associated with goddesses, they represent the underworld aspect of their cult: it is interesting that one representation of Epona[55] depicts her with a dog and a raven; the connection between the horse-goddess and the Otherworld has already been examined.

Other deities appear with dogs and ravens. A sculpture found at Moux in Burgundy[56] depicts a peaceful, bearded god dressed in Gaulish breeches and a cloak fastened at the shoulder (figure 7.10). He carries a billhook and three fruits in the crook of one arm and rests his other hand on a knotted club or stick; by his side sits a dog with pricked-up ears. On each of the god's shoulders perches a raven, its long sharp beak pointing towards his head. The inanimate attributes of the god proclaim him as a lord of nature, a pruner of foliage and a gatherer of fruit. His dog may simply be a companion, a guardian in the wild countryside, but the ravens present a symbolism which may reflect the underworld and thus the dog, in this context, may also be a chthonic motif.

Sequana and the water-birds

In 1963, investigations at a waterlogged site north-west of Dijon brought to light an important healing sanctuary, Fontes Sequanae, a spring shrine at the source of the river Seine. The site was particularly rich in votive objects, not only of metal and stone but also of wood, the oak heartwood of the Châtillon plateau. Dedications made by grateful or hopeful pilgrims show that the deity venerated here was called Sequana, goddess of the Seine; her bronze cult-image, recovered from the mud, depicts a serene deity wearing long robes and a diadem, her hands outstretched to welcome her suppliants (figure 8.10). The interesting point here is that she stands in a boat in the form of a duck, the prow fashioned as its beaked head and its tail forming the stern.[57] The duck is present here as a simple water symbol, indicative of Sequana's aquatic identity and of the healing powers of the spring-water. Of the many representations of pilgrims in stone or wood, some are shown bearing gifts to Sequana (figure 8.4), gifts that sometimes took the form of birds.

Figure 8.10 Bronze figurine of Sequana in her duck-prowed boat, first century AD, Fontes Sequanae, near Dijon. Paul Jenkins.

Other representations of ducks are recorded from free Celtic and Romano-Celtic Europe[58] but most of these occur as isolated figurines, there being no clue to their religious identity. An exception is the combined iconography of the water-bird and the sun, which was a tradition whose origins lay in the later European Bronze Age. In this period, solar symbols ride in boats with water-bird head terminals, on sheet bronze vessels and on jewellery, and sun-wheels and ducks appear together on armour. The association of the solar and water-bird symbols continued into the Celtic Iron Age, with duck-boats carrying suns on bronze pendants, and torcs decorated with wheels flanked by duck-like birds (figure 6.15).[59] In this context, the water-bird appears to be an attribute of a celestial deity. We know that, in the Celtic period, the sun- and sky-gods were complicated beings who were linked not only with the heavens but also with water and the underworld. Perhaps the water-bird was perceived as a suitable solar emblem because it was able both to fly and to swim, thus bringing together the elements of sky and water, both of which belonged to the celestial powers. To the pagan Celts, the sun and water were both related to healing, and this perception of the water-bird as a link between the two elements may have

213

resulted in the making of the image of Sequana, the curative goddess of Fontes Sequanae, riding in a duck-adorned boat.

Geese and cranes

In Celtic iconography, geese are most commonly associated with war: thus, because of their watchful and aggressive nature, these birds were perceived as appropriate emblems or companions for warrior-gods. The great freestanding stone goose, gazing alertly from the lintel of the Iron Age cliff-top temple of Roquepertuse in Provence guarded a shrine in which war-deities were venerated.[60] The bronze figurine of a Celtic war-goddess from Dinéault in Brittany[61] depicts a young female wearing a helmet, the crest of which is in the form of a goose which thrusts its neck forward in such a threatening manner that one can almost hear it hissing. In Iron Age Czechoslovakia, warriors were sometimes buried accompanied by geese,[62] as if the birds were considered lucky emblems of bravery and aggression which would enhance the image of the soldier in the next world.

Marsh-birds – egrets or cranes – had a close affinity with the supernatural world, as described in the Insular vernacular sources (see chapter 7). In iconography, the most important crane symbolism occurs on two monuments in the early first century AD, one from Paris, the second from Trier.[63] The two stones possess remarkably similar imagery, consisting of the association of a bull with three egrets. The Parisian monument (figure 8.11), dedicated to Jupiter in the reign of Tiberius by a guild of sailors, is made up of several stone blocks: on one a large bull stands in front of a willow-tree, two birds on his back and a third perched on his head; on an adjacent panel, a woodcutter hacks at the branch of a willow.[64] The inscription above the bull reads 'Tarvostrigaranus' (the Bull with Three Cranes); that above the man reads 'Esus' (Lord). The Treveran sculpture is virtually identical, in terms of the content of its imagery: here, on a single stone surface, a woodcutter chops at a willow-tree in which are a bull's head and three cranes or egrets. The motifs of tree, birds and bull are all related in life: cranes or egrets and willows both have water associations, and the birds love willows. In addition, egrets and cattle are symbiotically linked in that the birds feed on tics and other pests which infest the hides of the cattle. The whole symbolism of woodcutter, tree, birds and bull reflects a complex mythology of which we can know little but a possibility is that the Tree of Life is depicted, its destruction reflecting the seasonal 'death' of winter and the departure of the tree's spirit in the form of birds. The bull may represent new life and virility, the regenerating strength of spring and the awakening of the earth. The water element could equally reflect the life-force and fertility generated

214

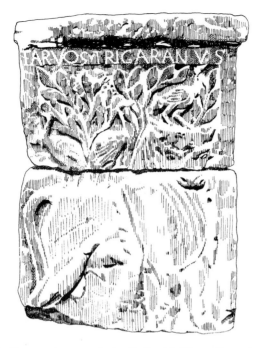

Figure 8.11 'Tarvostrigaranus', the Bull with Three Cranes, on a stone monument from Paris, early first century AD. Paul Jenkins.

by rivers and lakes. Tarvostrigaranus has no precise parallel outside Trier and Paris, but it is possible that a curious image from Britain may reflect similar symbolism. This is a small bronze figurine of a bull, once covered in silver-wash, from a fourth-century AD shrine at Maiden Castle, Dorset.[65] The bull originally had three horns (see pp. 222–3) and has the remains of three female figures on its back. In Irish vernacular legend, women on occasions metamorphosed into cranes (chapter 7), and it may be that, on this figure, women are substitutes for the marsh-birds associated on the Continent with Tarvostrigaranus, thus presenting iconographically a tradition well documented in the early Insular literature.

Doves of peace and healing

Like ravens, doves were perceived as oracular birds, perhaps on account of their distinctive call. In classical iconography and mythology, doves were the attribute of Venus, goddess of love, presumably because of the intimate behaviour of courting doves; the birds came to represent peace and harmony as well as sexual love. In the ancient world, the concept of

Figure 8.12 Romano-Celtic clay figurine of a dove, Nijmegen, Netherlands.
Paul Jenkins.

harmony was close to healing: bodily health and peace of mind were perceived to be related. It was perhaps partly for this reason that images of doves were offered to the Celtic healer-deities of thermal springs, particularly in Burgundy. Pilgrims offered multiple stone figures of doves, in groups of two, four or six, to the curative spirits presiding over shrines at Nuits Saint Georges, Beire-le-Châtel and Alesia.[66] At Forêt d'Halatte (Oise), at Essarois and Fontes Sequanae, pilgrims dedicated images of themselves carrying doves as gifts to the healing forces who resided in the springs.[67] At the great therapeutic cult establishment of Mars Lenus at Trier, images of young children held doves as presents for the healer-god, who was especially fond of children.[68] Apart from the association between doves and harmony, another reason for the presence of dove images at curative shrines could be that prophecy and healing were linked: the classical Apollo was both a healer and a prophetic god and, indeed, the Celtic Apollo was venerated at both Essarois and Beire-le-Châtel. Oracles, visions and dreams were all perhaps related to the healing process, which was brought about not simply by the treatment of physical symptoms but by methods which depended on holistic concepts whereby mind and body were inextricably bound together and needed to be treated together. Certainly there is evidence that priests at these shrines were also sometimes doctors, who performed surgery in addition to providing the link between the worlds of the profane and the spiritual.

POWER AND VIRILITY: BEARS, BOARS AND BULLS

All these creatures were revered and admired for their qualities of strength, dominance and unfettered potency. All three were represented in imagery, either alone or in association with a deity.

Bears

Bears were least commonly represented: a group of little jet amulets in the form of bears comes from northern Britain and dates to the Romano-Celtic period. An example at York accompanies a burial of the fourth century AD; another was buried with the body of a child at Malton (Yorks.), but it is too small to have been a toy; a third was found at Bootle (Lancs.).[69] There is evidence that particular divinities were occasionally perceived as having a close affinity with bears. Of these, the most important was the goddess Artio (figure 8.13), whose name means 'Bear', just as Epona's name refers directly to her equine associate. The

Figure 8.13 The bear-goddess Artio, on a Romano-Celtic bronze group from Muri, near Berne, Switzerland. Paul Jenkins.

217

name indicates that the identities of goddess and bear are so close that they are almost one. Artio, whom we met briefly in the earlier discussion on hunting (chapter 3), was venerated in Switzerland: here a devotee commissioned a bronze group consisting of an image of the goddess and her bear, below which is a dedication to her. Artio sits with her attributes of fruit, and facing her is a large bear who leans forward as if either to threaten the goddess or to take the fruit. Behind the bear is a tree, perhaps representative of the wild forest he inhabits.[70] Artio was the patron of bears, but she may also have protected the hunters or wayfarers who might encounter bears in the wood and be in danger from them. She was venerated outside Switzerland: among the Treveri of the Moselle, she was worshipped in the remote Bollendorf Valley, her name inscribed on the rocky sides of the defile.[71] Artio may have had an ambivalent role, both as guardian of bears and as protector of humans against them. The goddess was perhaps perceived, not as a personified bear herself, but as a mediator between human and animal, a means whereby fear could be overcome and the bear-hunt be successful. But she would also ensure that the species survived and that each bear taken would be replaced. Interestingly, the divine patron of bears was not necessarily female: Mercury Artaios was venerated at Beaucroissant (Isère).

Boars

These creatures were above all symbols of warfare and aggression. Images of boars, dorsal ridge erect, decorated weapons and armour; boar-headed trumpets brayed fearsomely on the battlefield (chapter 4). Although there is little faunal evidence from Iron Age sites to suggest that boar-hunting provided much food for Celtic communities, the animal must have been hunted for sport and for the 'blooding' of young warriors in preparation for battle. War and hunting were closely associated in the Celtic mind: the north British god Cocidius was equated both with Mars, Roman god of war, and Silvanus, the Italian nature-god. He was depicted on stone carvings with spears and boars.[72] Iconography indicates that boar-gods and goddesses were worshipped: the eponymous female divinity Arduinna was venerated by communities living in the Ardennes Forest. On a bronze statuette from the region,[73] she is depicted as a huntress, wearing a short belted tunic and carrying a short knife. But she is riding her boar companion and the weapon is not being used. We are perhaps witnessing a similar ambivalence in the attitude of Arduinna as is the case with Artio: she is a patroness of the animal, but her knife symbolizes her dominance and her ability to kill the boar if she so wishes. She is a protectress not only of the beast but also of its hunters. Another named boar- or pig-god was Mercury Moccus, worshipped among the Burgundian Lingones. The most important extant image of a boar-god comes from Euffigneix (Haute-Marne) and probably dates to the second or first century BC, before the Roman Conquest.[74] The image consists of a stone block which has been carved, as if by someone more used to working in wood, into the shape of a man, wearing a heavy torc round his neck. A huge eye symbol adorns each side of the stone, perhaps to avert the Evil Eye or to make the image all-seeing and thus all-powerful.[75] But most distinctive of all is the image of a boar which strides, bristles stressed, along the god's torso.[76] The deity is identified by means of the boar symbol; there is a very close affinity between anthropomorphic and zoomorphic imagery here, and one can almost imagine a scene of transmogrification from animal to human form (or the reverse). The metamorphosis of boars was a common theme in both the Insular and the Welsh mythological traditions (chapter 7).

The aggression of the boar, symbolized by the erect spines along its back, is a striking characteristic not only of the Euffigneix boar but also of many boar statuettes. Many of these figurines date to the pre-Roman period, and are discussed in chapter 6. One clear example of this deliberate exaggeration of the bristles can be seen on the huge bronze boar from Neuvy-en-Sullias (Loiret), which dates to around the time of the Roman Conquest (figure 5.9). This nearly life-sized figure is one of many bronzes (including other boars, a horse, a stag and dancers) which were deliberately buried as a hoard, perhaps for safety, to protect such sacred images from looting by the Romans, near to a place on which a Romano-Celtic temple was later built.[77] The same emphasis on the dorsal crest may be observed on a bronze plaque depicting a slain boar, from a shrine at Muntham Court, Sussex (figure 3.2),[78] perhaps the centre of a hunting cult. The representation of boars on Iron Age coins (figure 3.4)[79] all share the exaggerated symbolism of aggression and the semiological message of such representations is clear. Interestingly, it is the bristles rather than the boar's tusks which are chosen to reflect the animal's ferocious temperament. This is probably, at least in part, so that Celtic artists could have free rein to develop a naturalistic feature into something fantastic and ornamental.

Most curious of all boar images is a Gaulish figurine[80] which shows all the combative, pugnacious characteristics natural to boars but which is given supernatural status by the addition of three horns (figure 8.14). This triple horn is something which is found on images of bulls (p. 222) but is much more strange when applied to an animal that is hornless in life. This figure must have been made by an artist or commissioned by a patron who was familiar with the relatively common triple-horned bull and who wished to enhance the potency of the boar-image by endowing it with a symbol which itself conveyed the concepts of destruction and fertility.

Figure 8.14 Bronze figurine of a triple-horned boar, Cahors, Lot, France.
Paul Jenkins.

Bulls

The essence of a bull is its power, virility and aggression: its fearsome
horns and bellowing roar have endowed it with a clear but complex
symbolism but, interestingly, the force of the animal was perceived by
the Celts as entirely positive. Thus it was used as an image of fertility
and beneficence, and if there were a belligerent aspect to the bull cult,
the creature was seen as fighting on behalf of humankind against the
negative forces of disease, barrenness and death. That the Celts viewed
the sacred bull as a beneficial emblem is shown by the occurrence of bull
names: one tribe, the Taurini, named themselves the 'bull tribe'; the
town of Tarbes in southern Gaul was called 'bull town'; and in Galatia in
Asia Minor, the name Deiotarus has been interpreted as meaning
'Divine Bull'.[81]

No one deity was particularly associated with the bull, but it seems to
have fulfilled a sacred role in a number of cults. The fertility and
regenerative aspects of the beast are indicated above all by its link with
healing sanctuaries: images of bulls formed votive offerings at such
curative shrines as Tremblois, Fontes Sequanae and Forêt d'Halatte.[82]
The antlered god Cernunnos was associated with bulls: he was a god of
nature and abundance (see pp. 231–4) and the bull enhanced his role as
a beneficent provider. On a stone at Saintes, Cernunnos sits on a throne
supported by bulls' heads,[83] and on a relief at Reims (figure 8.21), the

god sits pouring grain out of a bag, which is consumed by a stag and a bull standing beneath him.[84] Here the two most potent zoomorphic images of virility are present: the stag represents the wild woodland and the bull the domestication of farm and field.

The image of the bull as a bringer of abundance may account for the presence of bull symbols on such objects as buckets and firedogs. Cattle were crucial to the Celtic economy (chapter 2) and this may have led to an association between the image and plenty. Bucket-escutcheons or handle-mounts in the form of bull heads are common on both Iron Age and Romano-Celtic sites in Britain and on the Continent: the great cauldrons from Brå (figure 2.6) and Rynkeby in Denmark are decorated with bull heads (chapter 6). There is a particularly interesting North Welsh group of bull bucket-ornaments, represented by examples from the Little Orme, Dinorben and Welshpool, with stylized faces, prominent snouts and jutting horns (figures 2.5, 7.14).[85] Such emblems may have been attached to vessels, not simply for decoration but to fulfil some magico-symbolic purpose, probably connected with the contents of the vessel.[86] Similar symbolism may have pertained to the bull heads on iron firedogs, such as those from Barton (Cambs.), Baldock (Herts.) and Capel Garmon in North Wales (figures 2.23, 5.6, 5.13). These firedogs were used for containing fires within the hearth space, and were thus linked with

Figure 8.15 Bronze bull, once triple-horned, Cirencester, Gloucestershire. Betty Naggar.

221

culinary activities – the roasting or boiling of meat. The Capel Garmon firedog dates to the first century BC or first century AD, and is arguably the most ornate and beautifully wrought piece of ironwork in existence. The interesting feature of the animal-head terminals is that, although they bear extravagant horns, the heads themselves are more reminiscent of horses than bulls, and they have manes. This last detail may not be significant since, in the 'Táin', the two great mythical Irish bulls are described as maned.[87] However, it may be that the Capel Garmon firedog was made with deliberately ambiguous zoomorphic symbolism, whereby elements of both horse and bull (both prestigious creatures for the Celts) were purposely incorporated in the imagery.

The possible ambiguity of the Capel Garmon piece is present in a different form on a series of curious bucket-mounts, which contain a composite element: at Thealby (Lincs.), the mount consists of a bull's head surmounted by that of an eagle; on an even more complex example from the river Ribble in Lancashire, the heads of a bull, an eagle and a man are combined.[88] Some kind of mythological or cult-story must be reflected by these curious images: it is tempting to link them with episodes in the early literature. In the 'Táin', there is an interchange between the great Brown Bull of Ulster and the raven-formed battle-goddess, the Morrigán.[89]

One category of bull image which is both distinctive and enigmatic is the triple-horned bull, of which there are many examples, notably in north-east Gaul, with a mere scattering of statuettes from Britain (figure 8.16).[90] The images are mainly in the form of small figurines of bronze, but clay ones are known and occasionally they occur in stone. Usually, the triple-horned bull is not associated with other cult imagery, but there are exceptions: at Beire-le-Châtel in Burgundy[91] a curative sanctuary contained several cult objects including images of a Celtic Apollo and a goddess of music, Ianuaria, as well as groups of stone doves. Here were found several stone images of the three-horned bull. The other important association is at Willingham Fen (Cambs.) where a bronze mace or sceptre was found, possibly associated with a shrine. On the mace are depicted a god with a wheel, a dolphin, eagle and the head of a triple-horned bull.[92] The wheel and the eagle are indicative of celestial symbolism and we know that in classical myth and religion, the sky-god Jupiter was closely linked with the bull. The triple horn is not easy to explain: triplication was a common form of image-making among the Celts,[93] which appears to have combined concepts of intensification and a deliberate veering away from naturalism. The bull itself is a power symbol, and its horns exemplified that power. The tripling of the horn at one and the same time augmented that power, rendered the image out of the ordinary (and therefore perhaps divine) and introduced the magical symbolism of the number three which was so dear to the Celtic

Figure 8.16 Clay three-horned bull, first century AD, from a child's grave at Colchester, Essex. Miranda Green.

spirit. So whether the triple-horned image occurred in company with a healing deity or the lord of the sky, it served the same purpose of increasing potency both for itself and for its cult associates.

The great bull image of Tarvostrigaranus has been discussed earlier when the theme of cranes was explored. The bull appears on two monuments, in Paris and Trier:[94] on the Paris stone (figure 8.11) a huge, heavily muscled bull stands before a willow, three marsh-birds on his back and head; above him is the dedication. Again the bull is associated with triplism, not in the horns but in the imagery of the three birds. The precise significance of the bull in this context is obscure, but the general imagery of willow, birds, bull and woodcutter (who hacks at the tree in both monuments) may represent a cyclical myth of the death of winter and the renewal of spring.[95] So the bull may once more be present in his virile role as promoter of fertility. The link between triplism and bulls, seen in the third horn and the three cranes, is also present on the pre-Roman Gundestrup Cauldron:[96] the iconography with which the silver plates of this cult vessel are decorated includes a great deal of bull symbolism. The animal here plays an essentially sacrificial role: on the baseplate a bull sinks dying to the ground under the attack of hunters and dogs (figure 5.1); on one of the side panels, the bull is again sacrificed to the knives of men, but here the creature is in triple form (figure 5.3).

SACRED SNAKES

In Celtic symbolism, the snake represented concepts evoked by its particular properties: snakes are essentially earthbound creatures who can slide in and out of impossibly narrow crevices in rocks and disappear below ground. Their carnivorous nature and the venom of some species must have led to their being regarded with fear and awe. The Old Testament vilifies snakes, linking Eden's serpent unequivocally with evil, condemned by God to eat the dust of the earth and to be shunned by all other creatures because of its sullying of humankind. Snakes possess the curious habit of sloughing their skin several times a year, being apparently 'reborn' in the process. They are fertile creatures: the male has a multiple penis, and the female gives birth to a prodigious number of young. Moreover, the very physical shape of the snake evokes the image of the phallus. Finally, the sinuous, rippling movement of the reptile as it flows along the ground has a resemblance to water and the river meandering through the meadowland. All these aspects of the snake stimulated a complex symbolism: to the Celts, it could represent the underworld, death, healing, renewal and fertility. It is interesting that the serpent played a similarly composite role in classical religion: the healer-god Asklepios/Aesculapius had a snake emblem, and he combined his curative function with a chthonic dimension.[97]

The serpent-goddesses

In the iconography, the snake is frequently the companion of a goddess, who herself has a clear identity as a spirit of fecundity, abundance or healing (figure 8.17). The Celto-Germanic mother-goddesses were invoked on dedicatory stones decorated with the image of a serpent curled round a tree (very like Satan in the Garden of Eden): this has been interpreted as a symbol of the Tree of Life, protected by the snake[98] who, like the tree itself, bridged the gulf between the upper and lower worlds. Both the tree and the snake were perceived to emerge from below ground to the upper air.

Several of the healer-goddesses possessed snake attributions or companions which must have reflected the rebirth aspect of curative cults. Visitors to the Burgundian sanctuary of Mavilly worshipped a goddess with serpents and a torch, the latter perhaps evocative of light and thus clear vision, at a shrine frequented by pilgrims with eye disease.[99] Sirona was venerated with her consort Apollo at the important healing

Figure 8.17 Bronze group of Apollo and Sirona, with a snake encircling the goddess's arm, Mâlain, Burgundy. Paul Jenkins.

sanctuary of Hochscheid near Trier, where her cult image represents her as a dignified, serene woman wearing a long robe and a diadem. She carries a bowl containing three eggs in one hand, and around her arm is entwined a serpent which reaches out its head to the eggs (figure 8.18). Here Sirona was clearly perceived not simply as a healer but also as a divinity of fertility and rebirth.[100] Her snake imagery is repeated on a bronze group depicting Sirona and Apollo and dedicated to them at Mâlain in Burgundy (figure 8.17): again, the serpent twists itself around the goddess's wrist.[101] Interestingly, another healing spring-goddess, Damona, worshipped with Apollo Moritasgus at Alesia, seems equally to have combined roles of healing and fertility: all that remains of Damona's cult image is a stone head crowned with ears of corn and a snake-encircled hand.[102]

The curative cult establishments, built at the sites of sacred springs, were both physically and symbolically associated with water, and this may be one reason for the adoption of the snake by both Sirona and Damona. Serpents and the symbolism of water occur also away from the therapeutic sanctuaries: in north Britain, an image of a local river-goddess,

225

Figure 8.18 Stone statue of the healer goddess Sirona, with a bowl of eggs and a serpent, second to third century AD, from a shrine at Hochscheid, Germany. Original height: *c.*1m 69cm. Paul Jenkins.

Verbeia, spirit of the river Wharfe, was venerated at Ilkley, and is represented by a stone figure of a woman grasping two snakes, which fall in rigid zigzag movements from her hands.[103]

The ram-horned serpent

This extraordinary product of the Celtic imagination is found in the iconography of north-west Europe both before and during the Roman period. The image is of a serpent, its head in the form of a ram with curling horns. The idea seems to have been to enhance the symbolism of the snake, a chthonic and regenerative motif, as we have seen, by the addition of an unnatural element. Horns represented force and, because of their shape and their association with bulls, billy-goats and rams, virility and the essence of male fertility. In addition, the ram was an important emblem of fecundity in classical religious imagery. As was the case with the triple-horned bull, the ram-horned snake was a cult image which broke through the confines of naturalism and formed an intensely potent composite symbol.

On the Gundestrup Cauldron, the ram-horned snake occurs three times, once with the wheel-god, once at the head of a Celtic army and once in the company of the antlered god (see p. 147). An examination of the abundant iconography of the Romano-Celtic period in north-east Gaul demonstrates that this snake was above all the associate of Cernunnos, the stag-god. Indeed, it is possible to trace a representation of the god and his horned snake back to the fourth century BC, when the north Italians of Camonica Valley carved on the rocks a huge antlered figure with torcs and a serpent, the two major attributes of Cernunnos.[104] In Romano-Celtic Gaul, the antlered god is depicted as very close to his serpentine companion: on a bronze image at Étang-sur-Arroux in Burgundy and on a stone sculpture at Sommerécourt (Haute-Marne), the body of Cernunnos is encircled by a pair of horned snakes which feed from fruit and corn-mash held in vessels on the god's lap. It is interesting that there is another stone from the same site which represents a goddess with a horned serpent, again eating from a bowl of food: she has a cornucopia and a pomegranate, both potent classical fertility motifs.[105] Again, at Yzeures-sur-Creuse (Indre-et-Loire), a carving depicts a youth whose ram-horned snake twines around his legs and rests its head against his stomach.[106] But this close affinity between antlered god and horned serpent reaches its climax in a portrayal at Cirencester in Gloucestershire (figure 7.18), where Cernunnos's body is merged with those of two ram-horned snakes which replace his own legs and rear up on each side of his head to eat the fruit or corn grains clustered by his ears.[107] The symbolism on a stele at Vendoeuvres (Indre) is slightly different: here Cernunnos is flanked by two human-headed snakes, thus reversing the transmogrification shown by the antlered god himself.[108]

Cernunnos is a peaceful god of nature and fruitfulness: his snakes appear to reflect similar qualities and perhaps intensified the god's role as a lord of renewal or rebirth. Other deities were also, on occasion, accompanied by these ram-horned snakes: the Celtic Mars, a beneficent healer and combatter of barrenness and disease rather than a warrior, was depicted with these composite reptiles. He appears, on a carving at the curative sanctuary of Mavilly (Côte d'Or), as an armoured soldier, bearing a Celtic shield and a spear. He is accompanied by a goddess who rests her hand on his shield, and by the side of his spear-shaft, a ram-horned snake rears up from the ground.[109] Far away from Burgundy, at Southbroom in Wiltshire, a hoard of bronze figurines included a statuette of a local Mars grasping two large ram-horned snakes by their necks.[110] The Celtic Mercury, too, adopted this hybrid creature, again perhaps as a promoter of healing and fertility: at Beauvais (Oise), the classical-looking image of Mercury is belied by the ram-horned snake carved on each side of the stone.[111] At the curative establishment of Néris-les-Bains (Allier), the Gaulish Mercury sits, like Cernunnos, while a huge ram-horned serpent reposes with its head in his lap; the god is accompanied by a nymph-like goddess, the spirit of the spring.[112]

The ram-horned snake was occasionally a companion of the sky-gods: its association with the wheel-god (a solar divinity) on the Gundestrup Cauldron has already been noted. This is repeated far away at Lypiatt in Gloucestershire (figure 8.19), where a Romano-Celtic devotee set up an altar to the sun-god on which were carved a solar wheel and a ram-horned snake.[113] It is well established that the Celtic sun-god possessed links with fertility, healing, death and resurrection,[114] and it is probable that the snake was chosen as a companion of the sun-god precisely because much of the symbolism associated with it was envisaged as relevant to the solar cult. It is worth noting that conventional snakes are often associated with the Celtic sky–sun-god.[115]

The serpent of the underworld

The association of the celestial powers with the symbolism of the horned snake has just been discussed. But in other iconography of the Celtic sky-god, the snake appears to play a different role, primarily as a chthonic symbol of the negative, dark forces of the underworld. The sculptured group on the summit of Jupiter–giant columns has been mentioned earlier in this chapter, when the cults related to horses were being considered (pp. 207–9). The iconography consists of a sky-horseman, armed with a thunderbolt and (sometimes) a solar shield, whose horse rides down a 'giant', semi-human monster whose legs are

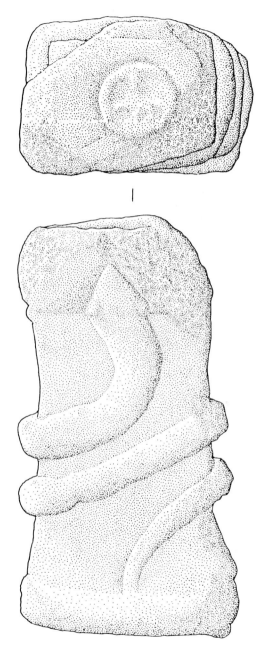

Figure 8.19 Stone altar encircled by ram-horned snake, Romano-Celtic, Lypiatt Park, Gloucestershire. Height: 15cm. Nick Griffiths.

replaced by serpents (figure 8.7). The artistic theme may owe something to classical imagery where, in the battle between the Olympian deities and the Titans of Earth, the chthonic giants are depicted with serpent-limbs.[116] The Celtic giant is huge, an earthbound creature, its contorted facial expression evocative of its stress and anguish, and its snake-legs enhance its chthonic identity. The giant is subjugated by the galloping horseman, but it is clear that the iconography represents a cult that is essentially dualistic, where there is interdependence and symbiosis between the elements of sun and earth, sky and underworld. Darkness is necessary as well as light, winter as well as summer, and without death, life cannot exist. All of these seeming antitheses are embodied by the zoomorphic imagery of the columns: celestial god and chthonic giant are thus identified; horse and serpent represent the two opposing yet mutually dependent poles of the sky-god's sphere of influence. The iconography (and perhaps the symbolism as well) reminds one irresistibly of St George and the dragon.

GOD MADE BEAST: CERNUNNOS AND THE HORNED ONES

The divine stag

To the Celts, the stag symbolized wild nature. Its alertness, speed and its aggression and potency during the rutting season made it an object of reverence, and its spreading, tree-like antlers seemed to epitomize the forest. Often the antlers are emphasized in iconography.[117] At Colchester (Essex), a small bronze stag was dedicated to Silvanus Callirius at a Romano-Celtic shrine.[118] The Celtic soubriquet means 'King of the Woodland'. The magnificent stag figurine from the late Iron Age hoard of Neuvy-en-Sullias (Loiret) is depicted with his antlers in velvet,[119] signifying that it is late springtime. Indeed, the autumnal shedding and spring growth of a stag's antlers may well have endowed the creature with a cyclical, seasonal symbolism, similar to that of deciduous trees.

The iconography of stags was closely associated with that of hunting. At Camonica Valley,[120] the divine stag was revered and hunted at the same time. He was also the companion of the solar god and his antlers were sometimes represented as curved round to form a circular, rayed sun.[121] The divinity of the stag at Camonica is powerfully indicated on a carving which dates to the beginning of the Iron Age in the seventh century BC,[122] and depicts a being who is half-man, half-stag. This image may portray the stag-god in metamorphosis, in the same way as Cernunnos himself (pp. 231–4).

The Romano-Celtic hunters display an ambivalent attitude to their stag victims (see also chapter 3): the sculpture at the high mountain sanctuary of Le Donon in the Vosges shows a god who is both hunter and benefactor of the forest and its inhabitants.[123] He stands, carrying the fruits of the wild woodland – pine-cones, nuts and acorns – in an open bag under his arm. He wears the pelt of a wolf as a cloak, his boots are ornamented with the heads of animals, and he carries the tools of his hunting activity: a long knife, a chopper and a spear. He is therefore a hunter, who kills the forest-dwellers and who wears the skins of his victims. But beside him is a stag, apparently a fearless companion on whose antlers the god rests his hand, in apparently benevolent protection. The deity is thus both slayer and guardian of the forest-dwellers; the stag is both victim and associate of the nature-god. Other hunter-divinities show the same ambivalence to their prey: Cocidius was a local god of north Britain, equated sometimes with the Roman Mars, sometimes with Silvanus. On a sculpture from Risingham, he appears as a hunter with his dog: nearby a family of deer – stag, doe and fawn – is grazing unconcernedly in the presence of Cocidius. The forest is represented by trees laden with acorns.[124] The simple carving at Treclun in Burgundy shows a similar scene, with dogs and stags.[125]

Cernunnos: the stag-god

The veneration of the stag and its close association with the supernatural led to the concept of a god whose identity could be represented by an image which blurred the boundaries between man and animal. That beasts – the stag in particular – were themselves considered divine is shown above all by the iconography of a deity who, though he is depicted in anthropomorphic form, none the less had zoomorphic features (figures 7.18, 8.20, 8.21). He was Cernunnos, the Horned One, distinguished by his possession of antlers. He was a powerful god, whose potency was enhanced by his adoption of the essence of his animal associate. Cernunnos's name appears only once, on a first-century AD stone at Paris, which depicts the head of an elderly, balding, bearded man wearing antlers with torcs hanging from them,[126] and with stags' ears. But the god himself was venerated before this period: at Camonica Valley, a site whose rock art abounds in stag imagery, a fourth-century BC image depicts a large standing figure of a god with antlers and torcs.[127] An Iron Age coin dating to about AD 20 depicts Cernunnos wearing antlers and with what seems to be a solar wheel symbol between them (figure 8.20).[128] On a late pre-Roman bronze statuette at Bouray (Seine-et-Oise), a god wearing a torc sits cross-legged on the ground: he bears no antlers but the fact that he possesses hooves is indicative of his stag symbolism.[129] The most important representation of Cernunnos dating from the free Celtic period is on the Danish Gundestrup Cauldron,[130] where an antlered deity sits cross-legged, one

Figure 8.20 Celtic silver coin with the head of Cernunnos, a sun symbol between his antlers, *c.* AD 20, Petersfield, Hampshire. By courtesy of the National Museum of Wales.

torc round his neck, another in his hand, accompanied by his stag, a ram-horned serpent and multifarious other creatures, both naturalistic and fantastic (figure 6.18).

Cernunnos flourished in the Romano-Celtic period, when he was represented by a large number of images, mainly in north-central Gaul, but also further west, at Saintes and even among the Dobunni of south-western Britain.[131] Many of the free Celtic and Romano-Celtic images have common characteristics: often the god is shown seated in a cross-legged position, as at Gundestrup, Reims (figure 8.21)[132] and Sommerécourt.[133] This may not be significant, since such a position would be natural and comfortable for people accustomed to sit on the floor, as, indeed, was observed by classical observers of the Celts.[134] Frequently the god is associated with torcs, sometimes two; he is often accompanied by one or more ram-horned snakes (see pp. 227–8); he has a stag and other animal associates.

The images of Cernunnos at Sommerécourt (Haute-Marne) and Étang-sur-Arroux near Autun,[135] the first of stone and the second of bronze, have two shared features of considerable interest for the interpretation of Cernunnos's cult: both show the god feeding horned serpents from bowls of food, and the animals curl themselves intimately round their benefactors. Both images have holes in their heads for the insertion and removal of separate antlers. This could be especially meaningful in that we might envisage a symbolism, reflecting the seasonal cycle of stags themselves, whereby the antlers were perhaps removed in the autumn and replaced in spring.

The Burgundian tribes, the Aedui and the Lingones, worshipped a Cernunnos who could be perceived as three-headed. The bronze figurine at Étang has one main head and two small subsidiary heads, one at each side. On a sculpture at Nuits-Saint-Georges, Cernunnos is three-faced; he is part of a triad of divinities.[136] On a carving at Beaune, he is again one of three deities, but here it is one of his companions who is three-headed rather than the stag-god himself.[137]

Cernunnos symbolizes abundance and prosperity and is the guardian of wild nature. He is Lord of Animals, who is often seen surrounded by many different creatures, a Noah-like figure of benevolence. This happens on the iconography of Gundestrup, Nuits-Saint-Georges and Beaune. The stele at Reims (figure 8.21) depicts Cernunnos feeding a

Figure 8.21 Stone relief of Cernunnos seated between Apollo and Mercury. Beneath the antlered god are a bull and stag eating from a sack of coins or grain, Reims, France. Height: 1m 30cm. Paul Jenkins.

233

stag and a bull from a bag of grain or coins; the god feasts horned snakes at Sommerécourt and Étang. At Cirencester (figure 7.18), two horned serpents rear up to eat from open bags by Cernunnos's ears.[138] The interweaving of god and serpents noted on the Gaulish monuments is even closer at Cirencester, as we have seen, where the snakes actually form Cernunnos's legs. The stag-god again has a purse on the image at Vendoeuvres.[139] Here there is an interesting variation on the snake symbolism in that the two reptiles flanking the stag-god have human faces, as if they have escaped the limitations of realism, just as Cernunnos himself has done. The role of the god as lord of natural abundance and fertility is extended to the role of healing: he was venerated at such healing sanctuaries as Néris-les-Bains.[140] At Reims, Cernunnos is flanked by the healer-god Apollo and the Celtic Mercury, a god of commercial success.[141]

It is possible that Cernunnos was a skin-turner or shape-shifter, able to vary his outward form from human to animal at will. His semi-zoomorphic images may present the god as in mid-change, to remind his worshippers of his particular powers, born of his affinity with the animal world. Many of the Norse gods could change form in this way: Loki, for instance, became at different times a mare, a hawk, a salmon and a seal.[142]

The horned ones: gods or devils?

Horns are obvious representations of aggression, of the ability to inflict pain and destruction. Although horns are not sex-specific, they also tend to symbolize the pugnacity displayed by male animals, especially in rut, and thus virility and fertility in general.

Horned images appear in Celtic and, indeed, in pre-Celtic iconography in Europe (figure 8.22). Certain animals, which have no horns in reality, were endowed with these attributes in the imagination of ancient European artists: horned birds, for instance, are common in Urnfield (later Bronze Age) imagery. We have already met Celtic horned serpents; horses could also be depicted with horns: a depiction dating to the fourth or third century BC, carved at Mouriès in Provence, shows a triple-horned horse. The heads decorating the late Iron Age Capel Garmon firedog (figure 5.13) are horned, like bulls, but resemble horses. One Gaulish image of a boar sprouts three horns. In the earlier discussion of bull imagery, allusion was made to the triple-horned bull, a common Romano-Celtic image. In all these instances, horns appear to have been added in order to endow the animals with sanctity, an element of the supernatural, and virile, aggressive force.

Anthropomorphic horned images formed part of the European craftsman's repertoire as early as the Bronze Age, when Danish male

Figure 8.22 Bronze bull-horned human head, first century AD, Lezoux, Puy-de-Dôme, France. Paul Jenkins.

figurines were adorned with horns.[143] These beings are ithyphallic and the presence of the horns probably enhanced their virility symbolism. Pre-Roman Celtic art endowed many half-human, half-divine images with horns: one of the rare representational stone carvings of the fifth to fourth century BC consists of a statue of a male deity at Holzerlingen in Germany.[144] The sculpture is a plain block of stone with a belt at the waist and the arms crossed on the chest, but the Janiform head bears a double-horned crown. Iron Age metalwork is sometimes decorated with horned figures: an example is the bucket-escutcheon at Boughton Aluph (Kent),[145] which is in the form of a male head with jutting bull's horns, a variation on the bull-headed bucket-mounts which are so common in the later Iron Age.

The association between horns and aggression is demonstrated by the use of horns to adorn Celtic helmets (figure 4.16): this tradition is mentioned by Diodorus Siculus,[146] who comments that Celtic warriors wore helmets decorated with animal crests or horns, to increase their stature and the ferocity of their appearance in battle. We can see this in iconography, for example on the Gundestrup Cauldron plate (figure 4.5) with its image of the wheel-god attended by a small figure wearing a horned helmet. Similarly, the carvings of Celtic armour in the early first century AD on the Orange Arch[147] include bull-horned helmets (figure 6.6). While horned images are relatively uncommon in Romano-Celtic Continental contexts, horned warrior-deities were popular images in Britain, especially in the Brigantian north (figures 8.23, 8.24).[148] I will take just one example of many, a small, roughly incised relief at Maryport in Cumbria.[149] He is naked, with a spear in his right hand, a shield in his left. What is especially interesting is the intense phallic

Figure 8.23 Stone bust of horned god, Moresby, Cumbria. Paul Jenkins.

symbolism of the piece: the god is ithyphallic and even his nose resembles an erect phallus, while the horns themselves are also phallic in form. Here war, destruction, aggression, virility and fecundity are all present in this one simple yet concentrated image.

Horns were not the sole prerogative of the war-gods, though they were above all associated with aggression. Certain divinities could be endowed with horns on certain occasions, to stress particular aspects of their natures. The Celtic Mercury was occasionally given horns: the shrine at West Uley in Gloucestershire was dedicated to Mercury.[150] Most of the many images from the sanctuary present the god in his usual classical guise but one depicts him with a prominent pair of horns. The stylized relief of Mercury found in a well at Emberton (Bucks.) presents an interesting example of an ambiguity in imagery which may be deliberate: the Graeco-Roman god often wears a *petasos* or cap with small wings sprouting from it. The Emberton Mercury bears excrescences on his head, but the carving is so stylized that it is difficult to tell whether these are horns or wings. In my opinion, this feature may well have been left deliberately vague and imprecise by the Celtic artist: the significance of the image perhaps lay in the eye of the beholder, a Roman seeing wings and a Celt horns. Physically, the difference between small wings and horns is very little, but the conceptual or symbolic shift is enormous.

Horns were given to the goddesses only infrequently, although horned female deities are known, for instance at Richborough in Kent and Icklingham in Suffolk.[151] The possession of horns by gods who were not warriors was probably meant to emphasize aspects of the fertility or prosperity of their cults. The addition of the attributes of a bull, ram or goat to an anthropomorphic image gave it the power of that animal, as surely as Cernunnos's antlers endowed him with the force of the wild woodland and the qualities of its most prominent creature, the stag. What is clear is that the horned beings did not represent the power of evil. In Christian contexts, horns have been associated with Satan. The reasons for this are interesting but strictly outside the scope of this book. A multihorned dragon is equated with Satan in chapter 12 of the Book of Revelation. Medieval Christians perceived the Devil as horned and hooved, perhaps because of the classical Pan, a lascivious nature-god who would be well known to medieval classicists. It may have been that the sexual excesses ascribed to this god, or the essence of unacceptable paganism, were epitomized, in Christian eyes, by the cults of animals. But certainly, as far as the Celts were concerned, evil connotations were entirely absent from their horned deities, although it is true that sexuality implied by fertility was undoubtedly part of the symbolism of the horned gods. The Celtic worshipper perceived horned or antlered divinities as bringers of abundance, where the growth of crops

Figure 8.24 Lead plaque of horned god, Chesters, Northumberland.
Miranda Green.

and increase of livestock were crucial to survival, and where infant mortality and disease were a constant threat. Moreover, the horned warrior-gods were venerated not simply as destroyers but also as protectors or guardians, not just against enemies in battle but against all the ills of humankind. The horned gods of north Britain[152] combined elements of aggression (perhaps against the Roman conquerors) with beneficent guardianship of their people. Ironically, the protective character of the Celtic horned and antlered gods bears a far greater resemblance to the beneficence of Christ than to the image of the Devil.

9

CHANGING ATTITUDES TO THE ANIMAL WORLD

It is an interesting paradox that, to an extent, the more 'civilized' a society becomes the worse is its attitude to animals. In its strictest sense, civilization means 'city-living' and it is true that the further removed one is from the natural world, the smaller may be one's sensitivity to it. Thus Keith Thomas, speaking of early modern England, comments that 'human civilization indeed was virtually synonymous with the conquest of nature'.[1] Many of the Greek and Roman philosophers, products of advanced ancient civilizations based upon the *polis* and the *urbs*, preached that man was the measure of all things, and thus that animals and all of nature were subordinate to humankind.[2] This attitude to creatures that are not human can be linked, in very general terms, to the treatment of some humans – women, groups of different ethnic origins and different classes, especially slaves – as inferior. This was certainly the case in the classical world and, indeed, in early modern England where, in the eighteenth century, racialists remarked that the orang-utan was closer to the negro than the negro to the white man.[3]

The notion that humans had a God-given right to treat the natural world and its animals as their possessions to do with as they pleased has, of course, a very ancient and biblical pedigree. In his creation of the world in the Book of Genesis, God gave the first humans dominion over all the beasts of the earth, the birds of the air and the creatures of the waters.[4] Moreover, it is not without significance that it was an animal – a serpent – which was directly responsible for Adam and Eve's fall from grace and their banishment from the Garden of Eden. After the Flood, God renewed the supremacy and authority of humankind over the animal world.[5]

Keith Thomas's scholarly exploration of the attitude of humans to animals and the environment in the early modern period of England (1500–1800)[6] provides a fascinating insight into the reasoning behind the unquestioning view, which is still held (in more or less modified form) in most societies all over the world, that animals existed solely in order to be exploited for the benefit of humans, at whatever cost to the

Figure 9.1 Triple-horned bronze human head, first century AD, Hafenturm, Germany. Paul Jenkins.

creatures themselves and for however trivial a cause. Between the sixteenth and eighteenth centuries, animals in Britain were considered as the absolute property of people to use as they wished: no moral issues were considered relevant, and the killing of animals for pleasure was regarded as totally acceptable. It was noted by English observers in the seventeenth century that this attitude contrasted sharply with the much more balanced treatment of beasts by some North American Indian tribes, for whom there was a 'tacit contract' between humans and animals, even though beasts were traditionally hunted for food and skins.[7] To Europeans at this time, there was a yawning and unbridgeable gulf between animals and humans. But during the sixteenth century the keeping of pets became established as a norm among the English middle classes,[8] although pet-keeping had been a fashion much earlier, among the aristocracy of the medieval period. This, together with riding, encouraged the establishment of two distinct categories of animals – those which were close to humans, like horses, dogs and other creatures living in and around the house, and those which were exploited for labour, food and sport, the farmyard beasts and the wild animals.

It was partly the close coexistence of the privileged first category which led to a greater understanding of animals. The second major factor, which did not emerge until the nineteenth century, was the work of the evolutionists of whom Charles Darwin was in the forefront.[9] His research made it impossible for the great divide between humans and animals to be maintained. But the superiority of humans over animals is still largely accepted. Most people are omnivorous and, of course, meat-eating is the primary purpose of present-day animal exploitation. In addition, there is still a hangover from past concepts of animals as uncouth, savage, 'uncivilized' creatures in the derogatory language used to describe humans of whom others disapprove. Hooligans and murderers are called 'animals' or 'beasts', and many names of animals are used in contemptuous descriptions: 'bitch', 'cat', 'cow', 'goat', 'shrew' and 'vixen' are but a few examples (the majority, interestingly, levelled at women).

This brief exploration of the realm of modern and early modern attitudes to animals serves to highlight the contrast beween the so-called 'civilized' world and that of the pagan Celts, who shared with the American Indians the regard for a maintenance of harmony and balance with the natural world and its creatures. The belief that beasts and humans are close and essential associates, joint owners of the earth, does not preclude exploitation or meat-eating, which occurred widely in the Celtic world, as previous chapters have shown. What does seem to have existed, however, is respect, and this appears to have resulted from the close link perceived between the natural and supernatural worlds. The world of the Celts was less anthropocentric than either that of modern peoples or of classical societies. This meant that animals were regarded as occupants of the landscape in their own right and were not there simply for the use of man. The strong ritual element in so many aspects of Celtic life involved with animals implies that beasts were valued and belonged to the gods. Activities such as hunting were only permissible if certain criteria were met, which included sacrifice and other ritual activities.

Anthropocentricity and the notion of animals as existing for the gratification of humans tends to go hand in hand with monotheism. This is especially true of such divine powers as the Jehovah of the Old

Testament who made man 'in his own image'. In societies where there is but one god, animals have at best a lesser place in the supernatural hierarchy. By contrast, in polytheistic systems, animals may frequently play a prominent role: this is as true of the religion of ancient Egypt as of the pagan Celts. In the Mediterranean cultures of Greece and Rome, there were many deities, but humankind was at the centre of the universe and, in contrast to the doctrines of Judaism and Christianity, man made the gods in his image: the physical representations of the classical gods and goddesses showed them as perfect specimens of manhood and womanhood.

Attitudes to animals in both ancient and modern societies are full of paradoxes, contradictions and ambiguities. For all the merciless exploitation of animals in early modern England, beasts were none the less perceived as having a religious or spiritual sense, even though they were generally denied souls. The birth of Christ, as chronicled in the New Testament, was associated with the beasts of his stable: 'the ox and ass and camel which adore'.[10] Psalm 148 alludes to the praise of the Lord by the animals. Whilst the Celts clearly revered animals and regarded many as sacred, they nevertheless subjected them on occasions to treatment which – to modern European sensitivities at least – seems truly barbarous, in the name of religion. Thus, the skinned and disembowelled dog buried with his Iron Age master at Tartigny in Gaul excites our compassion and revulsion.

A phenomenon associated with attitudes to a specific creature which, interestingly, spans space and time is the belief in the prophetic powers of ravens. This was well noted in the earliest Insular literature and was a tradition held also by the peoples of the classical world.[11] A pamphlet written in 1694 alluded to a Herefordshire raven which uttered a prophecy three times.[12]

The apparent similarities and yet also the differences between animals and humans have for long evoked strong views. Pet owners, especially the Victorians, have tended to anthropomorphize and sentimentalize animals, ascribing to them human personae rather than respecting them for themselves. Some aspects of animal behaviour – fidelity, protectiveness, affection, for instance – endear animals to humans and have long done so. Others – such as the killing instinct – may have the reverse effect. The Celts acknowledged the diverse qualities of animals and considered them sacred, partly because of their affinities with humans and partly for the opposite reason. It was precisely this paradox which enhanced the status of animals as supernatural beings.

NOTES

ABBREVIATION

C.I.L.   *Corpus Inscriptionum Latinarum*, Berlin, Georgium Reimarum, 1861–1943.

2 ANIMALS IN THE CELTIC ECONOMY

1 Strabo, *Geography* IV, 1, 2.
2 Davis 1987, pp. 155–68.
3 Wells 1990, pp. 437–76.
4 Reynolds 1987, p. 38.
5 Strabo IV, 4, 3.
6 Reynolds 1979, pp. 47–56; Fowler 1983, pp. 188–99.
7 Brunaux 1989, pp. 23–6.
8 Meniel 1987a, pp. 8–12.
9 Anati 1965, pp. 127–30.
10 Coles 1991.
11 Athenaeus IV, 36.
12 Fowler 1983, pp. 188–99; Davis 1987, pp. 169–95.
13 Cunliffe 1986, p. 72.
14 Grant 1989b, pp. 135–46.
15 Reynolds 1987, pp. 50–60.
16 Grant 1984a, pp. 102–19.
17 Haselgrove 1989, pp. 1–18.
18 Grant 1984a, pp. 102–19.
19 Fitzpatrick 1991.
20 Meniel 1987a, pp. 47–64; Meniel 1986b, pp. 115–22.
21 King 1978, pp. 207–32.
22 Noddle 1984, pp. 105–23.
23 Cunliffe 1986, pp. 126–35.
24 Grant 1989b, pp. 135–46.
25 Reynolds 1987, pp. 50–60; Grant 1984a, pp. 102–19.
26 Cunliffe 1986, p. 80.
27 Reynolds 1987, p. 24.
28 Cunliffe 1986, pp. 118–26.

29 Reynolds 1987, pp. 50–60.
30 Reynolds 1979, pp. 47–56; Meniel 1987a, pp. 12–15; Davis 1987, pp. 169–95.
31 Reynolds 1979, pp. 47–56.
32 ibid.; Reynolds 1987, pp. 40–4.
33 ibid.; Ross 1986, pp. 67–76.
34 Davis 1987, pp. 169–195.
35 Cunliffe 1986, pp. 126–135.
36 Grant 1984a, pp. 102–19.
37 Meniel 1987a, pp. 47–64.
38 For example, Strabo IV, 4, 3.
39 Caesar, *De Bello Gallico* VI, 22.
40 Tacitus, *Germania* V.
41 Piggott 1965, p. 235.
42 Kinsella 1969, pp. 49–50.
43 ibid., p. 54; Proudfoot 1961, pp. 94–122.
44 Piggott 1965, p. 235; Cross and Slover 1936, p. 326.
45 Darvill 1987, p. 190.
46 Ross 1986, pp. 67–76; Reynolds 1979, pp. 47–56; Meniel 1987a, pp. 16–20.
47 Grant 1989b, pp. 135–46.
48 Reynolds 1987, pp. 40–4.
49 Anati 1965, pp. 127–30.
50 Cunliffe 1986, pp. 126–35.
51 Coles 1991.
52 Mercer 1981, pp. ix–xxi.
53 Cunliffe 1986, pp. 126–35; Davis 1987, pp. 155–68.
54 Strabo IV, 4, 3.
55 Kinsella 1969, p. 54; Ross 1986, pp. 67–76.
56 Reynolds 1987, pp. 40–4.
57 *Geography* IV, 4, 3.
58 Jones and Jones 1976, pp. 56–63.
59 Piggott 1965, p. 235; Ross 1986, pp. 67–76.
60 Mac Cana 1983; Kinsella 1969, *passim*.
61 Kinsella 1969, p. 46.
62 Grant 1984a, pp. 102–19.
63 Meniel 1987a, pp. 47–64.
64 Reynolds 1987, pp. 40–4.
65 Meniel 1987a, pp. 8–12; Reynolds 1987, pp. 40–4.
66 Grant 1984a, pp. 102–19.
67 Reynolds 1979, pp. 47–56.
68 Meniel 1986b, pp. 115–22;, Meniel 1990, pp. 185–8.
69 Grant 1989b, pp. 135–46.
70 Grant 1984a, pp. 102–19; Meniel 1987a, pp. 47–64; Davis 1987, pp. 169–95.
71 Cunliffe 1986, pp. 126–35.
72 Davis 1987, pp. 135–68.
73 Anati 1965, pp. 127–30.
74 Reynolds 1979, pp. 27–8, 47–64.
75 Meniel 1987a, pp. 33–46; Cunliffe 1986, pp. 126–35; Grant 1984a, pp. 102–19.
76 Meniel 1990, pp. 185–8.
77 Meniel 1987a, pp. 33–46.
78 Cunliffe 1986, pp. 126–35.
79 Davis 1987, pp. 155–68.
80 Meniel 1987a, pp. 33–46.

81 Cross and Slover 1936, p. 326.
82 Ross 1986, pp. 67–76.
83 Reynolds 1979, pp. 47–56; Ross 1986, pp. 67–76.
84 Davis 1987, pp. 169–95; Reynolds 1979, pp. 27–8.
85 Meniel 1987a, pp. 21–4, figure on p. 24.
86 *De Bello Gallico* V, 12.
87 Grant 1989b, pp. 135–46; Cunliffe 1986, pp. 118–26.
88 Reynolds 1979, pp. 47–56.
89 Meniel 1987a, pp. 21–4.
90 Pliny, *Natural History* X, 27, 53, Meniel 1987a, pp. 65–78.
91 *Geography* V, 5, 2.
92 Green 1986, figure 72.
93 Ross 1986, pp. 67–76.
94 Jones and Jones 1976, p. 97.
95 Cunliffe 1986, pp. 126–35.
96 Anati 1965, pp. 127–30.
97 Meniel 1987a, pp. 25–31; Meniel 1986b, pp. 115–22.
98 Meniel 1986a, pp. 37–9.
99 Diodorus Siculus V, 28, 4.
100 Cunliffe 1986, pp. 126–35; Davis 1987, pp. 169–95.
101 Meniel 1987a, pp. 79–88; Grant 1984a, pp. 102–19; Grant 1989b, pp. 135–46; Reynolds 1987, pp. 50–60.
102 Fowler 1983, p. 170.
103 Reynolds 1987, pp. 50–60.
104 ibid., pp. 40–4.
105 Cunliffe 1986, pp. 126–35.
106 Fenton 1981, pp. 210–15.
107 ibid.
108 Ryder 1981, pp. 182–209.
109 Reynolds 1987, p. 28, figure 12; Anati 1965, figure on p. 117.
110 Haselgrove 1989, pp. 1–18.
111 Reynolds 1987, p. 28, figure 13.
112 Reynolds 1979, pp. 47–56; Cunliffe 1986, pp. 118–26.
113 Meniel 1987a, pp. 33–46.
114 Anati 1965, pp. 112–22.
115 Meniel 1986b, pp. 115–22.
116 Reynolds 1979, pp. 47–56.
117 Fowler 1983, p. 5; Reynolds 1979, pp. 27–8.
118 ibid., pp. 47–56.
119 Meniel 1987a, pp. 79–88.
120 Anati 1965, pp. 112–18.
121 Fowler 1983, p. 179.
122 *Geography* IV, 4, 3.
123 Meniel 1987a, pp. 47–64; Meniel 1986b, pp. 115–22; Grant 1989b, pp. 135–46; Davis 1987, pp. 169–95.
124 Grant 1975, pp. 378–408.
125 Frere 1978, p. 317.
126 Ryder 1981, pp. 182–209.
127 Reynolds 1987, pp. 50–60.
128 Reynolds 1979, pp. 27–8.
129 Cunliffe 1986, pp. 126–35.
130 Ryder 1981, pp. 182–209.

131 Diodorus Siculus V, 30, 1–2.
132 Delaney 1986, p. 19.
133 Meniel 1987a, pp. 47–64.
134 Ryder 1981, pp. 182–209.
135 Coles 1991.
136 Ryder 1981, pp. 182–209.
137 Davis 1987, pp. 155–68; Grant 1984a, pp. 102–19; Mercer 1981, pp. ix–xxi.
138 *De Bello Gallico* VI, 22.
139 *Geography* IV, 5, 2.
140 Meniel 1987a, pp. 65–78.
141 Kinsella 1969, p. 27.
142 Cunliffe 1986, pp. 118–26.
143 Reynolds 1979, pp. 27–8.
144 Meniel 1987a, pp. 12–15.
145 Reynolds 1987, pp. 40–4; Meniel 1987a, pp. 47–64.
146 ibid.
147 Davis 1987, pp. 169–95; Grant 1975, pp. 378–408.
148 *Natural History* XI, 97, 240.
149 Ryder 1981, pp. 182–209.
150 Ritchie and Ritchie 1985, p. 19.
151 Green 1989, pp. 42–4, and figure 17 on p. 185.
152 Delaney 1986, p. 22.
153 Robinson 1984, p. 119.
154 Ross 1986, pp. 67–76.
155 Diodorus Siculus V, 26, 3.
156 Athenaeus IV, 36.
157 Meniel 1986b, pp. 115–22; Grant 1989b, pp. 135–46; Reynolds 1979,
    pp. 47–56.
158 Meniel 1990, pp. 185–8.
159 Meniel 1987a, pp. 47–64.
160 ibid.
161 ibid., pp. 33–46.
162 ibid., pp. 47–64.
163 Meniel 1986b, pp. 115–22.
164 Cunliffe 1986, pp. 118–35; Grant 1984a, pp. 102–19.
165 Noddle 1984, pp. 105–23.
166 Grant 1989b, pp. 135–46.
167 Jones and Jones 1976, pp. 56–63.
168 Mac Cana 1983, p. 97.
169 Diodorus Siculus V, 28, 4.
170 Ross 1986, pp. 67–76.
171 Delaney 1986, p. 22.
172 Athenaeus IV, 36.
173 Meniel 1987a, pp. 65–78; Grant 1989b, pp. 135–46.
174 Brunaux 1988.
175 Ryder 1981, pp. 182–209.
176 *Geography* IV, 4, 3.
177 Reynolds 1987, pp. 50–60.
178 Meniel 1987a, pp. 65–78.
179 Diodorus Siculus V, 28, 4.
180 Green 1992a, p. 75.
181 Savory 1976, plate 1.

182 Cunliffe 1986, pp. 118–26.
183 Megaw 1970, catalogue no. 23.
184 *Geography* IV, 5, 2.
185 *Natural History* IV, 16, 104.
186 *De Bello Gallico* III, 13.
187 Ryder 1981, pp. 182–209.
188 Meniel 1987a, pp. 65–78.
189 Ross 1986, pp. 67–76.
190 Meniel 1987a, pp. 79–88.
191 Kinsella 1969, p. 147.
192 ibid., p. 148.
193 Meniel 1987a, pp. 79–88.
194 Ryder 1981, pp. 182–209.
195 Glob 1969, pp. 18–36.
196 Birley 1977, pp. 123–6.
197 Anon. 1980a, catalogue no. 6, 2.
198 Diodorus Siculus V, 32, 7.
199 Kinsella 1969, p. 178.
200 Collis 1984, pp. 163–5; Delaney 1986, p. 19.
201 Stead *et al.* 1986, *passim.*
202 Meniel 1987a, pp. 79–88; Meniel 1986b, pp. 115–22.
203 Diodorus Siculus V, 28, 4.
204 Reynolds 1979, pp. 47–56; Ryder 1981, pp. 182–209.
205 *Natural History* XI, 45, 126; Caesar, *De Bello Gallico* VI, 28.
206 Grant 1984a, pp. 102–19; Grant 1984b, pp. 221–8.
207 Armitage 1982, pp. 94–106.
208 Ryder 1981, pp. 182–209.

3 PREY AND PREDATOR

1 Caesar, *De Bello Gallico* VI, 21.
2 ibid., 28. Interestingly, a letter to *Current Archaeology* has pointed out the possibility that the intractable Chillingham wild cattle may be the descendants of the aurochs: see Macauley 1991.
3 Meniel 1987b, pp. 357–61.
4 Megaw and Megaw 1989, p. 174.
5 Meniel 1987a, pp. 89–100.
6 ibid., pp. 101–43.
7 ibid.
8 Duval 1987, pp. 22–9.
9 Anon. 1991a, p. 406.
10 Meniel 1987a, pp. 101–43.
11 Boucher 1976, figure 291; Green 1989, figure 10.
12 Meniel 1987a, pp. 89–100.
13 Strabo, *Geography* IV, 4, 3.
14 Meniel 1987a, pp. 8–12.
15 ibid., pp. 89–100.
16 ibid., pp. 101–43.
17 Megaw 1970, catalogue no. 37.
18 Anon. 1980b, pp. 245–6, no. 76.
19 ibid., p. 263, no. 116.

20 Olmsted 1979, plate 2C.
21 Green 1986, figure 15.
22 Megaw and Megaw 1989, pp. 160–2.
23 Arrian, *Cynegetica* XXIII.
24 Martial, *Epigrams* XII, 14; Hyland 1990, pp. 231–47.
25 Meniel 1984.
26 Meniel 1987a, pp. 89–100.
27 Meniel 1990, pp. 185–8.
28 Meniel 1987a, pp. 101–43.
29 King 1978, pp. 207–32.
30 Wait 1985, pp. 52–3.
31 Cunliffe 1986, p. 46.
32 Ross and Feacham 1976, pp. 230–7.
33 Green 1986, p. 184; Frere 1984, p. 296.
34 Anon. 1980a, no. 3.50; Megaw and Megaw 1989, pp. 33–4; Green 1986, figure 13; Green 1989, figure 56.
35 Megaw and Megaw 1989, pp. 30–2.
36 Anon. 1980b, p. 262, no. 116.
37 ibid., p. 279, no. 175.
38 Green 1989, figure 43.
39 Megaw 1970, no. 2; Green 1989, figure 54.
40 Anati 1965, pp. 1, 29, 89–90.
41 ibid., pp. 124–7.
42 ibid., p. 230.
43 ibid., p. 179.
44 *Cynegetica* XXIII.
45 *De Bello Gallico* VI, 27.
46 ibid. V, 12.
47 Green 1989, figure 42.
48 *Cynegetica* XXIII.
49 Meniel 1987a, pp. 89–100.
50 Meniel 1986a, pp. 37–9; Meniel 1989a, pp. 87–97.
51 Meniel 1987a, pp. 89–100.
52 ibid.
53 Meniel 1989a, pp. 87–97.
54 Wait 1985, pp. 122–53.
55 Meniel 1987a, pp. 101–43.
56 Anati 1965, p. 124.
57 Stead *et al.* 1986.
58 Athenaeus IV, 37.
59 See Ross 1986.
60 Anati 1965, pp. 124–7.
61 Meniel 1987a, pp. 101–43.
62 Meniel 1989a, pp. 87–97.
63 Meniel 1987a, pp. 101–43.
64 Meniel 1989a, pp. 87–97.
65 Wait 1985, pp. 122–53.
66 Cunliffe 1986, pp. 155–71; Grant 1989a, pp. 79–86.
67 Meniel 1987a, pp. 89–100, 101–43; Meniel 1986b, pp. 115–22.
68 Cunliffe 1986, pp. 126–35.
69 *Cynegetica* XXIII.
70 Brunaux 1988, pp. 95–7.

71 *Geography*, IV, 4, 3.
72 Diodorus Siculus V, 28, 4; 32, 7.
73 Collis 1984, pp. 163–72.
74 Delaney 1986, pp. 22–3.
75 Meniel 1987a, pp. 79–88.
76 ibid., pp. 89–100.
77 Wait 1985, pp. 122–53.
78 Cunliffe 1986, pp. 126–35.
79 Meniel 1986b, pp. 115–22.
80 *De Bello Gallico* V, 12.
81 Meniel 1986b, pp. 115–22.
82 Coles 1991.
83 Cunliffe 1986, pp. 126–35.
84 Grant 1989b, pp. 135–46; Anati 1965, pp. 130–2.
85 Meniel 1990, pp. 185–8; Grant 1984a, pp. 102–19.
86 Brunaux 1988, pp. 119–21.
87 Hyland 1990, pp. 231–47.
88 Green 1989, figure 56.
89 Megaw 1970, no. 2; Anati 1965, pp. 29, 89–90.
90 Megaw and Megaw 1989, pp. 30–2; Anati 1965, pp. 1, 63.
91 ibid., p. 236.
92 Strabo IV, 4, 3.
93 Megaw 1970, no. 37.
94 Anati 1965, pp. 119–24.
95 Megaw and Megaw 1989, pp. 84–8.
96 Jones and Jones 1976, p. 9.
97 *Geography* IV, 5, 2; Toynbee 1973, p. 104.
98 Isbell 1971, p. 33, lines 219–21.
99 Toynbee 1973, pp. 104–5.
100 Anati 1965, pp. 119–24.
101 *Cynegetica* XXIII.
102 *Geography* IV, 4.
103 Anon. 1978, pp. 57–60.
104 Green 1986, figure 72.
105 Grant 1989a, p. 84; Grant 1991, pp. 109–15.
106 Meniel 1987a, pp. 25–31.
107 *De Bello Gallico* VI, 28.
108 *Epigrams* XII, 14.
109 Meniel 1987a, pp. 89–100.
110 Anati 1965, pp. 124–7. There is a picture of a lassoed stag on page 206.
111 ibid., pp. 130–2.
112 Hodder 1987, pp. 62–3.
113 Green 1989, figure 42.
114 ibid., figure 43.
115 Webster 1986, pp. 15, 44.
116 *Cynegetica* XXIV.
117 Brunaux 1988, pp. 87–97.
118 *De Bello Gallico* VI, 16.
119 Diodorus Siculus V, 29, 4–5.
120 *Geography* IV, 4, 5.
121 Meniel 1987a, pp. 89–100.
122 Wait 1985, pp. 52–3.

123 Ross and Feacham 1976.
124 Green 1986, pp. 179–81; Ross 1968, pp. 255–85.
125 Green 1992a, p. 45.
126 Megaw and Megaw 1989, pp. 21–2.
127 Anati 1965, p. 230.
128 ibid., figure on p. 179.
129 Green 1989, figure 54.
130 Green 1986, figure 72.
131 See Wedlake 1982.
132 Green 1989, p. 100; Green 1992a, p. 62; Phillips 1977, no. 234, plate 63.
133 Jones and Jones 1976, pp. 3, 45–6.
134 Mac Cana 1983, pp. 50–4, 107.
135 Jones and Jones 1976, pp. 95–136.

4 ANIMALS AT WAR

1 Kinsella 1969, p. 155.
2 Meniel 1987a, pp. 25–31.
3 Diamond 1991, p. 275.
4 Davis 1987, pp. 155–68.
5 Diamond 1991, p. 275.
6 See Hyland 1990.
7 ibid., pp. 63–70.
8 Piggott 1965, pp. 177–208; Megaw 1970, pp. 13–14; Megaw and Megaw 1989, pp. 25–7.
9 Delaney 1986, pp. 21–2; Megaw 1970, p. 23; Piggott 1965, p. 216; Megaw and Megaw 1989, pp. 41–2.
10 Anon. 1980b, pp. 260–1, no. 115.
11 Piggott 1965, p. 198, figure 111,5; Megaw 1970, no. 10.
12 Anon. 1980a, no. 3.58; Megaw and Megaw 1989, p. 34.
13 Piggott 1965, p. 181, plate XXXI; Green 1989, figure 56.
14 Piggott 1965, plate XXIV.
15 Megaw and Megaw 1989, p. 27.
16 Megaw 1970, no. 17.
17 Ridgeway 1905, *passim*; Hyland 1990, pp. 20–2.
18 Brunaux 1988.
19 Hyland 1990, pp. 20–2, 170–3.
20 ibid., pp. 170–3.
21 Grant 1984a, pp. 102–19.
22 Megaw and Megaw 1989, p. 235.
23 Hyland 1990, pp. 87–100.
24 Grant 1989b, pp. 135–46.
25 Hyland 1990, pp. 20–2.
26 Caesar, *De Bello Gallico* IV, 2.
27 Davis 1987, pp. 155–68; Grant 1984a, pp. 102–19.
28 Hyland 1990, pp. 71–86.
29 Megaw and Megaw 1989, pp. 218–19.
30 Meniel 1987a, pp. 33–46.
31 Olmsted 1979, plate 3E.
32 Hyland 1990, pp. 130–4.
33 Ritchie and Ritchie 1985, pp. 34–6; Meniel 1987a, pp. 33–46.

34 Megaw and Megaw 1989, pp. 196–8; Piggott and Daniel 1951.
35 Ashbee 1989, pp. 539–46.
36 Green 1991a, figures 45, 89.
37 Butler 1974, pp. 16–17; Manning 1976, p. 31.
38 Meniel 1987a, pp. 33–46.
39 Meniel 1989a, pp. 87–97.
40 Brunaux 1988, pp. 95ff.
41 Anati 1965, pp. 142–8, plates on pp. 180, 208.
42 Grant 1984a, pp. 102–19.
43 Davis 1987, pp. 155–68.
44 Grant 1984a, pp. 102–19.
45 Polybius Histories III, 113–14; Tierney 1959–60, pp. 189–275.
46 Brunaux 1988, p. 103.
47 De Bello Gallico IV, 13, 15.
48 Brunaux 1988, p. 53.
49 Strabo, Geography IV, 4, 5.
50 Brunaux 1988, pp. 109–10.
51 Green 1989, p. 109; Espérandieu no. 105.
52 Duval 1987, pp. 42–64.
53 Megaw 1970, no. 194.
54 Green 1989, figure 62.
55 Olmsted 1979; Ritchie and Ritchie 1985, pp. 25–31.
56 Rodwell 1973, pp. 265–7.
57 Green 1991a, figure 90.
58 Green 1986, pp. 61–7.
59 ibid., p. 117.
60 Anon. 1991b, p. 34.
61 Geography IV, 4, 2.
62 Histories III, 113–14; Hyland 1990, pp. 170–3.
63 Hyland 1990, pp. 63–70.
64 ibid., pp. 71–86, 101–10.
65 Tacitus, Agricola 37.
66 Hyland 1990, pp. 157–69.
67 Agricola 37.
68 Histories II, 14–31; Ritchie and Ritchie 1985, pp. 34–6.
69 For example, De Bello Gallico IV, 24.
70 ibid. IV, 26.
71 ibid. V, 15.
72 ibid. VII, 14, 55.
73 ibid., 70.
74 ibid., 18; 80.
75 ibid. I, 48.
76 Ritchie and Ritchie 1985, pp. 34–6; Meniel 1987a, pp. 33–46.
77 Pausanias X, 19–23.
78 Ritchie and Ritchie 1985, pp. 34–6.
79 De Bello Gallico II, 17.
80 ibid. III, 20.
81 ibid. I, 15.
82 For example, I, 48; IV, 24.
83 ibid. VII, 4.
84 ibid., 64.
85 ibid., 65.

86 ibid., 66.
87 ibid., 71.
88 ibid., 76.
89 *Geography* IV, 4, 2.
90 Cheesman 1914, *passim*.
91 *De Bello Gallico* I, 15.
92 Hyland 1990, pp. 157–69; Holder 1980, *passim*.
93 *De Bello Gallico* IV, 6.
94 ibid. V, 48.
95 ibid. VII, 4.
96 Ritchie and Ritchie 1985, pp. 19–23.
97 Megaw 1970, p. 19; Davis 1987, pp. 155–68.
98 Anon. 1991a, pp. 155–62.
99 Megaw 1970, p. 14, and catalogue no. 1; Piggott 1965, pp. 179, 215.
100 *De Bello Gallico* IV, 24.
101 Piggott 1965, p. 215.
102 Ritchie and Ritchie 1985, pp. 31–4, figure 13.
103 Piggott 1965, pp. 238–41.
104 See Cunliffe 1986.
105 Megaw and Megaw 1989, p. 224, figure 379.
106 Ritchie and Ritchie 1985, pp. 19–23, figure 7.
107 Meniel 1987a, pp. 101–43.
108 Green 1986, p. 125; Cunliffe 1974, pp. 287–99.
109 Green 1986, p. 126; Dent 1985, pp. 85–92; Ritchie and Ritchie 1985, pp. 19–23, figure 8.
110 Tierney 1959–60, pp. 247ff; Athenaeus IV, 37.
111 Florus I, 37, 5; Piggott 1965, pp. 238–41.
112 Diodorus Siculus V, 29, 1–5.
113 *Histories* II, 23–4; Hyland 1990, pp. 71–86; Ritchie and Ritchie 1985, pp. 34–6.
114 Cunliffe 1986, pp. 83–5.
115 Dio Cassius LXXVI, 12.
116 *De Bello Gallico* IV, 24.
117 ibid. IV, 32.
118 ibid. V, 9.
119 ibid., 15.
120 ibid., 19.
121 ibid., 33.
122 Piggott 1965, pp. 238–41.
123 Cunliffe 1986, pp. 83–5; Brunaux 1988, pp. 106–7.
124 Piggott 1965, p. 240; Cross and Slover 1936, p. 136.
125 Kinsella 1969, p. 65.
126 ibid., p. 85.
127 Green 1992a, pp. 70–2.
128 Kinsella 1969, p. 155.
129 From Kinsella 1969, p. 145.
130 Diodorus Siculus V, 30, 2.
131 Olmsted 1979, plate 3E.
132 Abbaye de Daoulais 1987, pp. 132–3.
133 Anon. 1980b, p. 127, Abb. 19; Brunaux 1988, pp. 100–1; Ritchie and Ritchie 1985, p. 47, figure 26; Megaw and Megaw 1989, figure 290.
134 Megaw 1970, p. 17.

135 Brunaux 1988, pp. 106–7; Livy VII, 26.
136 Megaw and Megaw 1989, pp. 123–43.
137 Ritchie and Ritchie 1985, p. 38.
138 Anon. 1991a, p. 406.
139 Olmsted 1979, plate 3E.
140 Ritchie and Ritchie 1985, pp. 25–31.

5 SACRIFICE AND RITUAL

1 Grant 1991, pp. 109–15.
2 Wait 1985, pp. 122–53.
3 Hodder 1982, pp. 167, 171.
4 Grant 1984b, pp. 221–8.
5 Meniel 1987a, pp. 101–43.
6 Grant 1984b, pp. 221–8.
7 Beavitt 1989, pp. 173–80.
8 Brunaux 1988, pp. 116–17.
9 Anati 1965, pp. 171–8.
10 Brunaux 1988, p. 9.
11 Wait 1985, pp. 240–4; Brunaux 1989, pp. 23–6.
12 For example, Strabo, *Geography* IV, 4; Diodorus Siculus V, 31; Caesar, *De Bello Gallico* IV, 13; VI, 16; Tierney 1959–60, pp. 251, 269, 271–2.
13 Brunaux 1988, p. 103.
14 Cunliffe 1991.
15 Brunaux 1988, pp. 119–21; Petit 1989, pp. 99–110.
16 Wait 1985, pp. 122–53.
17 Brunaux 1988, pp. 119–21.
18 Beavitt 1989.
19 Brunaux 1989, pp. 23–6.
20 Brunaux 1988, p. 63; Wait 1985, pp. 240–2.
21 *De Bello Gallico* VI, 13.
22 Pliny, *Natural History* XVI, 95.
23 Meniel 1987a, pp. 101–43.
24 Grant 1989a, pp. 79–86.
25 Brunaux 1988, pp. 122–5.
26 ibid., pp. 119–21.
27 Wait 1985, pp. 122–53; Grant 1989a, pp. 79–86.
28 Grant 1984b, pp. 221–8.
29 Brunaux 1988, pp. 119–21.
30 Hodder 1987, pp. 185–211.
31 Meniel 1987a, pp. 101–43; Wait 1985, p. 244.
32 Brunaux 1988, pp. 119–21.
33 ibid., p. 79.
34 Wait 1985, pp. 122–53; Grant 1989a, pp. 79–86.
35 Wait 1985, pp. 122–53; Grant 1984b, pp. 221–8; Grant 1989a, pp. 79–86; Grant 1989b, pp. 135–46.
36 Cunliffe 1991.
37 Grant 1984b, pp. 221–8.
38 Cunliffe 1986, p. 46.
39 Grant 1984b, pp. 221–8; Grant 1991, pp. 109–15.
40 Ross 1968, pp. 255–85.

41 Wait 1985, pp. 78–82.
42 Green 1986, pp. 175–6.
43 ibid., pp. 175–6, 184.
44 Brunaux 1988, p. 139; Rybova and Soudska 1956; Piggott 1965, pp. 232, 234; Piggott 1968, p. 73.
45 Brunaux 1988, p. 40.
46 Green 1986, p. 133.
47 Petit 1989, pp. 99–110.
48 Brunaux 1988, pp. 28, 89–95.
49 *De Bello Gallico* VI, 19.
50 Green 1986, p. 125.
51 Meniel 1987a, pp. 101–43.
52 Grant 1991, pp. 109–15.
53 Brunaux 1988, p. 83.
54 Meniel 1987b, pp. 357–61; Meniel 1987a, pp. 101–43.
55 Meniel 1986a, pp. 37–9.
56 Meniel 1987a, pp. 101–43.
57 Meniel 1987b, pp. 357–61.
58 Meniel 1987a, pp. 101–43.
59 Meniel 1989a, pp. 87–97.
60 Meniel 1986a, pp. 37–9.
61 Grant 1989a, pp. 79–86.
62 Meniel 1987a, pp. 101–43.
63 Brunaux 1988, pp. 21–3, 28–9, 119–21.
64 Meniel 1987a, pp. 101–43.
65 ibid.; Brunaux 1988, pp. 28–9.
66 Wait 1985, pp. 166–90.
67 Ellison 1980, pp. 305–28.
68 Green 1986, p. 178; Anon. 1978, pp. 57–60.
69 Meniel 1987a, pp. 25–31, 101–43; Meniel 1989a, pp. 87–97.
70 Meniel 1987a, pp. 25–31.
71 Pryor 1990, pp. 386–90; Lynch 1991.
72 Turner 1982, p. 15.
73 Green 1976, p. 226.
74 Green 1986, pp. 175–6.
75 Rankov 1982, p. 392.
76 Wait 1985, pp. 78–82.
77 Cunliffe 1986, p. 46.
78 Grant 1989a, pp. 79–86.
79 ibid. Grant 1991, pp. 109–15; Cunliffe 1986, pp. 155–71.
80 Anon. 1978, pp. 57–60.
81 Turner 1982, p. 15.
82 Green 1976, p. 230.
83 Petit 1989, pp. 99–110.
84 Meniel 1987a, pp. 25–31.
85 Meniel 1989a, pp. 87–97.
86 Meniel 1987a, pp. 101–43; Meniel 1989a, pp. 87–97.
87 Megaw 1970, catalogue no. 35.
88 Meniel 1987a, pp. 101–43; Brunaux 1988, p. 123.
89 Brunaux 1988, p. 103.
90 Meniel 1987a, pp. 101–43; Meniel 1989a, pp. 87–97.
91 Brunaux 1988, p. 40.

92 Alcock 1972, pp. 136–53; Green 1986, p. 172; Wait 1985, pp. 166–90.
93 Meniel 1987a, pp. 101–43; Brunaux 1988, p. 83.
94 Green 1986, pp. 124–6.
95 Meniel 1989a, pp. 87–97.
96 Meniel 1987a, pp. 33–46, 101–43.
97 Meniel 1987b, pp. 357–61.
98 Petit 1989, pp. 99–110.
99 Wait 1985, pp. 52–3; Ross and Feacham 1976, pp. 230–7.
100 Wait 1985, pp. 122–53.
101 Grant 1989a, pp. 79–86.
102 Cunliffe 1986, pp. 155–71.
103 Cunliffe 1991.
104 Grant 1989a, pp. 79–86; Cunliffe 1986, pp. 155–71.
105 Grant 1984b, pp. 221–8.
106 Meniel 1987a, pp. 101–43; Meniel 1986a, pp. 37–9; Meniel 1989a, pp. 87–97.
107 Meniel 1987b, pp. 357–61.
108 Meniel 1987a, pp. 101–43.
109 Meniel 1989a, pp. 87–97.
110 Hodder 1987, pp. 185–211.
111 Cunliffe 1974, pp. 287–99; Green 1986, p. 180.
112 Brunaux 1988, pp. 119–21.
113 Meniel 1987a, pp. 101–43.
114 Downey, King and Soffe 1980, pp. 289–304; Green 1986, p. 180.
115 Wait 1985, pp. 166–90.
116 Green 1986, p. 181.
117 ibid.
118 Petit 1989, pp. 99–110.
119 Grant 1984b, pp. 221–8.
120 Wait 1985, pp. 52–3, 122–53; Grant 1989a, pp. 79–86; Cunliffe 1986, pp. 155–71.
121 Wait 1985, pp. 52–3.
122 Hodder 1987, pp. 156–62.
123 Grant 1991, pp. 109–15.
124 Meniel 1987a, pp. 101–43; Meniel 1989a, pp. 87–97; Brunaux 1988, pp. 119–25.
125 Meniel 1987a, pp. 101–43; Meniel 1989a, pp. 87–97.
126 Wait 1985, pp. 166–90; Alcock 1972, pp. 80–4, 136–53, 163; Harding 1974, pp. 96–112.
127 Wait 1985, pp. 166–90.
128 Green 1986, p. 178.
129 Meniel 1989a, pp. 87–97.
130 Meniel 1987a, pp. 101–43.
131 Meniel 1989a, pp. 87–97.
132 Grant 1989a, pp. 79–86.
133 Hodder 1987, pp. 185–211.
134 Wait 1985, pp. 122–53.
135 Cunliffe 1986, pp. 155–71.
136 Petit 1989, pp. 99–110.
137 Brunaux 1988, p. 40.
138 *Natural History* XVI, 95.
139 Meniel 1987a, pp. 101–43.
140 Green 1986, p. 180.

141 Meniel 1986a, pp. 37–9.
142 Meniel 1987a, pp. 101–43; Meniel 1989a, pp. 87–97.
143 Petit 1989, pp. 99–110.
144 Grant 1989b, pp. 135–46.
145 Wait 1985, pp. 122–53; Cunliffe 1986, pp. 155–71.
146 Meniel 1987a, pp. 101–43.
147 Cunliffe 1986, pp. 155–71; Grant 1984b, pp. 221–8.
148 Meniel 1989b, pp. 108–9.
149 Meniel 1987b, pp. 357–61.
150 Meniel 1986a, pp. 37–9.
151 Piggott 1965, pp. 232, 234.
152 Wait 1985, pp. 122–53.
153 Meniel 1987a, pp. 101–43.
154 Grant 1989b, pp. 135–46.
155 Green 1986, p. 181.
156 Frere 1984, p. 296; Hassall and Tomlin 1984, p. 337.
157 Meniel 1987a, pp. 101–43.
158 Green 1986, p. 133.
159 Beavitt 1989, pp. 173–80.
160 *De Bello Gallico* V, 12.
161 Meniel 1987a, pp. 23–4.
162 Grant 1989b, pp. 135–46.
163 Meniel 1987a, pp. 101–43.
164 Meniel 1989a, pp. 87–97.
165 Grant 1989a, pp. 79–86.
166 Green 1986, pp. 113–14, 126.
167 Meniel 1987a, pp. 101–43.
168 Green 1986, p. 181.
169 Grant 1989a, pp. 79–86.
170 Wait 1985, pp. 122–53.
171 Cunliffe 1986, pp. 155–71.
172 Ross 1968, pp. 255–85; Green 1986, p. 184.
173 Brunaux 1988, pp. 119–21.
174 Tait 1941, entry for 23 November 1827.

6 THE ARTIST'S MENAGERIE

1 Megaw and Megaw 1989.
2 ibid., p. 224.
3 ibid., figure 75.
4 ibid., p. 224, figure 379; Piggott and Daniel 1951, plate 59.
5 Megaw and Megaw 1989, p. 81; Anon. 1980a, catalogue no. 15.7.
6 Megaw and Megaw 1989, pp. 133–43.
7 ibid.
8 Kinsella 1969, p. 227.
9 Megaw and Megaw 1989, pp. 162–3.
10 Diodorus Siculus V, 30.
11 Olmsted 1979, plate 3E.
12 Green 1986, pp. 106–7.
13 Ritchie and Ritchie 1985.
14 Piggott and Daniel 1951, plate 61.

15 See Jope 1991.
16 Megaw and Megaw 1989, p. 223, figure 375.
17 Green 1991a, figure 90.
18 Duval 1987, pp. 42–63.
19 Jope 1991; Megaw and Megaw 1989, figure 46.
20 Green 1989, figure 58.
21 Grave 671. Piggott 1965, pl. 28a.
22 Gimbutas 1965, p. 328; Green 1991a, pp. 66–9.
23 Megaw and Megaw 1989, figures 368, 370.
24 Megaw 1970, nos. 60–1.
25 Megaw and Megaw 1989, p. 78.
26 Green 1986, p. 198.
27 Piggott 1965, pp. 198–9.
28 Megaw and Megaw 1989, pp. 93–100.
29 ibid.
30 ibid., pp. 144–5.
31 Ross 1967, pp. 234–42.
32 Savory 1976, plate VI.
33 Brunaux 1988, p. 79.
34 Stead 1985a, p. 36.
35 The exhibition ran from 1 May to 30 September 1991.
36 Megaw and Megaw 1989, p. 87
37 ibid., figure 307.
38 Megaw 1970, nos. 79–83.
39 ibid., no. 84.
40 Green 1991a, figure 55.
41 ibid., figure 54.
42 ibid., figure 73.
43 ibid., figure 56.
44 Megaw and Megaw 1989, figure 284.
45 Anon. 1991a, p. 375.
46 Olmsted 1979, pl. I.
47 ibid., plate 2B.
48 Green 1991a, figure 42.
49 Olmsted 1979, plate 3D.
50 Megaw and Megaw 1989, pp. 144–5, 160ff.
51 Green 1984, pp. 88–9.
52 Green 1989, pp. 92–3.
53 Olmsted 1979, plate 3E.
54 Olmsted 1979, outer plates A–D.
55 Planck 1982, pp. 105–72.
56 Olmsted 1979, outer plates E–G.
57 Olmsted 1979, outer plate G.
58 Green 1989, figure 56.
59 Benoit 1969, plates VIII, IX, XI.
60 Green 1989, figure 62.
61 Musée Archéologique de Nîmes.
62 Green 1989, p. 146.
63 Megaw 1970, no. 76.
64 Stead 1985b, pp. 40–2; Green 1986, p. 136.
65 Anati 1965, pp. 151–232.
66 Megaw and Megaw 1989, pp. 144–5.

67 Anon. 1980b, no. 175.
68 Green 1989, figure 57; Anon. 1980b, no. 76.
69 Foster 1977, pp. 26–8.
70 Green 1989, figure 60.
71 Szabó 1971, p. 68.
72 Green 1989, p. 141, figure 59.
73 Megaw and Megaw 1989, pp. 80–4.
74 Grave 507; Mohen, Duval and Eluère 1987, no. 26.
75 Green 1989, figure 65.
76 Anon. 1980b, no. 174.
77 Megaw and Megaw 1989, plate XVI.
78 Woolner 1965, pp. 27–44; Green 1991c. I am very grateful for information on the Horse from David Miles, Director of the Oxford Archaeology Unit.
79 Allen 1980, p. 141.
80 Duval 1987, pp. 44–50.
81 Allen 1980, pp. 139–40.
82 Green 1991a, pp. 116–19, figure 91.
83 ibid., pp. 133–6, and see chapter 8 of this book.
84 Allen 1980, nos. 241, 246–7; Green 1992b.
85 Zachar 1987, plate 201; Green 1991a, figure 41.
86 Green 1992b.
87 Green 1989, p. 20, figures 6, 7.
88 Green 1986, figure 3.
89 Green 1992b.
90 Davidson 1988, p. 50.
91 Allen 1976, pp. 265–82.
92 Ross 1967, p. 309.
93 Allen 1980, figure 23.
94 Green 1992b.
95 Allen 1980, pp. 133–4.
96 Boon 1982, pp. 276–82; Green 1986, figure 88.
97 Allen 1980, figure 28.
98 Green 1981, pp. 109–15; Green 1991a, figure 92.
99 Duval 1987, pp. 19–29.
100 Campbell 1976, p. 281.
101 Duval 1987, p. 29.
102 Ross 1967, p. 281.
103 Green 1989, frontispiece; C.I.L. XIII, no. 3026; Espérandieu, nos. 3132–7.
104 Ross 1967, pp. 279–92.
105 Hesiod, Works and Days, Opus 450.
106 Duval 1987, p. 19.
107 Green 1976, pp. 198–9, 205.
108 Megaw and Megaw 1989, pp. 160–3.

7 ANIMALS IN THE EARLIEST CELTIC STORIES

1 Green 1992a, pp. 18–21.
2 Jones and Jones 1976, p. 203.
3 Ross 1967, p. 301; Ross 1986, p. 114.
4 Mac Cana 1983.
5 Jones and Jones 1976, p. 3.

6 ibid., pp. 45–6.
7 ibid., pp. 117–18.
8 ibid., pp. 137–52.
9 ibid., pp. 177–9.
10 ibid., pp. 3–5, 124–5.
11 Ross 1967, pp. 297–353; O'Fáolain 1954; Mac Cana 1983, p. 104.
12 Ross 1967, p. 335.
13 Mac Cana 1983, pp. 50–4.
14 Jones and Jones 1976, pp. 61–3.
15 ibid., pp. 124–5.
16 Ross 1967, pp. 297–353.
17 Jones and Jones 1976, p. 116.
18 ibid., p. 131.
19 Sims-Williams 1990, pp. 57–81.
20 Jones and Jones 1976, p. 95.
21 ibid., pp. 56–63.
22 ibid.
23 ibid., p. 72.
24 Bromwich 1961, p. 26.
25 Mac Cana 1983, pp. 50–4.
26 O'Rahilly 1946, p. 279; Ross 1967, p. 220.
27 Diodorus Siculus V, 28, 4.
28 Ross 1967, pp. 297–353.
29 ibid.
30 ibid.
31 ibid.
32 Green 1992a, pp. 98–9; Campbell 1870–2, pp. 193–202.
33 Bromwich 1961, p. 26.
34 Jones and Jones 1976, pp. 124–5.
35 ibid., pp. 71–2.
36 Nutt 1906, pp. 325–39; Lambert 1979, pp. 141–69.
37 Ross 1967, pp. 234–96.
38 O'Fáolain 1954, pp. 27–39; Rolleston 1985, pp. 113, 139.
39 Giraldus Cambrensis, *Expugnatio Hibernica* I, 33.
40 Ross 1967, pp. 234–96; An Chraoibhín 1932, pp. 447f.
41 Green 1992a, pp. 98–9; O'Rahilly 1946, pp. 271, 279.
42 Ross 1967, pp. 302–78.
43 Krappe 1936, pp. 236–46.
44 Bergin *et al.* 1907, p. 31.
45 Green 1992a, p. 174; Mac Cana 1983, pp. 64–6.
46 Green 1986, p. 188.
47 Ross 1967, pp. 234–96.
48 O'Grady 1892, p. 250.
49 Ross 1967, pp. 234–96.
50 Strabo, *Geography* IV, 4, 6; Tierney 1959–60, p. 270.
51 Jones and Jones 1976, pp. 137–52.
52 ibid., p. 199.
53 O'Fáolain 1954, pp. 88–100.
54 Mac Cana 1983, pp. 50–4, 124.
55 Ross 1967, pp. 234–96.
56 Williams 1930, p. 45.
57 Jones and Jones 1976, pp. 115–16.

58 ibid., p. 32.
59 Ross 1967, pp. 121–3, 150–3.
60 Green 1992a, p. 195; Jones 1954, p. 134.
61 Page 1990, pp. 72–3.
62 Mac Neill 1904, pp. 192f.
63 Ross 1967, pp. 345–6.
64 Kinsella 1969.
65 Mac Cana 1983, pp. 50–4.
66 Ross 1967, pp. 297–353.
67 Mac Cana 1983, p. 117; Green 1992a, p. 207.
68 Ross 1967, pp. 297–353.
69 ibid.
70 Jones and Jones 1976, p. 48.
71 ibid., pp. 56–63.
72 ibid., p. 3.
73 Green 1992a, p. 82.
74 O'Rahilly 1946, pp. 120–2; Even 1953, pp. 7–9.
75 Jones and Jones 1976, p. 126.
76 ibid., p. 117.
77 ibid., pp. 6, 9–10.
78 ibid., pp. 56–63.
79 ibid., p. 27.
80 Giraldus Cambrensis *Topographica Hibernica* III.
81 Ross 1967, pp. 297–353.
82 de Vries 1963, pp. 136–7; Killeen 1974, pp. 81–6; Hennessy 1870–2, pp. 32, 55.
83 Jones and Jones 1976, pp. 9–10.
84 ibid., pp. 19, 22.
85 ibid., pp. 19–20.
86 Mac Cana 1983, p. 101.
87 Green 1992a, p. 72.
88 Jones and Jones 1976, pp. 118–19.
89 Mac Cana 1972, pp. 102–42; Mac Cana 1975, pp. 33–52; Mac Cana 1976, pp. 95–115; Sims-Williams 1990, pp. 57–81.
90 Ross 1967, pp. 297–353.
91 O'Fáolain 1954; Best 1905, pp. 18–35.
92 Jones and Jones 1976, pp. 124–5.
93 ibid., p. 225.
94 O'Grady 1892, p. 387.
95 Mac Cana 1983, pp. 41–2.
96 Jones and Jones 1976, pp. 56–63.
97 ibid., pp. 114, 117–118; Strachan 1937; Hamp 1986, pp. 257–8.
98 Mac Cana 1983, p. 90.
99 O'Fáolain 1954; Bhreathnach 1982, pp. 243–60; Lloyd *et al.* 1912, pp. 41–57.
100 Green 1992a, p. 139.
101 Kinsella 1969, *passim.*
102 Ross 1967, pp. 297–353.
103 ibid.; Murphy 1953, pp. 103–4.
104 An Chraoibhín 1932; Ross 1967, pp. 234–96.
105 Mac Cana 1983, p. 110.
106 Ross 1967, pp. 333–8.
107 Green 1992a, p. 68.

108 O'Rahilly 1946, pp. 318f.
109 Best and Bergin 1938, pp. 137–96.
110 Nutt 1906, pp. 325–39.
111 Ross 1967, pp. 234–96.
112 Mac Cana 1983, p. 86.
113 Green 1992a, p. 38.
114 Green 1986, pp. 170, 199.

8 GOD AND BEAST

1 A tradition noted, for example, in the cult of Asklepios at Epidaurus in Greece, where sacred dogs were kept within the confines of the shrine: see Jenkins 1957, pp. 60–76; Guthrie 1954, pp. 228, 246.
2 Thevenot 1968, pp. 67–9; Green 1989, figure 25.
3 ibid., figure 61.
4 Green 1986, pp. 159–60, figure 72; Wheeler 1932; Henig 1984, pp. 51–5; Collingwood and Wright 1965, nos. 305–8.
5 Wedlake 1982, *passim.*
6 Green 1992a; Webster 1986, p. 44.
7 Salviat 1979.
8 Green 1989, figure 30.
9 ibid., figure 31.
10 ibid., p. 83; Thevenot 1952, pp. 99–103; Thevenot 1957, pp. 311–14; Deyts 1976, nos. 13, 174; Espérandieu nos. 3633, 3385.
11 Green 1986, pp. 86–7; Green 1989, pp. 10–16; van Aartsen 1971; Hondius-Crone 1955.
12 Jenkins 1956, pp. 192–200; Wightman 1970, pp. 217, 223; Green 1989, pp. 28–9.
13 Jenkins 1956, pp. 192–200; Drury and Wickenden 1982, pp. 239–43, plate XVIII, 4.
14 Green 1989, p. 29.
15 Merrifield 1983, pp. 167–70, 180; Toynbee 1962, plate 76; Green 1986, pp. 189–202.
16 Green 1989, pp. 189–202.
17 Magnen and Thevenot 1953.
18 Green 1989, pp. 16–24.
19 Linduff 1979, pp. 817–37.
20 As at Rully and Santenay: Espérandieu nos. 2127, 7513.
21 Johns 1971–2, pp. 37–41.
22 For example at Chorey: Espérandieu no. 2046.
23 Oaks 1986, pp. 77–84.
24 As at Dalheim, Luxembourg: Thill 1978; Wilhelm 1974.
25 C.I.L. XIII, no. 5622.
26 Magnen and Thevenot 1953, no. 117.
27 For example at Allerey: Espérandieu no. 8235; Deyts 1976, no. 8.
28 Toussaint 1948, pp. 206–7.
29 Espérandieu nos. 4894, 1618.
30 ibid. no. 7290.
31 Suetonius, *Nero* 22.
32 Espérandieu no. 38; Thevenot 1968, pp. 56–7.
33 Diodorus Siculus V, 29, 4; Strabo, *Geography* IV, 4, 5.

34 Espérandieu no. 105; Benoit 1981, figure 49.
35 Green 1986, figure 58.
36 Green 1976, p. 218.
37 Green 1986, pp. 61–5; Green 1989, pp. 123–9; Green 1991a, pp. 133–6; Sterckx 1991.
38 Bauchhenss 1976, figure 1.
39 For example, at Neschers (Puy-de-Dôme); Pobé and Roubier 1961, no. 185; Green 1989, figure 53.
40 Thevenot 1951, pp. 129–41; Green 1989, pp. 116–19.
41 Lelong 1970, pp. 123–6.
42 Espérandieu no. 2978; Green 1989, figure 63.
43 Thevenot 1955.
44 Marache 1979, p. 3; Térouanne 1960, pp. 185–9; Thevenot 1968, pp. 65–9.
45 Thevenot 1951, pp. 129–41.
46 C.I.L. XIII, no. 1318.
47 Deyts 1983; Deyts 1985.
48 Green 1989, p. 149 and figure 96.
49 Green 1992a.
50 Ross 1967, pp. 302–78.
51 Green 1989, figure 25.
52 C.I.L. XIII, 4543; Espérandieu nos. 6000, 4568.
53 Green 1989, pp. 26–7.
54 ibid., p. 30; Linckenheld 1929, pp. 40–92; Green 1986, p. 89 and figure 37.
55 At Altrier: Espérandieu no. 4219.
56 Deyts 1976, no. 160; Green 1989, figure 45.
57 ibid., figure 16; Deyts 1985.
58 Green 1986, pp. 186–7.
59 Green 1991a, pp. 66 74.
60 Hodson and Rowlett 1973, pp. 157–91. Marseille, Musée Borély.
61 Musée de Bretagne, Rennes.
62 Megaw 1970, p. 17.
63 Paris: C.I.L. XIII, 3026; Espérandieu nos. 3132–7; Duval 1961, pp. 197–9. Trier: Espérandieu no. 4929; C.I.L. XIII, 3656; Wightman 1985, p. 178; Schindler 1977, p. 32, Abb. 91.
64 Green 1989, frontispiece and figure 44.
65 Green 1986, p. 191, figure 85.
66 Deyts 1976, nos. 50–2, 175–9; Espérandieu no. 3636, 1–3; Musée d'Alise Sainte Reine.
67 Musée Archéologique de Senlis; Deyts 1985; Thevenot 1968, pp. 149–64; Musée Archéologique de Châtillon sur Seine.
68 Wightman 1970, p. 213.
69 Green 1986, pp. 184–5, figure 81; Green 1978, pp. 23ff.
70 Boucher 1976, figure 291; Green 1989, figure 10.
71 Wightman 1970, p. 217; C.I.L. XIII, 4113, 5160.
72 Green 1989, p. 100.
73 Boucher 1976, figure 292.
74 Green 1989, figure 46.
75 Green 1991a, pp. 38–9, 109–10.
76 Pobé and Roubier 1961, no. 6; Espérandieu no. 7702.
77 Green 1989, figure 59; Espérandieu no. 2984; Megaw 1970, no. 238.
78 Green 1986, figure 73.
79 Green 1992b.

NOTES

80 Dayet 1954, pp. 334–5.
81 Green 1986, p. 179.
82 Musée Archéologique de Dijon 1973, no. 91; Deyts 1983; Musée Archéologique de Senlis.
83 Espérandieu no. 1319.
84 ibid. no. 3653.
85 Green 1986, p. 177; National Museum of Wales.
86 Hawkes 1951, pp. 172–99.
87 Kinsella 1969.
88 Green 1986, p. 169, figure 75.
89 Kinsella 1969.
90 Green 1986, pp. 190–2; Green 1989, pp. 180–2.
91 ibid., figure 81; Deyts 1976, nos. 21, 22, 44–6.
92 Green 1984, plate LXXXI; Green 1986, figure 84.
93 Green 1991b, pp. 100–9.
94 C.I.L. XIII, 3026; Espérandieu nos. 3132–7; Espérandieu no. 4929; C.I.L. XIII, 3656.
95 Green 1989, pp. 183–4.
96 Olmsted 1979.
97 Guthrie 1954, p. 246.
98 von Petrikovits 1987, pp. 241–54.
99 Ross 1967, p. 217.
100 Green 1989, figure 17; Schindler 1977, p. 33, Abb. 92; Dehn 1941, pp. 104ff.
101 Green 1989, figure 24.
102 Le Gall 1963.
103 Tufi 1983, nos. 30, 31, plate 9; Ross 1967, p. 217.
104 Bober 1951, pp. 13–51.
105 Espérandieu no. 4831.
106 Green 1989, pp. 92–3; Lambrechts 1942, pp. 21–32.
107 Green 1989, figure 39.
108 Espérandieu no. 1539.
109 Green 1989, figure 26; Espérandieu no. 2067; Deyts 1976, no. 284.
110 British Museum 1964.
111 Thevenot 1968, pp. 72–89.
112 Green 1989, p. 108, figure 21; Espérandieu no. 1573.
113 Green 1981, pp. 109–15.
114 Green 1991a passim, but especially, pp. 117–36.
115 Green 1986, p. 63.
116 ibid.; Green 1989, pp. 123–9.
117 Green 1986, figure 3.
118 ibid., p. 183.
119 Green 1989, figure 55; Pobé and Roubier 1961, no. 54.
120 Anati 1965.
121 Green 1991a, pp. 23, 55.
122 Green 1989, figure 54.
123 ibid., p. 100, figure 43; Espérandieu no. 7800; Hatt 1964, plates 150, 151.
124 Phillips 1977, no. 234.
125 Espérandieu no. 7633; Deyts 1976, no. 215.
126 C.I.L. XIII, 3026; Espérandieu nos. 3132, 3133.
127 Anati 1965; Green 1989, figure 35; Green 1986, figure 88.
128 Boon 1982, pp. 276–82.

129 Pobé and Roubier 1961, no. 11; Green 1989, figure 37.
130 Olmsted 1979; Green 1989, figure 1.
131 ibid., pp. 86–96.
132 Espérandieu no. 3653.
133 ibid. no. 4839.
134 Such as Diodorus Siculus V, 28, 4.
135 Thevenot 1968, pp. 144–9.
136 Planson and Pommeret 1986.
137 Espérandieu no. 2083; Green 1989, figure 79.
138 Green 1986, figure 86.
139 Espérandieu no. 1539; Thevenot 1968, p. 150.
140 Espérandieu no. 1566.
141 ibid. no. 3653.
142 Davidson 1988, pp. 212–13.
143 Glob 1974, p. 143.
144 Megaw 1970, no. 14.
145 Green 1986, pp. 197–9.
146 Diodorus Siculus V, 30.
147 Gros 1986, pp. 192–201.
148 Ross 1961, pp. 59ff.
149 Green 1986, figure 55.
150 Ellison 1977.
151 Green 1986, p. 198; Ross 1967, figure 103.
152 For example the horned head at Carvoran: Green 1986, figure 89.

9 CHANGING ATTITUDES TO THE ANIMAL WORLD

1 Thomas 1987, p. 25.
2 For example, Aristotle, *Politics* 1256a–b; Cicero, *De Natura Deorum* II, 14, 61–5.
3 Thomas 1987, p. 136.
4 Genesis, chapter I, verses 28–9.
5 ibid., chapter IX, verses 2–3.
6 Thomas 1987.
7 ibid., p. 23.
8 ibid., p. 110.
9 Darwin's *Descent of Man* was published in 1871.
10 From the Christmas carol 'In the Bleak Midwinter'.
11 Pliny, *Natural History* X, 14, 33.
12 Thomas 1987, p. 138.

BIBLIOGRAPHY

van Aartsen, J. (1971) *Deae Nehalenniae*, Rijksmuseum van Oudheden, Middelburg.

Abbaye de Daoulais (1987) *Aux Temps des Celtes: Ve-1er Siècle avant JC*, Association Abbaye de Daoulais, Quimper.

Alcock, L. (1972) *'By South Cadbury, is that Camelot'* . . . *Excavations at Cadbury Castle 1966–70*, Thames & Hudson, London.

Allen, D. F. (1976) 'Some contrasts in Gaulish and British coins', in P.-M. Duval and C. F. C. Hawkes (eds), *Celtic Art in Ancient Europe*, Seminar Press, London, pp. 265–82.

—— (1980) *The Coins of the Ancient Celts*, Edinburgh University Press, Edinburgh.

Anati, E. (1965) *Camonica Valley*, Jonathan Cape, London.

An Chraoibhín (1932) *Cailleach an Teampuill*, Bealoideas III, Dublin, pp. 447ff.

Anon. (1978) 'The Cambridge Shrine', *Current Archaeology* 61 (April), pp. 57–60.

Anon. (1980a) *Die Hallstattkultur*, Schloss Lamberg, Steier.

Anon. (1980b) *Die Kelten in Mitteleuropa*, Keltenmuseum Hallein, Salzburg.

Anon. (1991a) *The Celts*, catalogue of an exhibition held at the Palazzo Grassi, Venice, Bompiani.

Anon. (1991b) 'British Museum's new mounted warrior-god', *Minerva* 2(4) (July/August), p. 34.

Armitage, P. L. (1982) 'Studies on the remains of domestic livestock from Roman, Medieval and Early Modern London: objectives and methods', in A. R. Hall and H. K. Kenwood (eds), *Environmental Archaeology in the Urban Context*, Council for British Archaeology Research Report, no. 43, pp. 94–106.

Ashbee, P. (1989) 'The Trundholm Horse's Trappings: a Chamfrein?', *Antiquity* 63(240), pp. 539–46.

Bauchhenss, G. (1976) *Jupitergigantensäulen*, Württembergisches Landesmuseums, Stuttgart.

Beavitt, P. (1989) 'The ethnoarchaeology of sacrifice: some comments on the visible and the invisible with respect to human contacts with the spirit world in Borneo', in J.-D. Vigne (ed.), *L'Animal dans les pratiques religieuses: les manifestations materielles*, Anthropozoologica Troisième Numéro Special, Paris, pp. 173–80.

Benoit, F. (1969) *L'Art primitif Méditerranean de la Vallée du Rhône*, Publications des Annales de la Faculté des Lettres, Aix-en-Provence.

—— (1981) *Entremont*, Ophrys, Paris.

Bergin, O. *et al.* (1907) *Anecdota from Irish Manuscripts* I, Halle.

Best, R. I. (1905) 'The tragic death of Cú Roi mac Dári', *Eriu* 2, pp. 18–35.

Best, R. I. and Bergin, O. (1938) 'Tochmarc Etaine', *Eriu* 12, pp. 137–96.

Bhreathnach, M. (1982) 'The Sovereignty Goddess as Goddess of Death', *Zeitschrift für Celtische Philologie* 39, pp. 243–60.

Birley, R. (1977) *Vindolanda*, Thames & Hudson, London.

Bober, J. J. (1951) 'Cernunnos: origin and transformation of a Celtic divinity', *American Journal of Archaeology* 55, pp. 13–51.

Bökonyi, S. (1974) *History of Domestic Mammals in Central and Eastern Europe*, Akadémiai Kaidó, Budapest.

Boon, G. C. (1982) 'A coin with the head of the Cernunnos', *Seaby Coin and Medal Bulletin* 769, pp. 276–82.

Boucher, S. (1976) *Recherches sur les bronzes figurés de Gaule pré-romaine et romaine*, Ecole Français de Rome, Paris and Rome.

British Museum (1964) *Guide to the Antiquities of Roman Britain*, British Museum, London.

Bromwich, R. (1961) *Trioedd Ynys Prydein: The Welsh Triads*, University of Wales Press, Cardiff.

Brunaux, J.-L. (1988) *The Celtic Gauls: Gods, Rites and Sanctuaries*, trans. D. Nash, Seaby, London.

—— (1989) 'Les animaux et leurs hommes: G. Bataille, l'animal et le sacrifice', in J-D. Vigne (ed.), *L'animal dans les pratiques religieuses: les manifestations materielles*, Anthropozoologica Troisième Numéro Special, Paris, pp. 23–6.

Butler, D. (1974) *The Principles of Horseshoeing*, D. Butler, Texas.

Campbell, J. (1976) *The Masks of God: Primitive Mythology*, Penguin, Harmondsworth.

Campbell, J. F. (1870–2) 'Fionn's Enchantment', *Revue Celtique* 1, pp. 193–202.

Cheesman, G. L. (1914) *The Auxilia of the Roman Imperial Army*, Clarendon Press, London.

Coles, B. (1990) 'Anthropomorphic wooden figures from Britain and Ireland', *Proceedings of the Prehistoric Society* 56, pp. 315–33.

Coles, J. M. (1991) 'Drowned Celts and floundering archaeologists: the activities at Glastonbury and Meare', a paper presented at 'The Celts and their society', a conference held in Oxford (February).

Collingwood, R. G. and Wright, R. P. (1965) *The Roman Inscriptions of Britain*, Oxford University Press, Oxford.

Collis, J. (1984) *The European Iron Age*, Batsford, London.

Cross, T. P. and Slover, C. H. (1936) *Ancient Irish Tales*.

Cunliffe, B. W. (1974) *Iron Age Communities in Britain*, Routledge, London.

—— (1986) *Danebury: Anatomy of an Iron Age Hillfort*, Batsford, London.

—— (1991) 'Society, rituals and beliefs in southern Britain 600 BC–AD 50', a paper presented at 'The Celts and their society', a conference held in Oxford (February).

Darvill, T. (1987) *Prehistoric Britain*, Batsford, London.

Davidson, H. E. (1988) *Myths and Symbols in Pagan Europe*, Manchester University Press, Manchester.

Davis, S. J. M. (1987) *The Archaeology of Animals*, Batsford, London.

Dayet, M. (1954) 'Le sanglier à trois cornes du Cabinet des Medailles', *Revue Archéologique de l'Est et du Centre-Est* 5, pp. 334–5.

Dehn, W. (1941) 'Ein Quelheiligtum des Apollo und der Sirona bei Hochscheid', *Germania* 25, pp. 104ff.

Delaney, F. (1986) *The Celts*, Little Brown & Co., Boston and Toronto.

Dent, J. (1985) 'Three cart burials from Wetwang, Yorkshire', *Antiquity* 59, pp. 85–92.

Deyts, S. (1976) *Dijon, Musée Archéologique: Sculptures gallo-romaines mythologiques et religieuses*, Editions de la Réunion des Musées Nationaux, Paris.

—— (1983) *Les Bois Sculptés des Sources de la Seine*, XLIIè supplément à *Gallia*.

—— (1985) *Le sanctuaire des Sources de la Seine*, Musée Archéologique, Dijon.

Diamond, J. M. (1991) 'The earliest horsemen', *Nature* 350 (March), p. 275.

Downey, R., King, A. and Soffe, G. (1980) 'The Hayling Island Temple and religious connections across the channel', in W. Rodwell (ed.), *Temples, Churches and Religion in Roman Britain*, British Archaeological Reports (British Series), no. 77, Oxford, pp. 289–304.

Drury, P. J. and Wickenden, N. P. (1982) 'Four bronze figurines from the Trinovantian Civitas', *Britannia* 13, pp. 239–43.

Duval, P.-M. (1961) *Paris Antique*, Hermann, Paris.

—— (1987) *Monnaies Gauloises et Mythes Celtiques*, Hermann, Paris.

Ellison, A. (1977) *Excavations at West Uley: 1977. The Romano-British Temple*, CRAAGS Occasional Paper No. 3.

—— (1980) 'Natives, Romans and Christians on West Hill, Uley: an interim report on the excavation of a ritual complex of the first millennium AD', in W. Rodwell (ed.), *Temples, Churches and Religion in Roman Britain*, British Archaeological Reports (British Series), no. 77, Oxford, pp. 305–28.

Espérandieu, E. (1907–66) *Recueil Général des Bas-Reliefs de la Gaule romaine et pré-romaine*, Ernest Leroux, Paris.

Even, A. (1953) 'Histoire du cochon de Mac Da Tho', *Ogam* 5, pp. 7–9.

Fenton, A. J. (1981) 'Early manuring techniques', in R. Mercer (ed.), *Farming Practice in British Prehistory*, Edinburgh University Press, Edinburgh, pp. 210–15.

Fitzpatrick, A. P. (1991) 'Everyday life in the Later Iron Age of European Britain', a paper presented at the 5th Conference of the Institute of Field Archaeologists, University of Birmingham (April).

Flower, R. (1947) *The Irish Tradition*, Oxford University Press, Oxford.

Foster, J. (1977) *Bronze Boar-Figurines in Iron Age and Roman Britain*, British Archaeological Reports (British Series), no. 39, Oxford.

Fowler, P. J. (1983) *The Farming of Prehistoric Britain*, Cambridge University Press, Cambridge.

Frere, S. S. (1978) *Britannia: A History of Roman Britain*, rev. edn, Routledge, London.

—— (1984) 'Roman Britain in 1983: sites explored', *Britannia* 15, pp. 265–332.

Gimbutas, M. (1965) *Bronze Age Cultures of Central and Eastern Europe*, Mouton & Co., The Hague.

Glob, P. V. (1969) *The Bog People*, Faber & Faber, London.

—— (1974) *The Mound People*, Faber & Faber, London.

Grant, A. (1975) 'The animal bones', in B. Cunliffe (ed.), *Excavations at Portchester Castle, 1, Roman*, Reports of the Research Committee of the Society of Antiquaries, no. 32, pp. 378–405.

—— (1984a) 'Animal husbandry in Wessex and the Thames Valley', in B. Cunliffe and D. Miles (eds), *Aspects of the Iron Age in Central Southern Britain*, Oxford University Committee for Archaeology, Monograph no. 2, pp. 102–19.

—— (1984b) 'Survival or sacrifice? A critical appraisal of animal burials in Britain in the Iron Age', in C. Grigson and J. Clutton-Brock (eds), *Animals and Archaeology: 4. Husbandry in Europe*, British Archaeological Reports (International Series), no. 227, Oxford, pp. 221–8.

—— (1989a) 'Animals and ritual in Early Britain: the visible and the invisible', in J.-D. Vigne (ed), *L'Animal dans les pratiques religieuses: les manifestations materielles*, Anthropozoologica Troisième Numéro Special, Paris, pp. 79–86.

—— (1989b) 'Animals in Roman Britain', in M. Todd (ed.), *Research on Roman Britain 1960–1989*, *Britannia* Monograph Series, no. 11, Society for the Promotion of Roman Studies, London, pp. 135–46.

—— (1991) 'Economic or symbolic? Animals and ritual behaviour', in P. Garwood *et al.*, *Sacred and Profane*, Oxford University Committee for Archaeology Monograph, no. 32, pp. 109–15.

Green, M. J. (1976) *A Corpus of Religious Material from the Civilian Areas of Roman Britain*, British Archaeological Reports (British Series), no. 24, Oxford.

—— (1978) *Small Cult-Objects from Military Areas of Roman Britain*, British Archaeological Reports (British Series), no. 52, Oxford.

—— (1981) 'Wheel-God and Ram-Horned Snake in Roman Gloucestershire', *Transactions of the Bristol and Gloucestershire Archaeological Society*, vol. 99, pp. 109–15.

—— (1984) *The Wheel as a Cult Symbol in the Romano-Celtic World*, Latomus, Brussels.

—— (1986) *The Gods of the Celts*, Alan Sutton, Gloucester.

—— (1989) *Symbol and Image in Celtic Religious Art*, Routledge, London.

—— (1991a) *The Sun Gods of Ancient Europe*, Batsford, London.

—— (1991b) 'Triplism and plurality: intensity and symbolism in Celtic religious expression', in P. Garwood *et al.*, *Sacred and Profane*, Oxford University Committee for Archaeology Monograph, no. 32, pp. 100–9.

—— (1991c) 'Celtic drawing on the English landscape', a paper presented at the Ruskin School of Drawing and Fine Art in a series entitled 'Reasons for drawing', Oxford (October).

—— (1992a) *Dictionary of Celtic Myth and Legend*, Thames & Hudson, London.

—— (1992b) 'The iconography of Celtic coins', paper presented at the 11th Oxford Symposium on 'Coinage and monetary history', Oxford (April).

Gros, P. (1986) 'Une hypothèse sur l'Arc d'Orange', *Gallia* 44(2), pp. 192–201.

Guthrie, W. K. C. (1954) *The Greeks and Their Gods*, Methuen, London.

Hamp, E. P. (1986) 'Culhwch, the swine', *Zeitschrift für Celtische Philologie* 41, pp. 257–8.

Harding, D. W. (1974) *The Iron Age in Lowland Britain*, Routledge, London.

Haselgrove, C. (1989) 'The Later Iron Age in southern Britain and beyond', in M. Todd (ed.), *Research on Roman Britain 1960–1989*, *Britannia* Monograph Series, no. 11, Society for the Promotion of Roman Studies, London, pp. 1–18.

Hassall, M. W. C. and Tomlin, R. (1984) 'Roman Britain in 1983: inscriptions', *Britanna* 15, pp. 333–56.

Hatt, J. J. (1964) *Sculptures Antiques Régionales Strasbourg*, Musée Archéologique de Strasbourg, Paris.

Hawkes, C. F. C. (1951) 'Bronzeworkers, cauldrons and bucket-animals', in W. F. Grimes (ed.), *Aspects of Archaeology in Britain and Beyond*, Edwards, London, pp. 172–99.

Henig, M. (1984) *Religion in Roman Britain*, Batsford, London.

Hennessy, W. M. (1870–2) 'The Ancient Irish Goddess of War', *Revue Celtique* 1, pp. 32, 55.

Hodder, I. (1982) *The Present Past*, Batsford, London.

—— (1987) *Symbols in Action*, Cambridge University Press, Cambridge.

Hodson, F. R. and Rowlett, R. M. (1973) 'From 600 BC to the Roman Conquest', in S. Piggott, G. Daniel and C. McBurney (eds), *France Before the Romans*, Thames & Hudson, London, pp. 157–91.

Holder, P. A. (1980) *The Auxilia from Augustus to Trajan*, British Archaeological

Reports, Oxford.

Hondius-Crone, A. (1955) *The Temple of Nehalennia at Domburg*, Meulenhoff, Amsterdam.

Hyland, A. (1990) *Equus: The Horse in the Roman World*, Batsford, London.

Isbell, H. (1971) (trans.) *The Last Poets of Imperial Rome*, Penguin, Harmondsworth.

Jenkins, F. (1956) 'Nameless or Nehalennia', *Archaeologia Cantiana* 70, pp. 192–200.

—— (1957) 'The role of the dog in Romano-Gaulish religion', *Collection Latomus* 16, pp. 60–76.

Johns, C. M. (1971–2) 'A Roman bronze statuette of Epona', *British Museum Quarterly* 36(1–2), pp. 37–41.

Jones, F. (1954) *The Holy Wells of Wales*, University of Wales Press, Cardiff.

Jones, G. and Jones, T. (1976) *The Mabinogion*, Dent, London.

Jones, M. (1989) 'Agriculture in Roman Britain: the dynamics of change', in M. Todd (ed.), *Research on Roman Britain 1960–1989*, Britannia Monograph Series, no. 11, Society for the Promotion of Roman Studies, London, pp. 127–34.

Jope, M. (1991) 'Celtic art in relation to society', a paper presented at a conference, 'The Celts and their society', held in Oxford (February).

Killeen, J. F. (1974) 'The debility of the Ulstermen – a suggestion', *Zeitschrift für Celtische Philologie* 33, pp. 81–6.

King, A. C. (1978) 'A comparative survey of bone assemblages from Roman sites in Britain', *Bulletin of the Institute of Archaeology* 15, pp. 207–32.

Kinsella, T. (1969) *The Táin*, Dolmen, Dublin.

Krappe, A. H. (1936) 'Les Dieux au corbeau chez les Celtes', *Revue de l'histoire des religions* 114, pp. 236–46.

Lambert, P.-Y. (1979) 'La Tablette Gauloise de Chamalières', *Etudes Celtiques* 16, pp. 141–69.

Lambrechts, P. (1942) *Contributions à l'étude des divinités Celtiques*, Rijksuniversitaet te Gent, Brugge.

Le Gall, J. (1963) *Alésia. Archéologie et Histoire*, Fayard, Paris.

Lelong, C. (1970) 'Note sur une sculpture gallo-romaine de Mouhet (Indre)', *Revue Archéologique de Centre* 9, pp. 123–6.

Linckenheld, E. (1929) 'Sucellus et Nantosuelta', *Revue de l'histoire des religions* 99, pp. 40–92.

Linduff, K. (1979) 'Epona: a Celt among the Romans', *Collection Latomus* 38(4), pp. 817–37.

Lloyd, J. H. *et al.* (1912) 'The reproach of Diarmaid', *Revue Celtique* 33, pp. 41–57.

Lynch, F. (1991) Lecture given to the Prehistoric Society, 19 January 1991.

Macauley, A. (1991) 'Does the Aurochs still survive?', *Current Archaeology* 126, p. 251.

Mac Cana, P. (1972) 'Mongán mac Fiachna and Immram Brain', *Eriu* 23, pp. 102–42.

—— (1975) 'On the prehistory of Immram Brain', *Eriu* 26, pp. 33–52.

—— (1976) 'The sinless otherworld of Immram Brain', *Eriu* 27, pp. 95–115.

—— (1983) *Celtic Mythology*, Newnes, London.

Mac Neill, E. (1904) *Duanaire Finn I*, Irish Texts Society VII.

Magnen, R. and Thevenot, E. (1953) *Epona*, Delmas, Bordeaux.

Maltby, J. M. (1984) 'Animal bones and the Romano-British economy', in C. Grigson and J. Clutton-Brock (eds), *Animals and Archaeology: 4. Husbandry in Europe*, British Archaeological Reports (International Series), no. 227, Oxford, pp. 125–38.

Manning, W. H. (1976) *Catalogue of the Romano-British Ironwork in the Museum of Antiquities, Newcastle-upon-Tyne*, Department of Archaeology, University of Newcastle.

Marache, R. (1979) *Les Romains en Bretagne*, Ouest France, Rennes.

Megaw, J. V. S. (1970) *Art of the European Iron Age*, Harper & Row, New York.

Megaw, R. and Megaw, V. (1989) *Celtic Art. From its Beginnings to the Book of Kells*, Thames & Hudson, London.

Meniel, P. (1984) 'Contributions à l'histoire de l'élevage en Picardie: du Néolithique à la fin de l'âge du fer', *Revue Archéologique de Picardie*, numéro special.

—— (1986a) 'Etude des offrandes animales', *Revue Archéologique de Picardie* 3/4, pp. 37–9.

—— (1986b) 'Les animaux dans l'alimentations des Gaulois', in L. Bodson (ed.), *L'Animal dans l'alimentation humaine: les critères de choix. Actes du Colloque International de Liège. 26–9 Novèmbre 1986*, Bulletin de l'association l'homme et l'animal: Société de Recherche Interdisciplinaire, pp. 115–22.

—— (1987a) *Chasse et elèvage chez les Gaulois (450–2 Av J.C.)*, Editions Errance, Paris.

—— (1987b) 'Les Restes animaux des Necropoles du Mont Troté et des Rouliers', in J.-G. Rozey (ed.), *Les Celtes en Champagne: Les Ardennes au second âge du fer: Le Mont Troté, Les Rouliers*, Mémoires de la Société Archéologique Champenoise, no. 4, pp. 357–61.

—— (1989a) 'Les animaux dans les pratiques religieuses des Gaulois', in J.-D. Vigne (ed.), *L'Animal dans les pratiques religieuses: les manifestations materielles*, Anthropozoologica Troisième Numéro Special, Paris, pp. 87–97.

—— (1989b) 'A propos des restes animaux des fosses et des puits de Bliesbruck', in J.-D. Vigne (ed.), *L'Animal dans les pratiques religieuses: les manifestations materielles*, Anthropozoologica Troisième Numéro Special, Paris, pp. 108–9.

—— (1990) 'Archéozoologie du deuxième âge du fer dans la Moyenne Vallée de l'Oise', *Revue Archéologique de Picardie*, no. 8, pp. 185–8.

Mercer, R. (ed.) (1981) *Farming Practice in British Prehistory*, Edinburgh University Press, Edinburgh.

Merrifield, R. (1983) *London, City of the Romans*, Batsford, London.

—— (1987) *The Archaeology of Ritual and Magic*, Batsford, London.

Mohen, J. P., Duval, A. and Eluère, C. (eds) (1987) *Trésors des Princes Celtes*, Editions de la Réunion des Musées Nationaux, Paris.

Murphy, E. (1953) *Duanaire Finn*, Dublin.

Musée Archéologique de Dijon (1973) *L'Art de la Bourgogne Romaine Découvertes Recentes*, Musée Archéologique, Dijon.

Noddle, B. (1984) 'A comparison of the bones of cattle, sheep and pigs from ten Iron Age and Romano-British sites', in C. Grigson and J. Clutton-Brock (eds), *Animals and Archaeology: 4. Husbandry in Europe*, British Archaeological Reports (International Series), no. 227, Oxford, pp. 105–23.

Nutt, A. (1906) 'Tochmarc Etainne', *Revue Celtique* 27, pp. 325–39.

Oaks, L. S. (1986) 'The Goddess Epona: concepts of sovereignty in a changing landscape', in M. Henig and A. King (eds), *Pagan Gods and Shrines of the Roman Empire*, Oxford University Committee for Archaeology, Monograph no. 8, pp. 77–84.

O'Fáolain, E. (1954) *Irish Sagas and Folk-Tales*, Oxford University Press, Oxford.

O'Grady, (1892) *Silva Gadelica*, London.

Olmsted, G. S. (1979) *The Gundestrup Cauldron*, Latomus, Brussels.

O'Rahilly, T. F. (1946) *Early Irish History and Mythology*, Dublin University Press, Dublin.

Page, R. I. (1990) *Norse Myths*, British Museum Press, The 'Legendary Past'

Series, London.

Petit, J.-P. (1989) 'Bliesbruck et les grands ensembles de puits et de fosses cultuels de la Gaule Romaine', in J.-D. Vigne (ed.), *L'Animal dans les pratiques religieuses: les manifestations materielles*, Anthropozoologica Troisième Numéro Special, Paris, pp. 99–110.

von Petrikovits, H. (1987) 'Matronen und Verwandte Gottheiten', *Ergebnisse eines Kolloquiums Veranstaltet von der Göttinger Akadamiekommission für die Altertumskunde Mittel- und Nordeuropas*, Beihafte der Bonner Jahrbücher, Band 44, Köln/Bonn, pp. 241–54.

Phillips, E. J. (1977) *Corpus Signorum Imperii Romani: Great Britain. Vol. I, Fasc. 1. Corbridge, Hadrian's Wall East of the North Tyne*, British Academy, London, and Oxford University Press, Oxford.

Piggott, S. (1965) *Ancient Europe*, Edinburgh University Press, Edinburgh.

—— (1968) *The Druids*, Thames & Hudson, London.

Piggott, S. and Daniel, G. (1951) *A Picture Book of Ancient British Art*, Cambridge University Press, Cambridge.

Planck, D. (1982) 'Eine neuendeckte keltische Viereckschanze in Fellbach Schmiden, Remsmurr-Kreis', *Germania* 60, pp. 105–72.

Planson, E. and Pommeret, C. (1986) *Les Bolards*, Ministère de la Culture, Paris.

Pobé, M. and Roubier, J. (1961) *The Art of Roman Gaul*, Galley Press, London.

Proudfoot, V. B. (1961) 'The economy of the Irish Rath', *Medieval Archaeology* 5, pp. 94–122.

Pryor, F. (1990) 'Flag Fen', *Current Archaeology* 119 (March), pp. 386–90.

Rankov, N. B. (1982) 'Roman Britain in 1981', *Britannia* 13, pp. 328–95.

Reynolds, P. J. (1979) *Iron Age Farm*, British Museum, London.

—— (1987) *Ancient Farming*, Shire Archaeology, Princes Risborough, no. 50.

Ridgeway, W. (1905) *The Origin and Influence of the Thoroughbred Horse*, Cambridge University Press, Cambridge.

Ritchie, W. F. and Ritchie, J. N. G. (1985) *Celtic Warriors*, Shire Archaeology, Princes Risborough, no. 41.

Robinson, M. (1984) 'Postscript', in A. Grant, 'Animal husbandry in Wessex and the Thames Valley', in B. Cunliffe and D. Miles (eds), *Aspects of the Iron Age in Central Southern Britain*, Oxford University Committee for Archaeology, Monograph no. 2, p. 119.

Rodwell, W. (1973) 'An unusual pottery bowl from Kelvedon, Essex', *Britannia* 4, pp. 265–7.

Rolleston, T. W. (1985) *Myths and Legends of the Celtic Race*, Constable, London.

Ross, A. (1961) 'The Horned God of the Brigantes', *Archaeologia Aeliana* 39(4), pp. 59ff.

Ross, A. (1967) *Pagan Celtic Britain*, Routledge, London.

—— (1968) 'Shafts, pits, wells – sanctuaries of the Belgic Britons?', in J. M. Coles and D. D. A. Simpson (eds), *Studies in Ancient Europe*, Leicester University Press, Leicester, pp. 255–85.

—— (1986) *The Pagan Celts*, Batsford, London.

Ross, A. and Feacham, R. (1976) 'Ritual rubbish: the Newstead Pits', in J. V. S. Megaw (ed.), *To Illustrate the Monuments*, Essays presented to Stuart Piggott, Thames & Hudson, London, pp. 230–7.

Rybova, A. and Soudska, B. (1956) *Sanctuaire Celtique en Bohême Centrale*, Nakledatelství Ceskoslovenské Akademie Ved, Prague.

Ryder, M. J. (1981) 'Livestock products: skins and fleeces', in R. Mercer (ed.), *Farming Practice in British Prehistory*, Edinburgh University Press, Edinburgh, pp. 182–209.

Salviat, F. (1979) *Glanum*, Caisse Nationale des Monuments Historiques et des Sites, Paris.

Savory, H. N. (1976) *Guide Catalogue of the Early Iron Age Collections*, National Museum of Wales, Cardiff.

Schindler, R. (1977) *Führer durch des Landesmuseum Trier*, Selbstverlag des Rheinisches Landesmuseum, Trier.

Scott, E. (1990) 'In search of Roman Britain: talking about their generation', *Antiquity* 64(245) (December), pp. 953–6.

Sims-Williams, P. (1990) 'Some Celtic otherworld terms', in A. T. E. Matonis and D. F. Melia (eds), *Celtic Language, Celtic Culture. A Festschrift for Eric P. Hamp*, Van Nuys, California, pp. 57–81.

Stead, I. M. (1985a) *Celtic Art*, British Museum Press, London.

—— (1985b) 'The Linsdorf Monster', *Antiquity* 59, pp. 40–2.

Stead, I. M. *et al.* (1986) *Lindow Man: The Body in the Bog*, British Museum, London.

Sterckx, C. (1991) *Le Cavalier et l'Anguipède*, vol. III, partie I, Ollodagos: Actes de la Société Belge d'Etudes Celtiques, Brussels.

Strachan, J. (1937) *An Introduction to Early Welsh*, Manchester University Press, Manchester.

Szabó, M. (1971) *The Celtic Heritage in Hungary*, Corvina, Budapest.

Tait, J. G. (ed.) (1941) *Sir Walter Scott's Journal*, Oliver & Boyd, Edinburgh and London.

Teichert, M. (1984) 'Size variation in cattle from Germania Romana and Germania Libera', in C. Grigson and J. Clutton-Brock (eds), *Animals and Archaeology: 4. Husbandry in Europe*, British Archaeological Reports (International Series), no. 227, Oxford, pp. 93–103.

Térouanne, P. (1960) 'Dedicaces à Mars Mullo. Découvertes à Allonnes (Sarthe)', *Gallia* 18, pp. 185–9.

Thevenot, E. (1951) 'Le cheval sacré dans la Gaule de l'Est', *Revue Archéologique de l'Est et du Centre-Est* 2, pp. 129–41.

—— (1952) 'Maillets votifs en pierre', *Revue Archéologique de l'Est et du Centre-Est* 3, pp. 99–110.

—— (1955) *Sur les Traces des Mars Celtique*, vol. 3, Dissertationes Archaeologicae Gandenses, Bruges.

—— (1957) 'Sur les figurations du "Dieu au Tonneau" ', *Revue Archéologique de l'Est et du Centre-Est* 8, pp. 311–14.

—— (1968) *Divinités et Sanctuaires de la Gaule*, Fayard, Paris.

Thill, G. (1978) *Les Epoques Gallo-Romaine et Mérovingienne au Musée d'Histoire et d'Art, Luxembourg*, Musée d'Histoire et d'Art, Luxembourg.

Thomas, K. (1987) *Man and the Natural World*, Penguin, Harmondsworth.

Tierney, J. J. (1959–60) 'The Celtic ethnography of Posidonius', *Proceedings of the Royal Irish Academy* 60, pp. 189–275.

Toussaint, M. (1948) *Metz à l'époque gallo-romaine*, Paul Even, Metz.

Toynbee, J. M. C. (1962) *Art in Roman Britain*, Phaidon, London.

—— (1973) *Animals in Roman Life and Art*, Thames & Hudson, London.

Tufi, S. R. (1983) *Corpus Signorum Imperii Romani: Great Britain. Vol. I, Fasc. 3, Yorkshire*, British Academy, London, and Oxford University Press, Oxford.

Turner, R. C. (1982) *Ivy Chimneys, Witham: An Interim Report*, Essex County Council Occasional Paper No. 2.

de Vries, J. (1963) *La Religion des Celtes*, Payot, Paris.

Wait, G. A. (1985) *Ritual and Religion in Iron Age Britain*, British Archaeological

Reports (British Series), no. 149, Oxford.

Webster, G. (1986) *The British Celts and their Gods under Rome*, Batsford, London.

Wedlake, W. J. (1982) *The Excavation of the Shrine of Apollo at Nettleton Shrub, Wiltshire 1956–1971*, Society of Antiquaries, London.

Wells, P. S. (1990) 'Iron Age temperate Europe: some current research issues', *Journal of World Prehistory* 4(4), pp. 437–76.

Wheeler, R. E. M. (1932) *Report on the Excavations . . . in Lydney Park, Gloucestershire*, Oxford University Press, Oxford.

Wightman, F. M. (1970) *Roman Trier and the Treveri*, Hart-Davis, London.

—— (1985) *Gallia Belgica*, Batsford, London.

Wilhelm, E. (1974) *Pierres Sculptés et Inscriptions de l'Epoque Romaine*, Musée d'Histoire et d'Art, Luxembourg.

Williams, I. (1930) *Pedair Keinc y Mabinogi*, University of Wales Press, Cardiff.

Woolner, D. (1965) 'The White Horse, Uffington', *Transactions of the Newbury District Field Club* 11(3), pp. 27–44.

Zachar, L. (1987) *Keltische Kunst in der Slowakei*, Tatran, Bratislava.

INDEX